The Burden of Bad Ideas

HEATHER MAC DONALD

The Burden of Bad Ideas

HOW MODERN INTELLECTUALS MISSHAPE OUR SOCIETY

CHICAGO

Ivan R. Dee

2000

Most of the contents of this book appeared originally in *City Journal*, published
by The Manhattan Institute.

Library of Congress Cataloging in-Publication Data:
Mac Donald, Heather.
    The burden of bad ideas : how modern intellectuals misshape our society
/ Heather Mac Donald.
        p. cm.
    Includes index.
    ISBN 1-56663-337-0 (alk. paper)
    1. Political planning—United States.   2. Intellectuals—United States.
I. Title.
JK468.P64M23 2000
361.2'5'0973—dc21   00-034562

Contents

Introduction

I ONCE ASKED a mother on food stamps what she would do without them. "I'd get a husband," she replied matter-of-factly. Here was news, I thought—a tantalizing bit of evidence of welfare's corrosive effect on the inner-city family. But when I recounted this exchange in an article for one of the nation's most influential newspapers, the editor ordered me to leave it out. Quoting it, he said, would "stigmatize the poor."

This episode perfectly crystallizes my experience of writing on poverty and education. The reality I have observed again and again in welfare offices and urban classrooms across New York and elsewhere is so dissimilar from that presented in the mainstream media that I sometimes wonder whether their reporters and I occupy the same universe.

Maybe this is a matter of my background. I came to writing about urban problems and social policy an innocent, without a preconceived theory about the neighborhoods that have dominated domestic policy debate for almost half a century now. I wanted to know not only about people's experience growing up and living in the inner city but also their opinions about their communities' problems and government's efforts to solve them.

Three things struck me above all. First was the depth of dysfunction that I often saw—the self-destruction wrought by drugs and alcohol and promiscuity, the damage inflicted on children by a world from which the traditional family had largely disappeared (though throughout the most troubled neighborhoods I found individuals of extraordinary moral strength fighting for order). Second was the extent to which government programs shaped life in the ghetto, influencing the choices that individuals made and distorting the forms that social interaction took. Finally, I was continually amazed by the trenchancy with which those I interviewed could judge their situations and the policies that had gone into making them. If you want to know how well social policies are working, I learned, ask the poor—when their advocates aren't around.

After a couple of years visiting welfare hotels, public housing projects, and schools in that three-borough-wide band of educational failure known in New York as the Dead Zone, I increasingly understood that my initial lack of preconception accounted for the difference between what I saw and what the conventional press reported about the same subjects. I wanted to see firsthand as much as I could and then, as faithfully as I could, to render what I saw. Too many writers and commentators—it seems to me, at least—are in the grip of an inflexible ideology that prevents them from seeing clearly the reality in front of their eyes, if it doesn't square with theory.

It wasn't just journalists who held that ideology, of course. It informed the social policies that were misshaping inner-city life. That was the reason journalists often had such trouble accurately portraying the ghetto: they couldn't face the fact that the programs and principles they supported with such fervor didn't work. Or worse: these principles actually harmed the poor who were their supposed beneficiaries.

But what gives the ideology such hold over people as intelligent and engaged as my journalistic colleagues? It assures its adherents that they are compassionate and caring, merely by virtue of subscribing to it. It gives them a sense of specialness—even though its core ideas have formed the nation's elite orthodoxy for decades.

And indeed these orthodox ideas have permeated the nation's elite institutions so thoroughly that it is difficult to escape their sway. I was fascinated to observe—and to report on—how they had transformed such cultural bastions as the *New York Times* and the great philanthropic foundations that for more than a generation have helped set America's social and cultural agenda. I looked at how they had transformed our law schools, our education schools, our museums, even our public health schools—with further consequences for public health policy and for how schoolchildren are taught. And finally, I traced how this reigning intellectual orthodoxy affected the press's coverage of the shooting of Amadou Diallo by four New York police officers—and what effect this *cause célèbre* had on law enforcement in New York. The more I learned, the more I understood how it could be that the fact that something was true—a welfare mother's damning admission regarding welfare and family structure, say—came to matter less than maintaining certain false, but ego-massaging, ideas about poverty, social responsibility, and race.

What are these destructive and blinding ideas? First among them is the notion that the poor cannot be held responsible for their own behavior, because they are victims of an unjust and racist American society. Buttressing this idea are a series of corollaries: that government can assume the role of parents; that America's ineradicable racism and sexism require double standards for minorities; that reason is a tool of male oppression; and that education is not about knowledge but ethnic empowerment.

How do these ideas skew the presentation of reality in the mainstream press (beyond simply suppressing it, like the editor described above)? Late last year, the *New York Times* held up a young woman named Eve Engesser as a poster victim of New York's allegedly heartless policies toward the homeless. Miss Engesser faced eviction from her public shelter accommodation, as well as temporary separation from her children, because of her failure to follow the state's new shelter work requirements. The *Times* quoted a local minister approvingly: "They set these people up to fail," he fumed. "And then they sanction them when they do fail." But this is very far from the truth. "They" didn't set Miss Engesser up to fail; she created her own failure. She had her first child at age thirteen with another thirteen-year-old, who promptly disappeared. Her second child came four years later, by an equally temporary young man. In the tenth grade, she dropped out of school. Given these choices—and she could have made different ones in every case—poverty and even homelessness were virtual inevitabilities in Miss Engesser's life. The shelter's work rules didn't cause her plight. Her own self-destructive behavior did.

But the prevailing convention in welfare reporting and liberal discourse requires drawing a dark and impermeable veil over the alleged victim's past choices and treating her current problems as the product of malign social forces and callous Republican policies. The all-important imperative not to "stigmatize the poor" means ignoring any personal behavior that results in poverty, and treating someone who has had children out of wedlock, dropped out of school, developed a drug habit, committed crimes, or refused to follow workplace rules as the moral equivalent of her self-disciplined, law-abiding, job-holding neighbor, resolutely working her way out of poverty.

The result is a major disjunction between the actual causes of long-term poverty and the solutions favored by the liberal elites. More cash benefits and other government subsidies will not significantly improve the life chances of a boy raised by an unwed mother, with an endless stream of men trooping through his house, where drug parties keep him up at night, and whose mother does not have the self-discipline necessary to give children the moral and intellectual nurture they need to succeed.

No matter. The elites now contort themselves to discover new ways in which the poor are incapable of behaving responsibly. Public health professors and officials argue that racism and sexism, not self-destructive conduct, make poor women get AIDS. Federal bureaucrats and judges declare that thievery is evidence of disabling drug addiction, qualifying the thief for disability benefits. Those same wise men ascribe violence and academic failure in poor children to disability, to be rewarded with a steady stream of income until adulthood. High schools build day-care centers for teen mothers, on the theory that inner-city girls are destined to have out-of-wedlock babies, so why not make that reality more pleasant—in effect normalizing it—instead of stigmatizing it?

To me, it seemed obvious that if you insulate people from the consequences of their own self-destructive behavior, you're going to get a whole lot more of it. It's obvious to the poor themselves, too.

Only the elites don't get it. There are no harsher critics of the welfare system than the people within it; visit any welfare office, and you'll hear nothing but contempt for mothers who "keep having babies" while on the dole, or for people running around on "crazy checks"— disability payments for alleged mental or behavioral problems—when there's nothing wrong with them but their bad behavior. "Anything the government gives you and it's free, it's not good for you," a fifty-one-year-old woman in a homeless drop-in center in midtown Manhattan told me. "You get the program mentality and become a zombie." Somehow these homegrown critics never get quoted in the mainstream media. No space, apparently, given the more pressing need to hear from assorted advocates on the inadequacy of government poverty spending.

These essays record my travels through institutions that have been perverted by today's elite intellectual orthodoxy, from an inner-city high school that teaches graffiti-writing for academic credit—thus glorifying the school's racial sensitivity while sacrificing its students' future—to the Smithsonian Institution, now in thrall to a crude academic multiculturalism; from New York's Dantean foster care system to Ivy League law schools that produce "scholarship" urging blacks to view shoplifting, and pilfering from an employer, as political expression. These essays record, as well, the striking contrast between the irresponsibility of today's elite orthodoxy with that of the past. The great Gilded Age philanthropists, for example, promoted the values that made them so fabulously successful—self-discipline, education, and a powerful work ethic. They made no excuses for the poor, but held them to the same standards of behavior as themselves. The *New York Times*'s Hundred Neediest Cases appeal once unflinchingly lauded moral character and condemned indolence and dependency; today it treats welfare cheats as victims.

My purpose in these essays is to hold up reality in the most unvarnished way possible before the reader, to try to dispel the obfuscation that today's mainstream journalism, and today's elite ideology, has spread over it. I have tried, too, to take the reader into the institutions that generate and broadcast the new orthodoxy, and make him see just what constitutes wisdom there. I have tried to show how ideas that seem obviously dismissable nevertheless are molding the thought and actions of the next generation of lawyers, teachers, public health officials, and policymakers. The consequences fall upon the poor most directly; but insofar as the poor affect the whole of a city or a nation—in terms of crime or lost productivity or welfare costs—the consequences ultimately fall upon the rest of us, as well.

H. M.

New York City
June 2000

The Burden of Bad Ideas

The Billions of Dollars That Made Things Worse

IF THE PRACTICAL VISIONARIES who established America's great philanthropic foundations could see their legacy today, they might regret their generosity. Once an agent of social good, those powerful institutions have become a political battering ram targeted at American society. You can instantly grasp how profoundly foundations have changed by comparing two statements made by presidents of the Carnegie Corporation just a generation apart. In 1938 the corporation commissioned a landmark analysis of black-white relations from sociologist Gunnar Myrdal; the result, *An American Dilemma*, would help spark the civil rights movement. Yet Carnegie president Frederick Keppel was almost apologetic about the foundation's involvement with such a vexed social problem: "Provided the foundation limits itself to its proper function," Keppel wrote in the book's introduction, "namely, to make the facts available and then let them speak for themselves, and does not undertake to instruct the public as to what to do about them, studies of this kind provide a wholly proper and . . . sometimes a highly important use of [its] funds."

Three decades later, Carnegie president Alan Pifer's 1968 annual report reads like a voice from another planet. Abandoning Keppel's admirable restraint, Pifer exhorts his comrades in the foundation world to help shake up "sterile institutional forms and procedures left over from the past" by supporting "aggressive new community organizations which . . . the comfortable stratum of American life would consider disturbing and perhaps even dangerous." No longer content to provide mainstream knowledge dispassionately, America's most prestigious philanthropies now aspired to revolutionize what they believed to be a deeply flawed American society.

The results, from the 1960s onward, have been devastating. Foundation-supported poverty advocates fought to make welfare a right—and generations have grown up fatherless and dependent. Foundation-funded minority advocates fought for racial separatism and a vast system of quotas—and American society remains perpetually riven by the issue of race. On most campuses today, a foundation-endowed multicultural circus has driven out the very idea of a common culture, deriding it as a relic of American imperialism. Foundation-backed advocates for various "victim" groups use the courts to bend government policy to their will, thwarting the democratic process. And poor communities across the country often find their traditional values undermined by foundation-sent "community activists" bearing the latest fashions in diversity and "enlightened" sexuality. The net effect is not a more just but a more divided and contentious American society.

Not all foundations adopted the cause of social change, of course; but the overwhelmingly "progressive" large foundations set the tone for the entire sector—especially such giants as Ford, which got radicalized in the sixties, and Rockefeller and Carnegie, which followed suit in the seventies. Such foundations wield enormous financial might: a mere 2 percent of all foundations (or 1,020) provide more than half of the approximately $10 billion that foundations now give away each year, and in 1992 the 50 largest foundations accounted for more than one-quarter of all foundation spending. Though some conservative foundations have recently risen to prominence, Smith College sociologist Stanley Rothman has found that liberal foundations still outnumber conservative ones three to one, and that liberal policy groups receive four times as much foundation money and four times as many grants as their conservative counterparts. The Ford Foundation gave $42 million in grants to education and culture alone in 1994, while the Olin Foundation, the premier funder of conservative scholarship on campus, spent only $13 million on all its programs, educational and non-educational. Understanding the impact of foundations on American culture so far, therefore, means concentrating on the liberal leviathans.

In their early, heroic period, foundations provided a luminous example of how private philanthropy can improve the lives of millions around the world. Key institutions of modern American life—the research university, the professional medical school, the public library—owe their existence to the great foundations, which had been created in the modern belief that philanthropy should address the causes rather than the effects of poverty.

There was no more articulate exponent of the new philanthropic philosophy than Andrew Carnegie, a self-educated Scot who rose from impoverished bobbin boy in a textile mill to head America's largest coal and steel complex. He elaborated his theory of "scientific philanthropy," a capitalist's response to Marx's "scientific socialism," in *The Gospel of Wealth* (1889), an eloquent testament and a stinging rebuke to many a contemporary foundation executive.

The growing abyss between the vast industrial fortunes and the income of the common laborer, Carnegie argued, was the inevitable result of the most beneficial economic system that mankind had ever known. The tycoon, however, merely held his fortune in trust for the advancement of the common good; moreover, he should give away his wealth during his lifetime, using the same acumen that he showed in making it. The scientific philanthropist will target his giving to "help those who will help themselves," creating institutions through which those working poor with a "divine spark" can better themselves economically and spiritually. The "slothful, the drunken, [and] the unworthy" were outside his scheme: "One man or woman who succeeds in living comfortably by begging is more dangerous to society, and a greater obstacle to the progress of humanity, than a score of wordy Socialists," he pronounced.

Starting in 1901, Carnegie threw himself full-time into practicing what he preached. He created one of the greatest American institutions for social mobility: the free public library, which he built and stocked in nearly two thousand communities. He established the Carnegie Institute of Technology (now the Carnegie Mellon University); the Carnegie Foundation for the Advancement of Teaching, to provide pensions for all college teachers; a museum; a scientific research institute; a university trust; Carnegie Hall in New York City; the World Court building in the Hague; and a host of other major institutions. A Carnegie-commissioned report on medical education revolutionized medical training, sparking reforms that would give the U.S. the greatest medical schools in the world. Even so, his wealth grew faster than he could give it away. Finally, "in desperation," according to his biographer, he created the Carnegie Corporation in 1911.

During the early years of this century, the press kept tabs on a remarkable philanthropic rivalry: would Andrew Carnegie or John D. Rockefeller give away the most money? Rockefeller created overnight the great University of Chicago from a third-rate Baptist college in 1892. He established the renowned Rockefeller Institute for Medical Research and supported the education of Southern blacks. But he, too, could not make donations fast enough. So in 1909 he endowed a foundation that, in conjunction with the Rockefeller Institute, made medical history—eradicating hookworm here and abroad, establishing the first major schools of public health, developing the yellow fever vaccine, controlling a new strain of malaria, and reducing infant typhus epidemics. In later years the Rockefeller Foundation contributed to discoveries in genetics, biophysics, biochemistry, and in medical technologies like spectroscopy, X rays, and the use of tracer elements.

But the "scientific philanthropy" articulated by Rockefeller's personal advisor, Frederick Gates, contained a crucial—and ultimately destructive—innovation. The value of a foundation, Gates argued, was that it moved the disposition of wealth from the control of the donor into the hands of "experts"—precisely the opposite of Carnegie's view that the person who made the money would be its wisest administrator. Eventually, this transfer of control yielded the paradox of funds made by laissez-faire capitalists being used for the advocacy of a welfare state. Even during Rockefeller's lifetime, Gates's doctrine produced some odd moments. In 1919 Rockefeller prophetically wrote to his lawyer: "I could wish that the education which some professors furnish was more conducive to the most sane and practical and possible views of life rather than drifting . . . toward socialism and some forms of Bolshevism." But Rockefeller's attorney countered that donors should not try to influence teaching—or even consider a university's philosophy in funding it. The subsequent history of academia has proved the folly of that injunction, which Rockefeller unfortunately obeyed.

When the Ford Foundation flowered into an activist, "socially conscious" philanthropy in the 1960s, it sparked the key revolution in the foundation worldview: the idea that foundations were to improve the lot of mankind not by building lasting institutions but by challenging existing ones. Henry Ford and his son Edsel had originally created the foundation in 1936 not out of any grand philanthropic vision but instead to shelter their company's stock from taxes and to ensure continued family control of the business. When the foundation came into its full inheritance of Ford stock, it became overnight America's largest foundation by several magnitudes. Its expenditures in 1954 were four times higher than second-ranked Rockefeller and ten times higher than third-ranked Carnegie.

From its start, Ford aimed to be different, eschewing medical research and public health in favor of social issues such as First Amendment restrictions and undemocratic concentrations of power, economic problems, world peace, and social science. Nevertheless, Andrew Carnegie himself might have applauded some of Ford's early efforts, including the "Green Revolution" in high-yielding crops and its pioneering program to establish theaters, orchestras, and dance and opera companies across the country. But by the early 1960s, the trustees started clamoring for a more radical vision; according to Richard Magat, a Ford employee, they demanded "action-oriented rather than research-oriented" programs that would "test the outer edges of advocacy and citizen participation."

The first such "action-oriented" program, the Gray Areas project, was a turning point in foundation history and—because it was a prime mover of the ill-starred War on Poverty—a turning point in American history as well. Its creator, Paul Ylvisaker, an energetic social theorist from Harvard and subsequent icon for the liberal foundation community, had concluded that the problems of newly migrated urban blacks and Puerto Ricans could not be solved by the "old and fixed ways of doing things." Because existing private and public institutions were unresponsive, he argued, the new poverty populations needed a totally new institution—the "community action agency"—to coordinate legal, health, and welfare services and to give voice to the poor. According to Senator Daniel Patrick Moynihan, an early poverty warrior under Presidents Kennedy and Johnson, Ford "proposed nothing less than institutional change in the operation and control of American cities. . . . [Ford] invented a new level of American government: the inner-city community action agency." Ylvisaker proceeded to establish such agencies in Boston, New Haven, Philadelphia, and Oakland.

Most significantly, Gray Areas' ultimate purpose was to spur a similar federal effort. Ford was the first—but far from the last—foundation to conceive of itself explicitly as a laboratory for the federal welfare state. As Ylvisaker later explained, foundations should point out "programs and policies, such as social security, income maintenance, and educational entitlement that convert isolated and discretionary acts of private charity into regularized public remedies that flow as a matter of legislated right." In this vein, the foundation measured the success of Gray Areas by the number of federal visitors to the program's sites, and it declared the passage of the Economic Opportunity Act of 1964, which opened the War on Poverty and incorporated the Ford-invented community action agencies, to be Gray Areas' "proudest achievement."

Unfortunately, because it was so intent on persuading the federal government to adopt the program, Ford ignored reports that the community action agencies were failures, according to historian Alice O'Connor. Reincarnated as federal Community Action Programs

(CAPs), Ford's urban cadres soon began tearing up cities. Militancy became the mark of merit for federal funders, according to Senator Moynihan. In Newark, the director of the local CAP urged blacks to arm themselves before the 1967 riots; leaflets calling for a demonstration were run off on the CAP's mimeograph machine. The federal government funneled community action money to Chicago gangs—posing as neighborhood organizers—who then continued to terrorize their neighbors. The Syracuse, New York, CAP published a remedial reading manual that declared: "No ends are accomplished without the use of force. . . . Squeamishness about force is the mark not of idealistic, but moonstruck morals." Syracuse CAP employees applied $7 million of their $8 million federal grant to their own salaries.

Ford created another of the War on Poverty's most flamboyant failures—Mobilization for Youth, a federally funded juvenile delinquency agency on Manhattan's Lower East Side that quickly expanded its sights from providing opportunity to minority youth to bringing down the "power structure." Home base for the welfare-rights movement, the Mobilization for Youth aimed to put so many people on welfare that the state and city's finances would collapse. Its techniques included dumping dead rats on Mayor Robert Wagner's doorstep and organizing Puerto Rican welfare mothers for "conflict confrontations" with local teachers.

These programs were just warm-ups, however. When McGeorge Bundy, former White House national security advisor, became Ford's president in 1966, the foundation's activism switched into high gear. Bundy reallocated Ford's resources from education to minority rights, which in 1960 had accounted for 2.5 percent of Ford's giving but by 1970 would soar to 40 percent. Under Bundy's leadership, Ford created a host of new advocacy groups, such as the Mexican-American Legal Defense and Educational Fund (a prime mover behind bilingual education) and the Native American Rights Fund, that still wreak havoc on public policy today. Ford's support for a radical Hispanic youth group in San Antonio led even liberal congressman Henry B. Gonzales to charge that Ford had fostered the "emergence of reverse racism in Texas."

Incredibly, foundation officers believed that Ford's radicalization merely responded to the popular will. As Francis X. Sutton, a long-time Ford staffer, reminisced in 1989: "It took the critical populist up-surge at the end of the sixties to weaken faith that the foundation's prime vocation lay in helping government, great universities, and research centers. . . . As the sixties wore on, the values of the New Left spread through American society and an activistic spirit entered the foundation that pulled it away from its original vision of solving the world's problems through scientific knowledge." The notion that the 1960s represented a "populist upsurge," or that New Left values bubbled up from the American grassroots rather than being actively disseminated by precisely such rich, elite institutions as the Ford Foundation, could only be a product of foundation thinking.

The most notorious Bundy endeavor, the school decentralization experiment in the Ocean Hill–Brownsville section of Brooklyn, changed the course of liberalism by fracturing the black-Jewish civil rights coalition and souring race relations in New York for years afterward. Bundy had led a mayoral panel under John Lindsay that recommended giving "community control" over local public school districts to parents. The panel's report, written by a Ford staffer, claimed that New York's huge centralized school system was not sufficiently accountable to minority populations. Black and Puerto Rican children could not learn or even behave, the report maintained, unless their parents were granted "meaningful participation" in their education. Translation: parents should hire and fire local teachers and school administrators.

Ford set about turning this theory into reality with utmost clumsiness. It chose as the head of its $1.4 million decentralization experiment in three Brooklyn school districts a longtime white-hater, Rhody McCoy, who dreamed of creating an all-black school system, right up through college, within the public schools. McCoy was a moderate, however, compared to the people he tapped as deputies. Although the school board blocked his appointment of a militant under indictment for conspiracy to murder, he did manage to hire Les Campbell, the radical head of the Afro-American Teachers Association, who organized his school's most violent students into an anti-Semitic combat force. According to education scholar Diane Ravitch, McCoy had an understanding with racist thug Sonny Carson that Carson's "bodyguards" would intimidate white teachers until McCoy would diplomatically call them off.

Ford's experimental school districts soon exploded with anti-Semitic black rage, as militants argued that black and Puerto Rican children failed because Jewish teachers were waging "mental genocide" on them. The day after Martin Luther King's assassination, students at a junior high school rampaged through the halls beating up white teachers, having been urged by Les Campbell to "[s]end [whitey] to the graveyard" if he "taps you on the shoulder."

When the teacher's union struck to protest the illegal firing of nineteen teachers deemed "hostile" to decentralization, parent groups, mostly Ford-funded, responded with hostile boycotts. McCoy refused to reinstate the nineteen teachers, though ordered by the school board to do so. White teachers at one school found an anti-Semitic screed in their mailboxes, calling Jews "Blood-sucking Exploiters and Murderers" and alleging that "the So-Called Liberal Jewish Friend . . . is Really Our Enemy and He is Responsible For the Serious Educational Retardation of Our Black Children." McCoy refused to denounce the pamphlet or the anti-Semitism behind it. Nor did Ford publicly denounce such tactics—or take responsibility after the fact. McGeorge Bundy later sniffed self-righteously: "If private foundations cannot assist experiments, their unique role will be impaired, to the detriment of American society." But if the experiment goes awry, the foundation can saunter off, leaving the community to pick up the pieces.

Dean Rusk, president of the Rockefeller Foundation in the late 1950s, once described Ford's influence on other foundations: What the "fat boy in the canoe does," he said, "makes a difference to everybody else." And Ford's influence was never stronger than after it adopted the cause of social change. Waldemar Nielsen's monumental studies of foundations, published in 1972 and 1985, only strengthened the Ford effect, for Nielsen celebrated activist philanthropy and berated those foundations that had not yet converted to the cause. "As a result," recalls Richard Larry, president of the Sarah Scaife Foundation, "a number of foundations said: 'If this is what the foundation world is doing and what the experts say is important, we should move in that direction, too.'" The Rockefeller Brothers Fund, for example, funded the National Welfare Rights Organization—at the same time that the organization was demonstrating against Governor Nelson Rockefeller of New York. The Carnegie Corporation pumped nearly $20 million into various left-wing advocacy groups during the 1970s.

Many foundations had turned against the system that had made them possible, as Henry Ford II recognized when he quit the Ford Foundation board in disgust in 1977. "In effect," he wrote in his resignation letter, "the foundation is a creature of capitalism, a statement that, I'm sure, would be shocking to many professional staff people in the field of philanthropy. It is hard to discern recognition of this fact in anything the foundation does. It is even more difficult to find an understanding of this in many of the institutions, particularly the universities, that are the beneficiaries of the foundation's grant programs."

Did Ford exaggerate? Not according to Robert Schrank, a Ford program officer during the 1970s and early 1980s. Schrank, a former Communist, recalls the "secret anti-capitalist orientation" of his fellow program officers. "People were influenced by the horror stories we Marxists had put out about the capitalist system," he says; "it became their guidance."

Naturally, Henry Ford's resignation had no effect; the doctrine of independence from the donor had taken full root. As McGeorge Bundy coolly remarked: "He has a right to expect people to read his letter carefully, but I don't think one letter from anyone is going to change the foundation's course."

Today, the full-blown liberal foundation worldview looks like this: First, white racism is the cause of black and Hispanic social problems. In 1982, for example, Carnegie's Alan Pifer absurdly accused the country of tolerating a return to "legalized segregation of the races." The same note still sounds in Rockefeller president Peter C.

Goldmark Jr.'s assertion, in his 1995 annual report, that we "urgently need . . . a national conversation about race . . . to talk with candor about the implications of personal and institutional racism."

Second, Americans discriminate widely on the basis not just of race but also of gender, "sexual orientation," class, and ethnicity. As a consequence, victim groups need financial support to fight the petty-mindedness of the majority.

Third, Americans are a selfish lot. Without the creation of court-enforced entitlement, the poor will be abused and ignored. Without continuous litigation, government will be unresponsive to social needs.

Fourth, only government can effectively ameliorate social problems. Should government cut welfare spending, disaster will follow, which no amount of philanthropy can cure.

And finally, as a corollary to tenet four: at heart, most social problems are economic ones. In the language of foundations, America has "disinvested" in the poor. Only if the welfare state is expanded into "new areas of need," to quote Pifer, will the poor be able to succeed. This worldview is particularly noticeable in three key areas of foundation funding: the dissemination of diversity ideology, the "collaboratives" movement in community development, and public interest litigation and advocacy.

A worry for the liberal foundations in the 1970s, "diversity" became an all-consuming obsession in the 1980s. Foundation boards and staffs got "diversified," sometimes producing friction and poor performance. "Foundations were so anxious to show that they, too, had their black and Puerto Rican that hiring decisions entailed mediocrity," says Gerald Freund, a former program officer with the Rockefeller and MacArthur foundations. Some foundations, led by Ford, started requiring all grant applicants to itemize the racial and gender composition of their staff and trustees, sometimes to their great bewilderment. One organization dedicated to Eastern Europe was told that its funder expected more minorities on its board. No problem, replied a charmingly naive European ambassador; how about a Kurd or Basque trustee? He soon learned that that is not what funders mean by "minorities." Organizations that already represent a minority interest—an Asian organization, say—might be told to find an American Indian or a Hispanic board member. "It is stunning to me," laments the executive director of one of Washington's most liberal policy groups, "that it is no longer crucially important whether my organization is succeeding; the critical issue is the color complexion of my staff."

Universities have proved unswervingly devoted soldiers in the foundations' diversity crusade. It was in the sixties that Ford put its money behind black studies, setting up a model for academic ghettoization that would be repeated endlessly over the next thirty years. Today, many universities recall the Jim Crow South, with separate dorms, graduation ceremonies, and freshman initiation programs for different ethnic groups, in a gross perversion of the liberal tradition. Students in foundation-funded ethnic studies courses learn that Western culture (whose transmission is any university's principal reason for existence) is the source of untold evil rather than of the "rights" they so vociferously claim.

Lavishly fertilized with foundation money, women's studies—those campus gripe sessions peppered with testimonials to one's humiliation at the hands of the "patriarchy"—debased the curriculum further into divisive victimology. From 1972 to 1992, women's studies received $36 million from Ford, Rockefeller, Carnegie, Mott, and Mellon, among others. Foundation-funded research centers on women, such as the Center for Research on Women at Wellesley College, established with Carnegie money, sprang up on campuses nationwide. The Wellesley Center's most visible accomplishment is the wildly influential—and wholly spurious—report "How Schools Shortchange Girls," which claims that secondary education subjects girls to incessant gender bias. Not to be outshone, Ford produced a multilingual translation of the report for distribution at the Beijing global women's conference. Rockefeller, taking diversity several steps further, funds humanities fellowships at the University of Georgia for "womanists"—defined as "black feminists or feminists of color"—and supports the City University of New York's Center for Lesbian and Gay Studies.

Not content with setting up separate departments of ethnic and gender studies, foundations have poured money into a powerful movement called "curriculum transformation," which seeks to inject race, gender, and sexual consciousness into *every* department and discipline. A class in biology, for example, might consider feminine ways of analyzing cellular metabolism; a course in music history might study the hidden misogyny in Beethoven's Ninth Symphony—actual examples. One accomplishment of the curricular transformationists is to distinguish bad, "masculine" forms of thinking (logic, mathematics, scientific research) from good, "feminine" forms, which subordinate the search for right answers to "inclusiveness" and "wholeness." At the University of Massachusetts, Boston, the recipient of a Ford curriculum transformation grant, a course is not culturally diverse if it addresses "gender" one week and "social class" the next, according to the university's diversity coordinator. "We'd want the issues of diversity addressed every week," she says. Edgar Beckham, a program officer in charge of Ford's Campus Diversity Initiative, lets his imagination run wild in describing the enormous reach of diversity: "Every domain of institutional activity might be involved," he says—"buildings, grounds, financial aid." No domain, in other words, is safe from foundation intervention.

The big foundations pursue identity politics and multiculturalism just as obsessively in the performing and fine arts. Gone are the days when Ford's W. McNeil Lowry, described by Lincoln Kirstein as "the single most influential patron of the performing arts the American democratic system has ever produced," collaborated with such artists as Isaac Stern to find new talent. The large foundations now practice what Robert Brustein, director of the American Repertory Theater, calls "coercive philanthropy," forcing arts institutions to conform to the foundations' vision of a multicultural paradise—one that, above all else, builds minority self-esteem.

Foundations talk a good game of inclusion, but when it comes to artistic grant-making, their outlook is color-coded. I asked Robert Curvin, vice president for communications at Ford, what would be so wrong about giving a black child the tools to appreciate, say, a Schubert song. He replied that "all art and expression begins with one's own culture." "Traditionally," he added, "we did not recognize the tremendous value in conga drums. Now, we can't easily make these judgments [among different artistic forms]." Maybe not. But the view that black children are inherently suited for conga drums seems patronizing and false. Aren't American blacks as much the rightful heirs of the Western artistic tradition as other Americans?

Alison Bernstein, director of Ford's education and culture division, crystallized the liberal foundation perspective at the end of my interview with her. She had recently attended the New York City Ballet, where the audience, she noted, was "all white." Yet the success among blacks of *Bring In 'da Noise, Bring In 'da Funk*, the Tony-winning rap and tap tour through the history of black oppression, she said, shows that the "minority audience is out there." Why, she asked, isn't the New York City Ballet commissioning a work from Savion Glover, the tap prodigy behind *Bring In 'da Noise*? In other words, we can only expect blacks to come to the ballet for "black" choreography. In W. McNeil Lowry's time, her question would have been, how can we help minority students enjoy classical ballet, which will enrich them as human beings?

The second focus of the foundations' liberal zeal, the so-called "collaboratives" movement in community development, is emblematic of the thirty-year-long foundation assault on the bourgeois virtues that once kept communities and families intact. The idea behind this movement, which grows out of the failed community action programs of the 1960s, is that a group of "community stakeholders," assembled and funded by a foundation, becomes a "collaborative" to develop and implement a plan for community revitalization. That plan should be "comprehensive" and should "integrate" separate government services, favorite foundation mantras. To the extent this means anything, it sounds innocuous enough, and sometimes is. But as with the foundations' choice of community groups in the 1960s, the rhetoric of "community" and local empowerment is often profoundly hypocritical.

The Annie E. Casey Foundation's teen pregnancy initiative called Plain Talk is a particularly clear—and painful—example of the moral imperialism with which foundations impose their "progressive" values on hapless communities. In its early years, the foundation, the product of the United Parcel Service fortune, ran its own foster care and adoption agency. But when its endowment ballooned in the 1980s, the foundation jumped into the already crowded field of "social change."

Plain Talk set out to reduce unwanted teen pregnancies not by promoting abstinence but by "encouraging local adults to engage youth in frank and open discussions regarding sexuality," in the words of the project's evaluation report, and by improving teens' access to birth control. In Casey's view, the real cause of teen pregnancies is that "adults"—note, not "parents"—haven't fully acknowledged adolescent sex or accepted teens' need for condoms. The only problem was that the values of Plain Talk were deeply abhorrent to several of the communities (often immigrant) that Casey targeted. Incredibly, Casey regarded this divergence as a "barrier" to, rather than a source of, diversity. The evaluation report, prepared by Public/Private Ventures, a youth advocacy organization, refers with obvious disgust to the "deep-rooted preference for abstinence and the desire to sugarcoat the Plain Talk message that resurfaced repeatedly. . . . Stated simply," the report sighs, "the less assimilated, more traditional Latino and Southeast Asian cultures regard premarital sex among teenagers as unacceptable. They tend to deny that it occurs in their community and do not feel it is appropriate to discuss sex openly with their children." Foundation-approved diversity is only skin-deep: Asians and Hispanics qualify only if they toe the ideological line.

Project leaders were determined to stamp out all public expressions of dissent. When members of one collaborative were heard making "judgmental" statements about teen sexuality—in other words, that teens should not have sex—Casey recommended a "values-clarification workshop" with the Orwellian goal of teaching members how to "respect their differences." Likewise, when a young male member of the San Diego collaborative brought a homemade banner for a local parade that read "Plain Talk: Say No to Sex," the project manager promptly initiated a two-hour "team discussion" that eventually pressured the boy to accept a new banner: "Plain Talk: Say No to AIDS." Chastity isn't part of the agenda.

In the struggle between a massive colonizing force and small communities valiantly trying to hold on to their beliefs, there was never any question which side would triumph. Casey had millions of dollars; the communities just had their convictions. The evaluation states unapologetically that the "struggle" to force residents to accept Plain Talk goals was "long and sometimes painful." But eventually, says the report, people came to "recognize that while their personal beliefs are valid and acceptable, they must be put aside for the sake of protecting youth."

Plain Talk's moral imperialism might be easier to swallow were there any evidence that increasing condom availability and legitimating teen sex reduced teen pregnancy. But as such evidence does not exist, Casey's condescension toward immigrants' "deeply-rooted ways of thinking" about teen sexuality, ways that for centuries kept illegitimacy at low levels, leaves a particularly bad taste.

For all its self-congratulation for having involved residents in planning "social change . . . appropriate to the conditions in their particular communities," as the evaluation puts it, Plain Talk gives the lie to the central myth of all such community initiatives: that they represent a grassroots movement. The San Diego collaborative was led by a woman the evaluation report calls an "experienced sexuality educator with a special interest in AIDS awareness and prevention, . . . respected within the influential circle of community activists and agency representatives." The foundation couldn't have come up with an occupation more repugnant to the local churchgoing, Latino residents. But the "community leaders" favored by foundations do not represent the community; they represent the activists.

Yet for all its bold embrace of teen sexuality, Plain Talk was curiously unable to act on its own premises. At a Plain Talk retreat in

Atlanta, rumors flew of a "sexual encounter" among teens who apparently had absorbed the Plain Talk message far too well. But rather than asking non-judgmentally, "Did you use condoms?" or offering to provide condoms for the next orgy, the adults tried to squelch the rumors, realizing they would be fatal for the reputation of the initiative. They also attempted to establish a curfew for the next retreat, igniting weeks of battle from the teens. Adolescent "empowerment," once out of the bottle, is hard to put back in.

The collaborative movement suffers from another shortcoming: a foundation planning a collaborative doesn't have the slightest idea what exactly the collaborative is supposed to do or what its source of authority will be. Take Casey's inaugural project in social change, called New Futures. The astounding theory behind the initiative, echoing Ford's Gray Areas program, was that the greatest problem facing inner-city children is the discrete nature of government services such as education and health care. Not until all social programs are integrated can we expect children to stay in school, learn, and not have babies, reasoned the foundation. Accordingly, Casey gave five cities an average of $10 million each over five years to form a collaborative consisting of leaders from business, social service agencies, schools, and the community to lead the way toward "comprehensive," integrated services for junior high students.

No one, not even the foundation officers who cooked up the idea, knew what such services would look like. Casey's mysterious pronouncements, such as a suggestion to "integrat[e] pregnancy prevention, education, and employment strategies," left the local groups as befuddled as before. The "area of greatest difficulty," concludes the New Futures evaluation report in particularly opaque foundationese, "appeared to be translating crossagency discourse into tangible operational reform that would improve the status of youth"—in other words, the project was meaningless. A Ford project for comprehensive collaborative development ran into the same difficulty of making sense of its mission. "The notion of 'integrated, comprehensive development' is a conceptual construct not easily translated into active terms," states the first-year evaluation poignantly. "Participants have struggled with what, exactly, is meant by the term." If foundation officers thought in concrete realities, not in slogans, they'd have no trouble recognizing the silliness of the idea that "categorical services" are holding children back, when for centuries schools have concentrated solely on education, hospitals solely on health care, and employers solely on business, without untoward results for the young.

Little wonder that New Futures made things worse, not better. The project's "case managers," who were supposed to coordinate existing services for individual children, yanked their young "clients" out of class for a twenty-minute chat every week or so, sending the clear message that the classroom was not important. Students in the program ended up with lower reading and writing scores, higher dropout and pregnancy rates, and no better employment or college prospects than their peers.

The third significant area of funding, public interest litigation and advocacy, embodies the foundations' longstanding goal of producing "social change" by controlling government policy. Foundations bankroll public interest law groups that seek to establish in court rights that democratically elected legislatures have rejected. Foundations thus help sustain judicial activism by supporting one side of the symbiotic relationship between activist judges and social-change-seeking lawyers.

Foundations have used litigation to create and expand the iron trap of bilingual education; they have funded the perversion of the Voting Rights Act into a costly instrument of apartheid; and they lie behind the transformation of due-process rights into an impediment to, rather than a guarantor of, justice. Foundation support for such socially disruptive litigation makes a mockery of the statutory prohibition on lobbying, since foundations can effect policy changes in the courts, under the officially approved banner of "public interest litigation," that are every bit as dramatic as those that could be achieved in the legislature.

These days, however, foundation-supported lawyers defend the status quo as often as they seek to change it; after all, foundations helped create that status quo. Foundation money is beating back efforts to reform welfare, through such Washington-based think tanks as the Center for Law and Social Policy and the Center on Budget and Policy Priorities, whose director won a MacArthur "genius" award in 1996. The Ford Foundation, the Public Welfare Foundation, the Norman Foundation, and others support the Center for Social Welfare Policy and Law in New York City, a law firm that represented the National Welfare Rights Organization during the 1960s and 1970s, when that organization was conducting its phenomenally successful campaign to legitimate welfare and encourage its spread. Today, the center is using Ford money to sue New York City over its long overdue welfare anti-fraud program. The suit apocalyptically accuses the city of depriving needy people of the "sole means available to them to obtain food, clothing, housing and medical assistance," as if welfare were the world's only conceivable means of support.

Liberal foundations are straining to block popular efforts to change the country's discriminatory racial quota system. The Rockefeller Foundation and scores of other like-minded foundations are pumping millions into the National Affirmative Action Consortium, a potpourri of left-wing advocacy groups including the NAACP Legal Defense and Educational Fund, the Mexican-American Legal Defense and Educational Fund, the National Women's Law Center, and the Women's Legal Defense Fund. The consortium will undertake a "public education campaign" to defeat the California Civil Rights Initiative, the groundbreaking ballot measure that would allow ordinary people for the first time in history to vote on affirmative action. If passed, the measure would return California to the color-blind status intended by the federal Civil Rights Act of 1964.

The Edna McConnell Clark Foundation is among the staunchest foundation supporters of litigation and advocacy. David Hall McConnell, Edna's father, was a traveling book salesman who enticed customers with a free bottle of homemade perfume. When the perfume proved more popular than the books, the entrepreneurial McConnell started a perfume company in 1886 that became the world's largest cosmetic manufacturer, Avon. For its first twenty years, the Edna McConnell Clark Foundation supported such institutions as Lincoln Center, Smith College and Cornell University (to which it donated science buildings), the Columbia-Presbyterian Hospital, and the Woods Hole Oceanographic Institute. But in the 1970s the foundation, herded by its new professional managers, joined the stampede into activism.

No other foundation has had as dramatic an impact in shaping the debate over crime and punishment. Says Frank Hartman, executive director of the Kennedy School of Government: "I don't know what the conversation would be like in [Clark's] absence." The foundation has bankrolled the wave of prisoners' rights suits that have clogged the courts. But more important, Clark has tirelessly sponsored the specious notion that the U.S. incarcerates too many harmless criminals. In 1991 the Clark-supported Sentencing Project published a comparative study criticizing high U.S. incarceration rates, which sociologist Charles Logan likens to an "undergraduate term paper—one that was badly done." Nevertheless, the study was on page one of newspapers across the country, fueling editorials and congressional speeches about America's misguided prison policies. As Logan remarks, "Foundations are propaganda machines; that is the basis of their success."

The foundation also promotes the theme that American justice is profoundly racist. It supports the Equal Justice Institute in Alabama, which sues on behalf of prisoners claiming victimization by race. The Clark-funded Sentencing Project promotes the proposed federal Racial Justice Act, which would impose racial ceilings on sentencing. By injecting race into the debate over crime, McConnell Clark is doing a great public disservice. In an era of jury nullification on the basis of racial sympathy, white racism hardly seems the criminal justice system's major problem. Moreover, the first thing you will hear in any inner-city neighborhood is "Get the dealers off the streets," not "The penalties for dealing crack are discriminatory."

The McConnell Clark Foundation has one spectacular success to show for its effort to change government policies: it has helped make New York City's homeless policies the most irrational in the nation. The foundation has been the most generous funder of the Legal Aid Society's Homeless Family Rights Project, which has been suing the city for over a decade to require immediate housing of families claiming homelessness in a private apartment with cooking facilities.

Should the city fail to place every family that shows up at its doorstep within twenty-four hours (a requirement without parallel in any other city in the U.S.), Legal Aid sues for contempt, penalties, and—of course—legal fees, on top of the $200,000 McConnell Clark gives it each year.

The Clark-bankrolled project has found an eager partner in the presiding judge, Helen Freedman, who has hit the city with over $6 million in fines. She has ordered the city to pay every allegedly homeless family that has to stay more than twenty-four hours in a city intake office between $150 and $250 a night—an extraordinary windfall. James Capoziello, former deputy general counsel in the city's Human Resources Administration, calls the litigation "one of the most asinine instances of judicial misconduct and misuses of the judiciary" he has ever seen. Says one homeless provider in the city: "It is a crime to spend scarce resources for having to sleep on the floor. With $1 million in fines you could run a fifty-unit facility for a year."

There is considerable irony to Clark's support for homelessness litigation, since it helped create the problem. According to Waldemar Nielsen, Clark funded one of the lawsuits that led to the deinstitutionalization of the mentally ill, a primary cause of homelessness today. Moreover, Clark bankrolls an array of advocacy groups responsible in large part for New York's tight housing market—groups like New York State Tenant and Neighborhood Information Services, the most powerful advocate for rent regulation in the state. Thanks to such groups, New York is the only city in the country to have maintained rent control continuously since the end of World War II, leading to one of the lowest rates of new housing construction and highest rates of abandonment in the nation.

McConnell Clark also supports organizations that campaign against the city's effort to sell its huge portfolio of tax-defaulted housing, which it operates at an enormous loss. Jay Small, director of one such organization, the Association of Neighborhood Housing Developers, believes that once the city takes title to housing, the property should never revert to private ownership but should become "socially owned." Years after the Soviet collapse, the notion that the city should become a bastion of socialized housing is hardly forward-looking.

For some of the groups McConnell Clark supports, housing is just the opening wedge to a broader transformation of society. "Ultimately, the solution to the housing crisis is to change property relations," argues Small. He explains that he is using "a code word for socialism." Rima McCoy, co-director of the Clark-funded Action for Community Empowerment, also takes an expansive view of social relations. She was asked in 1995 whether housing was a right. The question astounded her: "That anyone could even ask that kind of question—do people have an inalienable right to housing?—is just a product of our current climate," she replied, "which would have the middle class believe that the poor are the source of the current problems in the U.S."

Of course, even within the large liberal foundations, even within so seemingly monolithic a place as the Ford Foundation, there have always been pockets of sanity, where a commonsense approach to helping people and promoting stable communities has reigned. And there are some signs of more recent countercurrents to the prevailing "progressive" ethic—the Ford and Casey foundations, for example, both trumpet their fatherhood initiatives. Yet the impulse toward the activism that over the past thirty years has led the great liberal foundations to do much more harm than good remains overwhelming. In a pathetic statement of aimlessness, the president of a once great foundation recently called up a former Ford poverty fighter to ask plaintively where all the social movements had gone.

The mega-foundations should repress their yearning for activism once and for all. The glories of early twentieth-century philanthropy were produced by working within accepted notions of social improvement, not against them. Building libraries was not a radical act; it envisioned no transformation of property relations or redistribution of power. Andrew Carnegie merely sought to make available to a wider audience the same values and intellectual resources that had allowed him to succeed. Yes, the world has changed since Carnegie's time, but the recipe for successful philanthropy has not.

[1996]

Behind the Hundred
Neediest Cases

ON DECEMBER 15, 1912, the *New York Times* ran a highly unorthodox headline: SANTA CLAUS PLEASE TAKE NOTICE! HERE ARE NEW YORK'S
100 NEEDIEST CASES. The equally unorthodox story began: "Fathoms
deep beneath the exhilaration and joyousness of Christmas there is a
world of desolation and hunger which few of the dwellers in light and
air have had time or chance to realize; the world of famine in the
midst of plenty, of cruel heart and body hunger with bounty in sight,
but not in reach." There followed one hundred short case histories of
what the *Times* called the "uttermost dregs of the city's poor," culled
from the files of the city's three largest charity organizations.

The response was immediate: food, blankets, toys, and clothing
poured into the *Times's* offices, along with offers of adoption, employment, and medical care. The "Hundred Neediest Cases" appeal
became an instant Christmas tradition, growing exponentially from its
first $3,630.88 to reach nearly $5 million annually today.

Behind this growth lies a profound change, however. The prototypical needy case in the first decades of the appeal was a struggling
widow or plucky orphan; today's is more likely to be a single mother
of five who finds her welfare check inadequate. This change reflects
one of the century's most momentous cultural developments: the
transformation of elite opinion regarding poverty and need. The elite
once held the poor to the same standards of behavior that it set for it-

self: moral character determined the strength of a person's claim for assistance. Those who worked and struggled and yet were overwhelmed by adversity deserved help; the idle and dissolute did not. Over time, though, elite opinion came to see the cause of poverty not in individual character and behavior but in vast, impersonal social and economic forces that supposedly determined individual fate. In response, need became the sole criterion for aid, with moral character all but irrelevant. The Neediest Cases appeal concludes this century an agnostic regarding individual responsibility and a strident advocate of the welfare state. The story of how it got there traces the rise of moral relativism among opinion and policy makers, the triumph of the entitlement ethos, and the transformation of the *New York Times* itself into a proponent of victimology and double standards.

At the heart of the first Neediest Cases appeals lay a crucial moral distinction between the deserving and the undeserving poor. *Times* publisher Adolph Ochs started the appeal to channel the charitable impulse of the Christmas season toward the truly needy, as certified by the charity organizations that distributed the donations. Those who tried to make a career out of poverty or refused to help themselves would not get aid. Unapologetic about its moral approach, the *Times* opened its 1913 appeal with this admonition: "Because the Christmas spirit is strong within you, do not give to the professional beggars on the streets, unworthy, all of them, and often criminals." Such "indiscriminate giving" only encouraged pauperism. The *Times* proposed to educate readers into a deeper understanding of poverty.

The distinction between the deserving and undeserving poor was particularly relevant to early twentieth-century New York. It was a world where upright individuals could work extraordinarily hard—as factory hands, seamstresses, and laundresses—and still be poor. Misfortune was everywhere. Tuberculosis and other diseases crippled or killed entire families. Mental illness sent children and adults alike to "institutions." Most important, no government safety net existed; private charity was the sole external resource available to the poor.

The first case histories reflected these hard realities, with tuberculosis, in particular, a leitmotif. What is most striking about the articles is their moral fervor, often shading into sentimentality. They made strong emotional appeals, emphasizing family values and individual courage. A case headlined YOUNG WIFE'S CHEERLESS FUTURE from 1913 is typical in accentuating the pathos of its subject: "In a large department store a pale, toil-worn woman stands all day behind the glove counter. Despite her cheerless life and an apparently hopeless future, she is always courteous to customers, patient and obliging. Her husband is in a hospital, an advanced case of tuberculosis. There are three delicate children at school." The young wife is on the verge of a physical collapse, her wages insufficient to pay the rent and provide food. The article asks for assistance until thirteen-year-old Katherine, the oldest of the children, is "ready to help."

Case 92 from 1912 struck another familiar theme—the orphan "little mother": "A girl of 19 is being father and mother both to a cluster of little brothers and sisters, six in number, and her next youngest brother, now 16, is helping her as much as he can. She spends her days in a shop and her nights at home as a cook, dressmaker, and nurse to her little family." Such stories were lessons in the virtues of perseverance and responsibility.

Widows also dominated the first decades of the appeal, their plight described with unabashed emotionalism. A twenty-year-old widow from 1912, for example, too frail from childbirth to support herself, is "resisting with all her might and main the impulse to send her child to an institution because it is the one beautiful and wonderful thing left to her of her starved and chilled romance." This emphasis on the innocence and worthiness of the charity recipients prevailed for the next four decades.

Throughout the twenties the *Times* held firmly to its moralized view of poverty and asserted the rectitude and purity of its beneficiaries, even when, as sometimes happened, a Hogarthian world of social squalor peeped out from behind them. A 1921 case headlined GOT MEALS FROM ASHCANS described two "ragged, unwashed" sisters, seven and five years old, who fed themselves from garbage cans. Abandoned by their parents, they were passed around among relatives living "in crowded shant[ies]" who didn't want them: "At first the relatives put them on the floor at night and let them cry themselves to sleep. Later they put them along the wall on chairs which served as beds for more important members of the household. When sound asleep, Doris and Fanny would be lifted out and placed on the floor, to make the chair beds available for the real owners. They are undernourished and suffering from severe skin troubles due to the ashcan diet. . . ." Yet the story concluded: The "good stuff in [the sisters] is indestructible. They are still two sweet, good-tempered, bright little girls."

Some social problems remained taboo for decades. A case from 1921 stands out for its rarity, as well as for its discreet circumlocutions about illegitimacy: "Mildred, very young and inexperienced, left the city telling her family and friends that she had work in another city. Several months later she returned, explaining that it had been unsatisfactory. She now has a position which barely enables her to support herself. Leaving her parents, she goes out alone, on one excuse or another, as frequently as she can, and visits a place were she sees Shirley, a tiny, blue-eyed baby. Mildred's earnings are so small that she can only partially pay for the child's board. She is greatly worried over money, and feels her position keenly. So far she has concealed everything from her family and her friends, but she has almost made up her mind to take Shirley home with her and let people think what they will. She wants to do what is right, but the situation is extremely perplexing." Nineteen twenty-one being a different era, Mildred's case elicited a marriage proposal from a sympathetic reader.

In 1921 an illegitimate birth was a crisis. For decades thereafter, a reference to a broken promise of marriage accompanied any mention of illegitimacy in the pages of the appeal. The illegitimate children were always sent to a foster home, on the assumption that an unmarried mother was an inappropriate parent.

In its early years the Hundred Neediest Cases exerted an enormous pull on New Yorkers' imaginations, even finding its way into novels of the time. The appeal was highly individualized: contributors could earmark their donations for a specific case, and each case listed a specific amount needed—at most, several hundred dollars. Donors therefore had a sense of making an immediate difference in individual lives.

The stock market crash of 1929 passed without mention in the Neediest Cases appeal, but the Great Depression most definitely did not. The appeal's response to the depression is a telling moment in its early history. On the eve of the welfare state's birth, the fund stressed its own voluntary nature: "The fate of these hundred cases rests entirely with the conscience of the reader. There is no compulsion to give." Rather than using the depression as a lever for its fund-raising, the charity drive sharply distinguished its purpose from that of the public welfare programs just then being launched. The Neediest Cases, the *Times* said in 1933, were "victims not of economic storms but of life itself," having "been stricken with still greater misfortune [than unemployment]." The paper worried that the "ill, the helpless, the deserted ones" would be overlooked in the nation's massive response to joblessness.

And indeed, the cases from the thirties were no different from those of the preceding two decades. As ever, the paper stressed the moral qualities of the recipients. A case from 1933 crystallized the genre: "No combination of troubles, it seems, can quench the spirit of Selina G. At 71 she is sick in a hospital ward. After a lifetime of struggle, she thinks up 'last lines' to speak to the welfare visitor: 'Good-bye. I'll see you next week. That is if I don't elope.' . . . A half century ago, while she was still a young bride, Selina had to support her husband, whose lungs had become affected by his work in a tannery. She did this for the twenty years he lived, a confirmed invalid. She kept on supporting herself by domestic service until stomach ulcers forced her to stop two years ago. . . . Then she was taken to the hospital, a very sick old woman and a little frightened, though she tried to hide that with her badinage."

As public relief programs grew in scope, however, the fund had to confront its relationship to them. "It will be asked, quite understandably, why private charity should be necessary in these days when the government is providing relief on so vast a scale," acknowledged the *Times* in 1937. The answer to this question, posed almost yearly over the next two decades, was in constant flux. Sometimes the *Times* would explain that the fund attended to matters of the spirit while public relief tended to material needs; other times, that the fund helped those who did not qualify for public assistance; and at yet others, that the fund provided specialized services (such as rehabilitation and medicine) unavailable publicly. But no matter how the *Times* defined the fund's role vis-à-vis welfare, up through the sixties it always presented public relief as an act of remarkable generosity on the part of the public, not as an entitlement.

If the appeal's sunny disposition toward public relief appears refreshingly innocent today, that is because welfare did not represent the same constellation of problems as it does now. "We didn't worry about long-term dependency back then," recalls Arthur Gelb, a former *Times* managing editor, who wrote the Neediest Cases profiles in 1944 and 1945. Today Gelb oversees the appeal as president of the New York Times Company Foundation. The forties were a more innocent world, he says: "The stigma of going on relief was so great that it was inconceivable to stay on. People kept their heads high." Even the movies reinforced the ideal of independence, Gelb recalls: "All the heroes had an idea: get out of poverty, get a job, because you have to earn a living on your own." The appeal itself constantly lauded the work ethic.

In December 1942 the *Times*'s front page rang with news of battles between the Allies and the Axis powers in Tunisia and Burma. Locally, juvenile delinquency in New York City schools was rising, a fact attributed to the war. Opening the 1942 drive, the *Times* posed its regular question: "'Is it possible,' you may ask, 'that in these days of public relief and war employment there are still those who need my aid?'" Its answer this time—and from then on—stressed the fund's newest priorities: counseling and therapy. "Psychological problems," the paper said, "are often more pressing than physical ones." For the first time, in 1942 the *Times* included the cost of counseling in the amount requested for each case.

The rise in juvenile delinquency certainly confirmed a growing spiritual malaise. But in contrast to older models of social work, which had stressed the moral reformation of the poor, the Hundred Neediest Cases increasingly incorporated trendy psychoanalytic explanations for, and responses to, social problems. Lack of "self-fulfillment" was starting to take its place among recognized personal ills. A 1942 case was headlined BEGINNING TO FIND HERSELF; another case described an aspiring artist burdened with a guardian aunt, wholly unsympathetic to her artistic hopes, who believed that the girl's proper place was at the lingerie counter of a department store.

A few cases began to anticipate, faintly, today's pervasive social dislocations. One described a baby found bruised, with a swollen forehead. The mother, picked up roaming the streets, claimed that the child had injured herself. The unemployed father had "irresponsibly" deserted the family, said the *Times*. But both society's and the *Times*'s response to such problems remained firmly moral, rooted in notions of individual responsibility. The mother was committed to an asylum, the child put up for adoption—both actions based on recognition of the mother's unfitness. In those days the *Times* did not shrink from labeling parents irresponsible or incompetent.

The postwar years saw the triumph of the psychoanalytic model. Contemporary thinking about family relations found its way into the drive, particularly the newly fashionable problem of "overly strict" child rearing, which reflected the emerging elite condemnation of traditional families. The case histories presented illegitimacy and juvenile delinquency as products of repressive childhoods, and social workers taught parents to give their straying children more freedom as an antidote to "rebellion."

Other family dramas unfolded in the Neediest Cases: a mother in 1949 was "terrified of becoming the kind of mother [her] mother was"; a periodically abandoned wife and mother was counseled to gain a "more objective view of her marriage" with an eye toward divorce. Social ties were starting to loosen—divorce was growing more prevalent, children more unmanageable. In one 1949 case a twenty-one-year-old woman, who "never felt she had a real home" because her parents had divorced, had an illegitimate son after her lover broke his marriage promise. Six years later the son had become a troublemaker and petty thief. According to the *Times*, a "psychiatric examination showed that his problems stemmed largely from a need for more attention from his mother." On the advice of the Brooklyn Bureau of Social Service, the mother quit her job and went on public assistance so as to give her son the "companionship he craves."

Such wrongheaded intervention in the lives of troubled families would go on to have a long history in the Neediest Cases. To take one example from our own day, a story in early 1996 headlined THERAPY HELPS A PROTECTIVE MOTHER COPE told an unintentionally heartbreaking tale of traditional values destroyed by liberal elites. A Guyanese single mother was allegedly causing "stress" in her son with her "rigid rules" against jeans and sneakers—rules more appropriate, the *Times* noted with alarm, for a British private school. Then the mother started having her own "stress" and discovered, through therapy, that she had repressed her memories of childhood sexual abuse— the Holy Grail of counseling. Now, presumably freed from the demons that had erupted in so cruel a dress code for her son, the mother has loosened her restrictions on him. The counseling—by an older but no wiser Brooklyn Bureau of Community Service, now renamed—succeeded: he now sports an earring and baggy pants, the *Times* reported proudly.

As if in recognition of the changing emphasis of the fund, the *Times* in 1949 stopped listing the amount needed for each case, explaining that a dollar amount could not be put on the "psychological help" that the charitable agencies now provided. The earlier notion that a reader could provide the entire amount needed to help a specific individual get through a specific crisis gave way to the idea of more generalized, permanent assistance for ongoing social ills.

The year 1949 marked one more milestone for the appeal. The *Times* cast aside its long-standing convention of distinguishing the "deserving" from the "undeserving" poor: "What a bleak world it would be if we helped only those who were thoroughly blameless! A good many of us make our own bad luck, and we suppose that some of the people represented in the Neediest Cases would not be in trouble now if they had managed their lives differently. It may even be appropriate once in a while, when help is asked, to recall Lord Chester-field's words: 'Do not refuse your charity even to those who have no merit but their misery.'"

One can only guess why the *Times* acknowledged the self-made bad luck of some of the Neediest Cases. Most likely the changing nature of the caseload simply forced itself upon the paper's attention. While the classic pure victims—widows and orphans—still generously leavened the appeal, they were matched by more troubling cases of family disintegration and irresponsibility—relatively innocuous compared with the raging social pathologies that would show up two decades later, but nevertheless noticeably different from the uplifting stories of triumph over adversity that dominated the first appeals.

Nineteen fifty-six was a year of extraordinary prosperity at home and increasing tension abroad. Cold-war consciousness infused even the appeal itself. The "health of a democratic society like ours" depends on voluntary assistance, wrote the city and state welfare directors in their statement on private philanthropy, a feature of the appeal since the Great Depression.

That same issue of the *Times* also contained a full-page ad for Elvis Presley's "latest and greatest" album, signaling the explosive arrival of the youth culture that peacetime prosperity had spawned. The 1956 Neediest Cases Fund documented the underside of that culture with an unprecedented amount of juvenile delinquency and gang activity. Children were growing disturbed and unmanageable.

By the sixties, all hell had broken loose. Truancy, delinquency, failure at school, illegitimacy, and parental abandonment pervaded the cases. The first case in 1965, headlined WAITING, described two children, two and three years old, who had been deserted by their mother in front of a candy store. "My mummy said to wait here," the three-year-old explained. In another case an eleven-year-old with a shiftless, rowdy father was described as fitting the "familiar pattern of the pre-delinquent." A father was arrested for molesting a neighbor's child. Several of the cases had attempted suicide, some in their teens.

The prosperity of the 1950s reached still greater heights in the 1960s, yet suddenly everybody seemed to be talking about poverty. In

1962, Michael Harrington published *The Other America*, which set the stage for the federal War on Poverty by arguing that America had ignored millions of poor people who had been victimized by the same forces that were making most Americans prosper. New York mayor John Lindsay launched his own local war on poverty when he came into office in 1965. It included a demand, announced on the first day of the 1965 Neediest Cases appeal, for federal job-training money for women who were "family heads"—signaling the start of a fateful campaign to normalize and destigmatize the unmarried welfare-dependent mother.

In the midst of this ferment over poverty, the Neediest Cases Fund made a startling, if only implicit, acknowledgment: welfare dependency had become a problem. In their annual statement on behalf of the appeal, the state and city welfare commissioners argued that "the rehabilitation of dependent people requires the skilled help of the voluntary agency staffs, the pioneers in this field." Suddenly, the fund's purpose was no longer to assist the helpless but to wean the dependent off government aid—a monumental shift, which passed without further mention. Its implications, though, were huge: rather than eliminating poverty, the massive public effort to end it had worsened it, at least among younger, able-bodied people.

For all the social disintegration that was showing up in the appeal, one taboo remained—against the normalization of illegitimacy. As in past years, when women profiled in the appeal had an illegitimate child, the assumed next step was putting the child up for adoption. In one 1965 case, for example, a social worker was said to be helping an unwed nineteen-year-old mother "face up to the decision she must make" to relinquish her baby. But this long-standing social consensus was under attack. Already 90 percent of the 311,000 children in the city receiving public assistance were without a male parent in the household.

By 1969 the Hundred Neediest Cases Fund had hit the rock bottom of social squalor. The appeal itself recognized that the era was one of "growing social disorganization." Welfare was spiraling out of control both in the city and nationwide, thanks to the welfare-rights movement. New York's rolls were rising at a monthly rate of seventeen thousand—triple what Mayor Lindsay's budget had forecast. Crime, too, was out of control; the National Commission on the Causes and Prevention of Violence called American cities a "mixture of fortresses and places of terror."

The *Times*'s fund put faces on these troubling trends. In one case a drug-addicted mother had disappeared two years previously, the father was bringing women home and locking out his two teenage children overnight, the daughter was pregnant by an older man, and the mother, recently released from jail and back in touch, wanted the son to come live with her. In another case the ten-year-old daughter of a heroin-addicted father and a paroled drug-dealer mother said she remembered strange teenagers shooting up in her kitchen. An out-of-wedlock son of a nineteen-year-old mother, who was herself illegitimate and had lived "on the streets" since she was fifteen, languished in a foster home, hostage to the mother's refusal to give him up for adoption. Truancy and delinquency were rampant, and more and more of the profiled teen mothers were keeping their children and going on public assistance. The underclass had taken over the fund in a big way.

As the social and moral disintegration mounted, the *Times* made a profound change in its editorial line on the Neediest Cases Fund. Gone were the holiday paeans to the generosity of ordinary citizens; gone, too, was the paper's honesty about self-induced misfortune. Instead, this was the moment that the *Times* turned sour and became an apologist for the welfare state. The editorial opening the 1969 campaign began: "The fifty-eighth annual appeal for New York's Hundred Neediest Cases arrives at a moment in this country, state and city when there is some confusion about the poor among us and what they desire. Much of this talk has been ill-informed and theoretical, taking the harsh line that penury and despair are self-induced and that financial aid is going to the lazy and undeserving." The *Times* insisted that the appeal represented people "trapped in prisons of circumstance."

This one editorial contained in miniature the agenda for the cultural elite for the next two decades: first, to deny that welfare had become a trap and that conditions in the inner city reflected a moral, as much as an economic, decline; second, to disparage as greedy, unfeeling, and possibly even racist those who questioned the welfare status quo; and third, to insist that individuals acted not of their own free will but because of environmental conditions beyond their control.

The modern era of the Neediest Cases had begun. From now on, the appeal would evolve into an increasingly strident and political platform for welfare advocacy. The moral certainties of the first decades of the appeal dissolved into a dogmatic "open-mindedness" about the various "life-style choices" that resulted in apparent need.

The format of the Hundred Neediest Cases appeal changed radically after 1972. That was the last year the *Times* printed profiles of all the cases simultaneously. It was also the last year the appeal was called the "Hundred Neediest Cases"; thereafter it became just the "Neediest Cases" and presented only one or two profiles at a time sporadically over many weeks. The *Times* never acknowledged or explained the change, but the nature of the few cases presented in 1972 may suggest a reason. Just one conveys the unprecedented degradation that now confronted *Times* readers: "Jennie" was a pregnant seventeen-year-old who had been raped by one of her mother's live-in "men friends." One brother was in jail for pushing heroin; the other two used drugs; she herself started using at age thirteen. Drugs had probably already affected her unborn child. She had attempted suicide. Catholic Charities was going to help her apply for public assistance so that "she will be free of her family and not have to depend on her friends." No mention was made of adoption: social service agencies by then embraced the view that single mothers should get public support to raise their illegitimate children.

Such social pathologies certainly were a challenge to the charitable impulse. For many years thereafter, instead of spotlighting the recipients, the appeal ran stories primarily on the agencies that distributed Neediest Cases money. One such profile, describing how the Community Service Society worked to divert youth in the South Bronx from the "delinquent-labeling process of the juvenile courts," seemed oblivious to the fact that some *Times* readers would deem the label "juvenile delinquent" perfectly appropriate for a teen criminal and wouldn't appreciate efforts to return such thugs to the streets.

A new Neediest Cases genre sprang up in the early seventies: bellyaching by the agencies about government cuts. Gone were the days of gratitude for public welfare; now the appeal regularly berated the public and the government for stinginess in supporting the poor. In 1973, as the front page followed the course of the Arab oil embargo, the appeal quoted Marina S. Heiskell, chair of the Community Service Society of New York, as saying: "We have witnessed an unbelievable trend of government cutbacks in health and welfare programs. The age-old public hostility toward the poor has not decreased, and alienation among groups—young and old, black and white, rich and poor—have [sic] even grown. At a time when there is more and more for us to do, we are faced with less and less to do it with."

Editorially the paper echoed the agencies' complaints: "Government funds, which were never plentiful," it moaned, "are dwindling." Just three years previously, the state and city welfare directors had noted with satisfaction government's "unprecedented" commitment, "in effort and in funds, to the alleviation of . . . mass deprivation." It was now taboo to mention that by any historical measure, welfare spending was extraordinarily high.

In 1975, the depth of New York City's financial crisis, the agencies reiterated their complaints against government budget cuts. Welfare benefits were too low, complained a director of the Community Service Society (though, of course, high welfare benefits were one cause of the city's budget crisis); the vice president of the Federation of Protestant Welfare Agencies, Joyce P. Austin, charged that the public was blind to the effect of the budget cuts. By now the appeal had become as much a mechanism for trying to boost public funding of the social service agencies as for inspiring private giving.

By 1981 the blame-the-government theme of the appeal had become explicitly political. Joyce Austin singled out President Reagan for "sweeping" and "unprecedented" cuts in food stamps, welfare, subsidized housing, and job-training services, she said, that "support the very essentials of life," as if government services, not individual initiative, support life.

During the seventies and early eighties, the *Times* generally refrained from such blame-the-government tirades. No more. The 1996 appeal opened editorially with as sensational a statement of the theme as the most radical agency directors might make: "The children, the sick, the elderly and the poor, who make up the most defenseless elements of New York City's population," the paper charged, "have suffered brutal blows from cutbacks in government services in recent years. The signs of trouble are as visible as the homeless in the streets, the abandoned buildings and the abused children in the headlines." The imagery equated welfare cutbacks with physical assault, and indeed the editorial went on to blame fatal child abuse on inadequate government welfare spending. Wholly absent was any sense of individual responsibility for creating or solving social problems.

The fund's spokesmen and recipients blame the public as well as the government for creating or contributing to poverty—despite unprecedented spending on the poor and the unprecedented openness of today's economy and society. On the fund's seventy-fifth anniversary in 1986, Thomas DiStefano, head of the Catholic Charities of Brooklyn, declared that the problems facing the poor have not changed over the years: "Many people are still burdened by poverty, discrimination, and injustice," he said—in other words, society's supposed racism and lack of justice are responsible for individual need. The then-president of the fund from the *Times*, Fred Hechinger, called "the plight of the homeless . . . a mark of public shame," his assumption being that public hard-heartedness is to blame, not advocate-driven policies that keep disturbed people from getting needed medical care.

In the new Alice-in-Wonderland world of the Neediest Cases appeal, charity heads, echoed by the *Times*, belittle the efficacy of the private charity they are soliciting. "It's naive and disingenuous for anyone to say that private charities can fill the gap [of congressional welfare cuts]," sniffed Megan E. McLaughlin, head of the Federation of Protestant Welfare Agencies, in 1995. Such talk suggests how little private charity seems to matter to these private agencies, which have come to rely more and more on government funding and to view themselves as handmaidens of the welfare state. Adolph Ochs, the founder of the Neediest Cases Fund, would have found this contempt for private initiatives astounding. Upon buying the *Times* in 1896, Ochs declared his philosophy: the paper would be devoted to sound money, low taxes, and "no more government than is absolutely necessary to protect society, maintain individual and vested rights, and assure the free exercise of a sound conscience."

Not only do the Neediest Cases charities value government welfare spending more than private donations, but much of their current charitable work, as profiled in the appeal, consists of signing up people for government assistance or fighting to restore benefits. Donors to the fund, therefore, pay twice: first, their donation is used to *obtain* welfare; then their taxes are used to *pay* welfare. A 1995 profile of the Community Service Society, for example, described a fifty-three-year-old Vietnam veteran who had lost his welfare benefits for failure to comply with the finger-imaging requirement. The veteran claimed he hadn't been informed of the requirement—a universal explanation among welfare recipients whenever they are penalized. The Community Service Society represented the veteran on appeal and won his benefits back.

And who are the victims who appear in the profiles today? Drug abuse still rages through the cases—a boyfriend on crack sets fire to the house of his companion, an unwed mother; a girl who began using drugs at age fifteen has five children by age eighteen; a grandmother cares for the abandoned children of her addicted daughter. The *Times* has even found a place for the victims of middle-class disorders. As one especially memorable profile opened, "The anorexia began during a cruise to the Bahamas."

Though the fund still profiles elderly widows, disabled breadwinners, and handicapped children, an overwhelming number of contemporary cases stem from one simple fact: having children out of wedlock. Take away illegitimacy and much of the Neediest Cases caseload would disappear. From the out-of-wedlock births in the appeal follows a predictable string of setbacks, including welfare dependency, homelessness, drug use, and often prostitution. The convention of mentioning a thwarted intention to marry has long since withered away; today many of the appeal's illegitimate births could be immaculate conceptions, for all the mention of a father.

Today's typical case is a garden-variety welfare mother. One unwed mother of four left New York for rural Florida when her relationship with her children's father broke up. She didn't like it there ("It was like Mayberry," she explains) and returned to Harlem. After a brief stint living with a son, she declared herself homeless and got a city-subsidized apartment in the Bronx, where she lives on welfare. Though it's a tight fit in the apartment, the *Times* reassures its readers, the family is managing. This saga, in the woman's view and the *Times*'s, demonstrates true grit: "It's like you have to fight to survive. That's what makes New York New York, I guess," she announces. Presumably as proof of her strong passion for justice, the *Times* notes glowingly that she lectures subway passengers for not giving money to a panhandling couple claiming AIDS.

As this case suggests, worthiness is now quite a flexible concept for the appeal. A measure of how far we have come from the virtuous widows and orphans of Adolph Ochs's time is the case of a Puerto Rican woman who, despite admitting to $10,000 of welfare fraud, now lives in a subsidized apartment on food stamps, welfare payments, and child support. Luz Pena's story epitomizes the *Times*'s current value-free approach to need. In the first half of the century, her successful bilking of the welfare system would have placed her in Ochs's category of "professional beggars"; now, however, the fund views her as needy because the deduction of restitution from her welfare check leaves just $80. Pena is emblematic of modern social welfare theory, wherein the sole criterion for assistance is material want; playing by the rules is no longer relevant.

The *Times* considers no one's opportunities so golden that the failure to take advantage of them is condemnable. Consider a 1996 profile of a seventeen-year-old with a drinking problem. The story begins with a deliberate attempt to jolt the reader: "Jennifer M. did not drink much in the mornings, maybe a swig of vodka at home or a beer on her way to school, just enough to make a teenage alcoholic feel that she could face the day." Jennifer began drinking at age fourteen, while on scholarship at a Brooklyn prep school. "'It was more of a party thing,' she said. 'We were young. It was fun. . . . The 10th and 11th grades were a blur to me.'" Now in a rehab program, she has had several relapses—smoking marijuana with friends and nearly drinking herself into a coma at a club—but had been clean for three months at the time of the article.

Jennifer's story is indeed a sorry affair, and it is good that she is getting help. But her predicament is not a fact of nature but a product of her reprehensible behavior, made all the worse by her squandering a free prep-school education. The *Times* treats the situation as if individual will or responsibility never entered the picture. Had the paper cast the story in terms of a fall and redemption, had it acknowledged the moral challenge Jennifer faced, it would have made a more sympathetic—and certainly a more honest—case. But in the *Times's* world, all victims look alike.

Even when modern cases seem to echo the early ones, they do so in an oddly dissonant key. The "little mother"—a young girl bereft of her mother, struggling to raise her brothers and sisters—was a mainstay of the early appeal and proved particularly moving to the *Times's* readers. A similar situation in the 1996 appeal—a fourteen-year-old orphan named Kenya Eubanks, being raised by her twenty-one-year-old sister—sounds familiar until you read on: the older sister has a three-year-old illegitimate child; both girls are on public assistance. In an earlier age the assumption would be that such a household needs adult supervision: the elder sister is already struggling with Kenya's boy problems and failure to do her homework. In today's climate the social worker got them their own apartment. In such a situation the chance that Kenya will herself reach age eighteen without having had a child seems small.

The Neediest Cases Fund still accomplishes wonderful things: it rehabilitates the disabled, sends handicapped children to camp, and buys glasses for nearly blind widows. But its unwillingness to render judgment on self-destructive behavior is part of a moral climate that has done real and lasting harm to the poor. Elite opinion contributed to the creation of today's underclass and must take some responsibility for reforming it. It is not enough to change welfare programs, to let responsibilities devolve to states and localities, to emphasize work over entitlement. We must once again start to draw moral distinctions in our public discourse—to praise virtue and blame vice. In this all-important task of cultural renewal, the *Times* continues to stand squarely in the way, stubbornly clinging to the destructive views it has done so much to disseminate.

[1997]

Public Health Quackery

FROM THE TIME of the Roman Empire until well after the discovery of the tuberculosis bacterium in 1882, many of the best medical minds believed that "miasmas"—invisible vapors emitted from the earth—caused killer infections such as typhus, diphtheria, and malaria. Though the bacteriological revolution of the late nineteenth century routed that theory, a new miasma theory has lately sprung up in schools of public health, holding that racism and sexism, though as unmeasurable as the ancient miasmas, cause AIDS, cancer, drug addiction, and heart disease. Indeed, according to public health professors, living in America is acutely hazardous to women and minorities, so shot through is the United States with sickness-producing—even fatal—injustice and bigotry.

You might be inclined to dismiss such a claim as just one more silly but harmless emanation from the ever more loony academy. Trouble is, government health agencies such as the Centers for Disease Control and Prevention (CDC) and the National Institutes of Health (NIH) take the academic miasmaticians very seriously, funding their activities and busily investigating on their own the health effects of "patriarchy" and racism. Though such politicized inquiries divert money from needed health education and research, their most pernicious effect is on the concept of individual responsibility, once a cornerstone of public health efforts. Government and academic miasmaticians now argue that members of designated victim groups are incapable of controlling such destructive behavior as promiscuous unprotected sex and intravenous drug use. In other words, some of the very people who claim to be solving public health problems have embraced an ideology that can only make them worse.

The command center of the modern miasma movement is at the Harvard School of Public Health, with Associate Professor Nancy Krieger at the helm. Shown on her Web page sporting a tie and vest (a preemptive strike, no doubt, against the patriarchy), Krieger is a magnet for government money, which underwrites a flood of her articles on racism, sexism, and health. In 1996, major national newspapers reported Krieger's research, funded by the National Heart, Lung, and Blood Institute, claiming that racism causes hypertension in blacks. Never mind that her data showed no correlation between bias and blood pressure: working-class blacks who reported no biased treatment had the highest blood pressure, for example, while those who did report discrimination had the lowest. These results simply prove the existence of "internalized oppression," according to this master miasmatician. Blacks who say they are not discriminated against are in fact the most victimized of all, because they have been brainwashed into denying their oppression.

Behind all their talk of racism and sexism, Krieger and her colleagues' real prey is individual responsibility. Traditional epidemiology looks at both individual risk behaviors and the environment to determine the source and pattern of disease. But the modern miasmaticians assert that to study individual risk behaviors, such as drug use or smoking, "blames the victim"—at least when that victim is poor, female, or black. When such victims get sick, society is to blame. And so the public health revisionists are generating a remarkable body of excuses for the most avoidable and dangerous behaviors, particularly those relating to HIV/AIDS.

Typical is an article by Nancy Krieger and Sally Zierler, another prolific radical teaching at Brown's School of Public Health. Writing in the 1997 *Annual Review of Public Health*, the authors argue that "enormous public force," rather than their own bad decisions, causes minority women to get HIV. To Krieger and Zierler, HIV is like an airborne disease; if you're a woman living in a certain neighborhood, you have little choice but to become infected.

The first element of "public force" that makes women get HIV, according to Krieger and Zierler, is . . . Ronald Reagan. Reagan's military buildup and tax cuts for the rich created the conditions for the spread of HIV; the racism of "white Europeans" fanned the epidemic, for racism makes women use drugs, a high-risk behavior for HIV. "In response to daily assaults of racial prejudice and the denial of dignity," they write, "women may turn to readily available mind-altering substances for relief." Racism also causes promiscuous unprotected sex. "Seeking sanctuary from racial hatred through sexual connection as a way to enhance self-esteem . . . may offer rewards so compelling that condom use becomes less of a priority," the authors explain.

Since individual women have no control over whether they get HIV, public health officials should not seek individual behavior change. Rather, the authors demand that government assist in racial and gender "empowerment," by—among other odd new public health strategies—increasing racial pride and awareness of ancestry among blacks, monitoring the race of elected officials, and examining "sexual fulfillment" and "sexual identity" among women.

The facts on which the miasmatics base their belief system can be remarkably flimsy. Take for instance the assertion of Margaret Ensminger, a professor of health policy and management at the Johns Hopkins School of Hygiene and Public Health, that there is "not a lot of evidence to support the idea that if poor people changed their behavior, their health would get better." Her evidence to the contrary includes the *Upstairs, Downstairs* television series, in which the wealthy flee the plague, and the death rate on the *Titanic*—2 percent of first-class female passengers and 44 percent of lower-class women, she alleges. Even if such "evidence" were not partly fictional, it is irrelevant to the question of whether the behavior of today's poor helps cause their health problems.

Other academic miasmaticians try to generate more conventional proof that the American economic and social system makes people lethally sick. A study in the June *Journal of the American Medical Association* is typical. A group of public health and sociology professors at the University of Michigan, with funding from the National Institute on Aging, looked at whether smoking, drinking, sedentariness, and obesity explained the earlier mortality among the poorer and less well educated compared with the better-off. Having found that these four behaviors do not explain all the difference, the researchers seize gleefully on their desired results: "heightened levels of anger and hostility" resulting from economic inequality, along with the "stress of racism, classism, and other phenomena related to the social distribution of power and resources," are killing people. Hence, public health officials should focus not on individual risk behaviors to improve health but rather on the far more important health effects of "socioeconomic stratification." As in much miasmatic research, the leap from data to conclusion is premature. The Michigan researchers leave unexamined a host of relevant risk factors, including drug use, sharing unclean needles, promiscuity, violence, diet, taking medication reliably, seeking medical care when needed, and genetic predisposition to disease.

In fact, the evidence for the paramount role of individual behavior in health is overwhelming. A CDC study from 1977, before the onset of modern miasmatism, estimated that "lifestyle" plays more than twice the role in premature death than does environment—50 percent of premature deaths result from behavior, compared with 20 percent from genes, 20 percent from environment, and 10 percent from inadequacies in health care. More recently, former secretary of Health and Human Services Louis Sullivan estimated that improving health behaviors around just the top ten causes of death could cut premature deaths among blacks by 40 percent to 70 percent.

Even the miasmatics' own research clearly demonstrates the relevance of behavior to health. Take a study by Brown's Sally Zierler comparing the risk factors for rape with those for HIV in women, a study funded by the National Institute of Allergy and Infectious Disease. Zierler's goal is explicit: she seeks to "shift the burden of responsibility [for avoiding HIV], and thereby public health policy, from women as individuals to their broader social context."

Yet Zierler's data demonstrate a strong correlation between behavior and risk. Women with HIV were more likely to report adult rape if they had had sex before the age of fifteen rather than waiting until at least age eighteen, if they had an average of three or more partners per year, or if they were bisexual. Clearly, the greater the promiscuity, the greater the chance of rape, a conclusion borne out by another of Zierler's data: rape is five times more likely among adult women with HIV who reported a previous sexually transmitted disease. Sexual history, in other words, *does* matter on the question of rape, especially since most rapists know their victims. Alcohol and drugs matter, too. The study showed that using them increased the chance of rape, and women with HIV who first injected drugs before the age of sixteen were eleven times more likely to report rape than were women with HIV who never injected drugs.

Of course, Zierler would not accept her data's inescapable message that behavioral choices count, because, to her, shooting drugs and engaging in promiscuous sex are not choices but unavoidable responses to poverty and racism. Her conclusion? Men are to blame for HIV: "Studies are needed that investigate the role of men as sexual partners," she decides, "and more generally, as people who shape the conditions and impose the experiences that increase women's exposure and susceptibility to HIV and its morbidity."

Even though the miasmatic dismissal of behavior's role in health rests on a purely ideological, rather than scientific, basis, the academic miasmaticians have easily convinced government health officials that individual responsibility is a sham. In a recent article on AIDS in the British journal *Social Science and Medicine*, Carolyn Beeker, a research sociologist at the CDC, argues that "virtually no behavior is under the complete and voluntary control of individuals."

At a philosophical level, Beeker may well be right. But she is not referring to the conditions for free will but to such mundane issues as "talking to a partner about condoms, avoiding anal intercourse, or leaving a sexually abusive situation." These behaviors, Beeker asserts, are not "isolated voluntary acts, but part of socially conditioned, culturally embedded, economically constrained patterns of living."

This doctrine is particularly pernicious regarding AIDS. In all but a few tragic cases, HIV is communicated by very specific individual behavior—frequent unprotected intercourse with infected partners, anal intercourse, shooting drugs with infected needles. It lies within an individual's power to avoid the disease, and public health efforts should focus on changing behavior, on the one hand, and on protecting the public through testing and partner notification, on the other—traditional public health measures that have been all but discarded for AIDS.

But Beeker and many of her colleagues at the CDC have no such tried-and-true responses in mind. The solution to AIDS, they say, lies not in behavior change but in nothing less than a revolution in male-female relations. The CDC has targeted for eradication "gender roles which define women as subordinate to men." Beeker also decries "women's dependence on their partners for sexual satisfaction." No wonder the public health profession was sad to see Jocelyn Elders, President Clinton's onanism-promoting surgeon general, booted from the job.

In this climate, it's not surprising that many government HIV "interventions" look more like women's studies consciousness-raising sessions than anything the founders of public health would recognize. The CDC, drawing on its annual $2.5 billion stream of tax dollars, funded an "intervention" for young pregnant poor women to promote their sense of "communal mindedness" and "enhance their negotiating skills." Beeker admits that it was "not clear" whether the participants' "communal competence" actually increased—nor, according to Beeker, does any evidence exist that "community empowerment" reduces risk better than a behavioral approach. Still, "empowerment" models continue to flourish.

The government has snatched up leading academic miasmaticians for research on racism and health. The CDC and the National Center for Health Statistics, for example, have given Harvard's Nancy

Krieger $92,392 for an ongoing study of the social determinants of cancer for four different racial and ethnic groups. The National Institute for Child Health and Human Development is about to fund her study on how to include socio-economic data in routine health statistics. Krieger, who often seems like the government's official voice of miasmatism, wrote up a 1994 NIH conference called "Measuring Social Inequalities in Health" for the leading federal public health journal, *Public Health Reports*. Hitting all the major miasmatic themes, her article reported that the conference recommended collecting socio-economic data as part of routine health reporting, so as to show "how the economic structure of the United States, and not simply individual behaviors or 'lifestyles,'" underlies racial and ethnic differences in health. But not just any socio-economic data would do. "Most measures of socio-economic position have been based upon the model of the white European heterosexual nuclear family," Krieger complained. Since such measures ignore "nontraditional (such as lesbian and gay) households," they are patently inadequate.

Such contemporary public health initiatives as needle exchanges for drug users, condom distribution in schools, and the war on Big Tobacco embody the miasmatic assumption that individuals, especially from designated victim groups, have no control over their self-destructive actions. The American Public Health Association, the largest such group in the world, has lobbied Washington for federal funding of needle exchanges; President Clinton's Advisory Council on HIV/AIDS, a miasmatic hotbed, huffily condemned the administration's recent reluctant decision to stay out of the needle business. The administration's silence, the council said, was "particularly shameful" in light of the health disparities among racial groups. In other words, went the implication, blacks can't be expected to refrain from drug use and so should instead be helped to use drugs "safely"—a remarkable perversion not only of public health traditions but of much else.

Even without federal funding, needle exchange thrives in cities across the country. Along with needles, Bridgeport, Connecticut, also passes out leaflets helpfully advising drug users how to smoke crack correctly and suggesting a temporary "slowdown" if the user starts coughing up "dark stuff." Of course, officially sanctioned free needles often end up back in circulation on the streets, when users sell them for more drug money, according to Rodney Hopson, a federally funded health researcher at Duquesne University.

The public health profession's mania for showering condoms upon Americans, from schoolchildren on up, reflects the same rejection of individual self-control. A 1995 editorial in the *American Journal of Public Health* called "our society's failure" to place condom vending machines in convenience stores and public bathrooms and our failure to encourage "aggressive marketing of condoms" a "national tragedy." As emeritus professor Monroe Lerner of the Johns Hopkins School of Hygiene and Public Health argues, the federal public health bureaucracy now assumes that people have "no impulse control, no sense of personal responsibility." It expects young people in particular, he says, to engage in "promiscuous sexual relations." As for the schools of public health, "don't expect any plea from them to observe a more traditional morality, where young people don't go to bed with each other before they are married." Lerner, who helped push the field into more political arenas during the 1960s, a development he now regrets, acerbically summarizes the past three decades of public health thinking: "The words *sin* and *deviance* have vanished from the vocabulary."

From its inception, of course, public health has had a special concern for improving the health of the poor. But the miasmatic exemption of the poor from individual responsibility is a dangerous new twist. "There's new elements in the discourse," enthuses CDC community psychologist May Kennedy. "The commitment to social justice at the CDC is just now becoming explicit." Expressing the same view is Paul Geltman, a professor of pediatrics at Boston Medical Center and an advisor to the Massachusetts Department of Health. "[There's] absolutely been an increase in political consciousness in public health in recent years," he says.

Why? One reason is the ever larger number of sociologists, community psychologists, and anthropologists now in the field. Lacking medical or scientific training, they see public health as a vehicle for social change. "Those of us who were activists in the 1960s are now professors," Brown's Sally Zierler, herself a doctor of public health, explained in an interview. "This is a way of continuing the work." Zierler and her radical colleagues use their academic credentials to "authorize" themselves, she says: now "we are working from the inside." Zierler marvels over her group's ascension: "In the 1950s we would have been blacklisted," she says. "We couldn't have had the agenda we have and be hired."

But an equally important reason for the rise of the miasmaticians is the dominance of identity politics in every other area of public discourse. In declaring that racism and sexism determine the very fundamentals of life for women and minorities, the miasmatics parrot their colleagues in the rest of the academy. It was just a matter of time before public health picked up the jargon and conclusions of multiculturalism.

Not that the miasmatics have completely swept the field. At the opposite end of the public health spectrum are the genetic researchers, with their ever more impressive breakthroughs in finding the genetic and molecular determinants of disease. The geneticists are anathema to the miasmatics, because finding genetic correlates for disease obviates the need for the gender and race revolution. Midway between the geneticists and the miasmatics is "risk factor epidemiology," which studies the relation of both individual behavior and environmental factors to disease. Though far less precise in its causal conclusions than genetic epidemiology, risk factor "epi" is nevertheless a model of scientific rigor compared with the miasmatics.

Few traditional epidemiologists will publicly challenge the race-and-gender crowd. Even so, it is not hard to detect a certain chip on the miasmatic shoulder. "The gatekeepers of epidemiology," Zierler says scornfully, "are white male M.D.s"—three of the most damning words in a miasmatician's vocabulary. The miasmaticians claim, quite falsely, that all the power and funding lie with high-tech genetic epi. "One of the issues in this environment," explains Denise Herd, a professor of Multicultural Health at Berkeley's School of Public Health, "is that medicine is the elite field. Sometimes you get socially conscious doctors, but if not, biological science is perceived as more relevant to public health than social science."

Nothing could be more odious to a miasmatician than a preference for hard science. To them, "biomedical" is a term of derision, for it implies a focus on an individual human being (rather than on power relations in society) by a detached observer with implicitly superior knowledge. This is far too individualistic, Western, and male a concept for the miasmaticians. Science's status, according to Harvard's Nancy Krieger, grows out of cold war paranoia and McCarthyism rather than out of its breathtaking intellectual insights. The CDC's Carolyn Beeker recommends as an antidote to this repressive scientism that the researcher act as "advocate, collaborator, or mentor"—in other words, as political activist.

Nothing better demonstrates the miasmatics' contempt for traditional science than the citations in their published research. A partial citation list for an article in the *American Journal of Preventive Medicine* by Nancy Krieger and Diane Rowley, an assistant director for science at the CDC, includes (among more traditional material): strident feminist bell hooks [sic] ("Ain't I a Woman: Black Women and Feminism"); equally strident and unscholarly literary theorist Michelle Wallace ("Black Macho and the Myth of the Superwoman"); novelist and race critic Toni Morrison; lesbian poet Adrienne Rich; radical feminist commentator Barbara Ehrenreich; and *The New Our Bodies, Ourselves: A Book by and for Women*, by the Boston Women's Health Book Collective. What scientific evidence do Krieger and Rowley submit for the completely unempirical charge of widespread "racism in medical school"? A "personal communication": perhaps, in other words, a whine from a friend. Equally revealing is what counts as noncontroversial fact, needing no footnote: Krieger and Rowley state that in the U.S., "women are routinely treated as sex objects and face the daily harassment of street remarks." How do they know?

This cavalier approach to fact pervades all miasmatic research on racism and sexism. The CDC has so far spent roughly $3 million conducting a three-city "ethnographic" (i.e., nonscientific) study of black women's experiences with racism and sexism. The study uses the Krieger fail-safe method for finding racism: if a black woman says she has been discriminated against, she has. If she says she has not, she *really* has, because that means she has low levels of racial pride, a sure sign of discrimination.

What about misperception problems? I asked Diane Rowley. What if that allegedly racist bank teller or welfare worker treats everyone brusquely, or what if the allegedly brusque behavior is simply businesslike? No problem—the CDC falls back on folk wisdom. "There's a saying," Rowley explains: "Black people are paranoid, but in most cases it is justifiable paranoia."

The miasmaticians' blame-the-male research manifests equal indifference to fact. Hortensia Amaro of Boston University's School of Public Health used a National Institute on Drug Abuse grant to show that men are to blame for involving women in drugs. She interviewed thirty-five drug users, but her resulting psychohistories hardly support the image of the helpless or put-upon female.

For example, Lisa, a twenty-year-old mother of two, says: "Well, getting high, I've always kept a drug dealer next to me. I mean, I got my kids' father, who I love, but he won't give me drugs. And I love my drugs, too. And drugs just means a little bit more to me than he did." A mother of three with a $100-a-day heroin and cocaine habit used to get money from her U.S. veteran partner. "But I was still hustling, you know, lying, stealing, and cheating, and prostituting with him, but he didn't know it. . . . I got to the point where not only I was stealing out of the store, I was robbing people, um, I was prostituting. You know, I was doing things I said I would never do." Other women admit to staying with men they don't like just to get drugs. One woman introduces her mother, a former heroin user, to cocaine; others start using drugs not with men but with their girlfriends.

Such morally equivocal stories do nothing to shake Amaro off the trail. She concludes bathetically: "Men who go to jail [as had 49 percent of the women in her study], men who do not take care of them or their children, and men who disappoint them fill the lives of these women." Therefore, gender relations need to change before women can be expected to avoid drug use. But of course, these women should have disappointed themselves by their reckless behavior toward their children. To blame men for their predicament is a moral dodge.

What does the government intend to do with all the treatises on sexism, racism, and health it keeps subsidizing or authoring? Its intentions are unclear. But those of academic miasmaticians are more definite. "I want . . . people [to] understand that they're complicit in oppression," Brown's Sally Zierler announces. Zierler wants everyone to acknowledge his role in making poor people get HIV and use drugs: "It can be transformative to realize your complicity," she says: ideally, you go through a "hierarchy" from "guilt to anger to real commitment." And then, with a whole cadre of people who understand that individual responsibility is an oppressive concept, who knows what major societal changes will be possible?

All this is a far cry from the public health profession's distinguished past, with its multiplicity of practical improvements to the quality of ordinary life. As new populations flooded into the cities in both Europe and America in the nineteenth century, urban aristocrats and plutocrats looked around and said, "The poor are living in wretched and often lethal conditions; we have a responsibility to improve those conditions." The middle- and upper-class movements for sanitary and housing reform—creating air shafts in crowded tenements and closed drainage systems in the streets—and for unadulterated milk and clean water represented the first great wave of Victorian reform and a monumental advance in social consciousness. In subsequent decades, public health pioneers would zealously sleuth out the source of infectious disease in swamps and slums, often falling ill themselves, while spreading the gospel of cleanliness.

The early sanitary reformers on both sides of the Atlantic recognized that new sewage and drainage systems, though essential to removing the lethal "miasmas," could not alone solve sickness and early death in the slums. The habits of the poor needed changing, too. John Simon, London's first medical health officer, expressed sentiments typical of the time in his 1848 First Annual Report: "Among the influences prejudicial to health in the City of London, as elsewhere, must be reckoned the social condition of the lower classes," he wrote. "The filthy, or slovenly, or improvident, or destructive or intemperate, or dishonest habits of these classes, are cited as an explanation of the inefficiency of measures designed for their advantage. . . . It is too true that, among these classes, there are swarms of men and women who have yet to learn that human beings should dwell differently from cattle; swarms, to whom personal cleanliness is utterly unknown." While the city fathers must improve public sanitation and the like, he concluded, no real improvement in the health of the slums is possible without "improving the social condition of the poor."

That meant not just economic improvement but, equally important, a change in behavior. In France, René Louis Villerme, a member of the hygiene department for the French Royal Academy of Medicine, similarly called in 1821 for moral regeneration, not the redistribution of wealth, as a key to improving the health of the poor. In the same vein, American statistician Lemuel Shattuck argued in his 1850 *Report of the Sanitary Commission of Massachusetts* that drunkenness and sloth among the poor were destroying their health. Since such lack of personal responsibility puts everyone at risk, he concluded, it was as much the state's duty to raise the moral level of the poor as to build the infrastructure for civic cleanliness.

The science and technology of public health grew far more sophisticated in the late nineteenth century, but the moral tone of the field persisted. An 1883 article in the *Journal of the American Medical Association* declared: "Public health . . . is the companion of orderly habits and pure morals." No one doubted the individual's responsibility to practice elementary sanitation, for many of the most important public health reforms continued to be low-tech behavior change. Early in the twentieth century, the Public Health Service eliminated typhoid in the rural South with its clean privy campaign, cut death rates from infectious diseases by advocating trash-can lids to keep out flies, and ended trachoma, a highly contagious, blinding eye infection, in Appalachia by the advocacy of soap and water and separate towels for different family members.

Many public health pioneers had a fervent commitment to improving social welfare. But they would have found it inconceivable to argue that seeking individual behavior change is against the interest of the poor or nonwhite. Too much evidence existed of the importance of personal habits to health, and the field has usually respected evidence.

So the pioneers would be especially horrified by the modern miasmatic policy toward sexually transmitted diseases, which, unlike the epidemic diseases of the past, still plague an astoundingly high number of Americans. Two principles—the protection of the public and the advocacy of individual restraint—governed public policy regarding venereal diseases (VD) for most of this century, up until the advent of AIDS. During World War I, for example—when venereal disease constituted such a military disaster that, given the option of eliminating all wounds or eliminating VD, every army commander would choose to wipe out VD, according to then–Surgeon General W. C. Gorgas—the only real hope was changing individual behavior. As Gorgas concluded: "It is the individual action and the individual beliefs of our people affected that are finally going to control the disease." Hence, he advised, the sexual morals of the male population must be elevated to the same plane as that of the female population.

In addition, the army tried hard to protect the public by monitoring behavior. It tested extensively, it searched out and treated all the sexual contacts of the infected patient, and it isolated the patient for treatment, methods that for decades were considered the best public health practice.

The government-sponsored All-America Conference on Venereal Diseases in 1921 similarly exemplifies the traditional public health worldview. The conferees rejected the contention of the Freudian psychological section that, because "disastrous consequences [follow from] repression of the sex instinct," the conference should avoid recommending continence as a disease-preventing measure. The conference committee, while noting "the complexity of the question of the relation of continence to the total well-being of the individual," nevertheless resolved that "the dangers and disadvantages to the individual and the race which ensue upon the infringement of continence in the unmarried man or woman are so serious that they outweigh the possible physiologic disadvantages of sexual abstinence." After all, the conferees agreed, "the prevention of contact between infected and uninfected individuals is the first principle of prophylaxis" (i.e., prevention).

However obvious this "first principle" may seem, the prevention of sexual contact between infected and uninfected individuals plays no part in today's AIDS prevention efforts. Public health authorities have never dared suggest that infected people should refrain from intercourse with the uninfected, or that the infected should exercise sexual restraint. Equally outside the realm of today's public health discourse is the All-America Conference's view that if an infected person is likely to continue spreading the disease, the doctor's duty of confidentiality is over. At that point, resolved the conference, the doctor must "exercise whatever means are at his command" to protect the public health—presumably, quarantine (a traditional, if extreme, public health measure) or publicizing the patient's infected status.

But today, at least 40 percent of persons infected with HIV do not tell their sex partners of their status, and nearly two-thirds of those do not regularly use condoms—suggesting that the government's laid-back prevention philosophy is not working. Yet until recently, public health authorities placed patient confidentiality far above their duty to protect the good of all. Caving in to gay activists, they abandoned the elementary practice of reporting the names of the infected to a central registry; and they have never emphasized the individual's obligation of disclosure. The CDC stopped testing newborns for HIV several years ago, when threatened with legislation that would require it to notify mothers if their babies tested positive. The CDC put the mother's rights of confidentiality above the innocent baby's need for immediate treatment, a reversal of public health traditions. Only a political backlash against "AIDS exceptionalism"—the exempting of AIDS from conventional public health measures—has begun to return some common sense to AIDS policy through legislation.

As a result of aggressive public health sleuthing and the social stigma against promiscuity, VD was way down by the late 1940s. But starting in 1957, on the eve of the sexual revolution, it began to rise. Today, the U.S. leads the industrialized world in sexually transmitted diseases, with 10 million to 12 million new cases a year. And the response of the public health community is, in essence, Way to go! Asked whether we should recommend abstinence to prevent AIDS and other sexually transmitted diseases, Boston University's Hortensia Amaro says: "No, that would be to shut down the voice, the internal voice of sexuality." That Amaro advises the Massachusetts Department of Health on HIV prevention does not give one hope for ending the problem anytime soon in that state.

Like Amaro, the CDC and indeed the entire public health profession are big believers in the "internal voice of sexuality." A CDC poster at the 12th World AIDS Conference in Geneva this July announced incredulously that "only" 56 percent of teens interviewed in a phone survey in three American cities said they had a condom with them at the time of the interview, and only 32 percent reportedly took a condom with them the last time they left the house. And at last year's annual American Public Health Association conference, a researcher from the Medical College of Ohio in Toledo reported her surprise when, in a survey of college freshmen at an unnamed southeastern state university, "only" 61 percent of respondents reported having had "voluntary intercourse." Struggling for an explanation, she hypothesized that they must have come from a "fundamentalist background."

In perhaps the most momentous reversal of historic public health practice, some modern miasmaticians view traditional morality as the very cause of sexually transmitted disease. In a remarkable article in the June *American Journal of Public Health*, a group of sociologists at the University of Chicago blame Americans' disapproval of premarital, extramarital, and homosexual sex for our high sexually transmitted disease rate. Such regressive attitudes impede effective public health campaigns, the authors claim.

Schools of public health are doing all they can to combat such dangerous sexual morality. For example, the public health department in New York University's school of education offers a whole course on "Alternative Lifestyles." The aim of the course is to question the "personal feelings" individuals may have toward non-traditional families and "intimate living relationships." Just to make sure students understand the backwardness of the heterosexual family, the department provides a cradle-to-grave curriculum on homosexuality, from "Gay and Lesbian People: Adolescents" to "Gay and Lesbian People: Aging." The agenda of these courses is politics, pure and simple, focusing on how "professionals may assist gay and lesbian people in affirming their identities, securing their rights, and coping with stress." Will anyone discuss the health risks of the promiscuous homosexual "lifestyle"? Unlikely.

The government's health agencies are also doing their best to counter regressive old-fashioned attitudes. The NIH have a whole set of guidelines on the recruitment of lesbians as subjects for clinical research, part of a spurious and wastefully expensive congressional mandate to ensure gender and race "diversity" in clinical trials. The lesbian guidelines, like the race and gender quotas, turn out to be nothing more than a Full Employment for Lesbians Act. According to the NIH, researchers must "reassure" prospective lesbian trial participants "that lesbians have been involved in the writing of the project and analysis of data." Researchers should also "include 'out' lesbians in all staff and research levels and establish a local lesbian advisory committee for further advice."

Given these views, it's no surprise that the federal public health bureaucracy's prevention strategies for HIV and other sexually transmitted diseases are so muddy, involving "skill-based training that increases, through modeling and practice, decision-making and communication skills that support reduction of sexual risk behaviors," as the CDC puts it. In this characteristic verbiage, only one thing is clear: the CDC is not about to call for testing, monitoring, partner notification, or, heaven forbid, abstinence. For the CDC, the teen "sexual partner" is a given; the only negotiable part is the amount of "communication" one has with that "partner."

The CDC has spent approximately $12 million on a five-year, five-city teen sexually transmitted disease prevention project, featuring condom demonstrations on dildos in a church in Nashville and condom ads on buses and billboards. A layman might assume that the CDC would measure the success of the program by changes in the sexual disease or pregnancy rates. But no: instead, the agency measures self-reported "risk-reduction" behavior. Yet surely, the bottom line for $12 million in tax dollars ought to be actual disease and pregnancy reduction, not merely whether condom use increased.

What really excites public health professionals today is not reducing teen pregnancy, and certainly not reducing teen sex, but "empowering" girls. I asked Andrea Solarz, a community psychologist at the Institute of Medicine, a division of the National Academy of Sciences, about the institute's teen pregnancy prevention approach. "It's not 'Just say no,'" she replied. "We're more likely to do an intervention that empowers teens to negotiate the process of decision, that empowers girls to make the choices they want to make." If that means intercourse, fine.

The fatuousness of the miasmatics should not obscure the continued importance of public health, from the unsung labors of municipal health departments in testing water supplies and monitoring infectious diseases to the fight against terrifying new antibiotic-resistant bacteria in hospitals. Even in such politically conquered institutions as the CDC and NIH, serious, vital science is still being done. But the field increasingly identifies itself by the most radical elements within it. The keynote speaker at the American Public Health Association's annual meeting this November will be Jesse Jackson; the association's miasmatic caucuses—from socialist to lesbian, gay, and bisexual—already plan a show of force. This self-indulgent pursuit of a gender and race revolution squanders the great legacy of public health, whose most enlightened practitioners sought to balance public and private responsibility for health.

[1998]

Law School Humbug

LAW SCHOOLS across the country have taken on a new function: cleansing students' souls. The taint to be extirpated, of course, is racism and sexism, and in many classes the sometimes dramatic measures needed to root out such blights have driven away the more mundane task of teaching legal analysis.

"I was going home crying every day," says Linda P., a law student at New York University. The source of her unhappiness was her "Race and Legal Scholarship" course. "No matter what I said, the response was: you don't know because you're white. Some students wouldn't speak to me after class. It scared me, because I thought I was this big liberal, and I was treated like the devil."

Linda's professor, Paulette Caldwell, practices the hottest form of legal scholarship today: critical race theory. While therapeutic courses such as Caldwell's remain a small portion of the curriculum at most law schools, the theory behind them has nevertheless shaken up the legal academy. Only "feminist jurisprudence" rivals critical race theory in influence and sheer sex appeal; both fashions are cut from the same cloth.

The impact of critical race theory and feminist jurisprudence doesn't stop at the ivy-clad walls of the legal academy. Feminist jurisprudence has revolutionized the law of sex discrimination and rape. Courts across the country, persuaded that legal practice is deeply racist and sexist, are conducting costly studies of their own alleged biases. Both movements are trying to limit First Amendment guarantees in order to protect female and minority sensibilities; their first success, beyond campus speech codes, has been in the workplace. These repercussions are all the more remarkable when you consider that critical race theory and feminist jurisprudence are fundamentally antithetical to the very notion of law.

Back in the law school classroom, Linda P. is not the only student crying these days. Law professors in many schools boast that their courses have reduced students to tears, sent them fleeing to the dean, and created crosscurrents of hostility in the classroom—proof that the professors are "touching a nerve." Frances Lee Ashley, a University of Tennessee law professor, faced numerous charges from students that her "Discrimination and the Law" class was simply a forum for white-bashing, that she favored black students, and that the class exacerbated racial tensions. Ashley was unrepentant. "If teachers intend to open this scary space," she writes in the *California Law Review*, "they need to be ready to make it reasonably safe and bearable for all members of the enterprise. As a teacher in a predominantly white but desegregating institution you [cannot] consistently do the right thing if by that you mean behavior that allows the average white student to avoid any feeling of being personally accused or defensive when matters of race are discussed."

Charles Jones, a professor at Rutgers-Newark Law School, asks students in his critical race theory seminar to write an essay about race relations, challenging, among other things, "the assumption that blacks, Jews, and Latinos are allies." When a black student wrote about her indelible dislike of white people, Jones knew he had struck gold. He asked the student to read her essay aloud in class; an Italian-American woman burst into tears and fled the room. Fortunately, critical race teachers are prepared for such disruptions. "Getting in touch with your feelings is difficult," explains Jones. "We let [the Italian-American woman experience] out her grief. She sat out a class or two, and when she came back, she wouldn't talk." It was a useful lesson, Jones concludes: "She was naive to think there's not a lot of cross-racial hatred." (However open-minded critical race teachers may be about "cross-racial hatred," it is difficult to imagine this story coming out as it did had a white student written of his dislike for blacks.)

The core claim of both critical race theory and feminist jurisprudence is that law is merely a mask for white male power relations. Law, in other words, is indistinguishable from politics; the purported objectivity and neutrality of legal reasoning is a sham.

However crude the multicultural trappings of these theories, their fundamental argument has a respectable pedigree. For over a century, American legal scholars have challenged the traditional distinction between legislative and judicial action. According to the traditional view, legislators make the law; judges merely apply it. Judicial decisions, this tradition holds, are determined by preexisting legal rules, not by the judge's own whims.

The stakes riding on the accuracy of this conception are enormous. For if rules do not in fact determine the outcome of cases, if judges inevitably enjoy such enormous interpretive discretion that they are virtually creating law as they go along, then the legitimacy not just of the judiciary but of governmental power itself is thrown into doubt.

The first American thinker to question the conventional understanding of law was also America's greatest legal scholar: Justice Oliver Wendell Holmes, whose ideas foreshadowed virtually all of twentieth-century American jurisprudence. Holmes was reacting against the late-nineteenth-century view of law as a fixed system of unchanging, quasi-Platonic principles.

Bunk! replied Holmes; "law is no brooding omnipresence in the sky." To equate it with a set of timeless legal principles ignores the fact that judges have always transformed the law in accord with changing opinions and social conditions. In fact, argued Holmes, there *are* no legal principles in any meaningful sense. Law is simply a prediction of "where the axe [of the state] will fall."

By the twenties and thirties, Holmes's skepticism about legal rules had expanded into one of the most powerful movements in American legal scholarship. The "Legal Realists" developed detailed exposés of the malleability of legal reasoning in every kind of judicial decision making. Since precedent can always be found on either side of a case, they claimed, judicial decision making and even fact-finding are often determined by unconscious, irrational factors or by the judge's political and economic beliefs. Legal rules, in other words, don't determine outcomes; judges do.

Men of letters as well as the law, the Legal Realists produced a witty and urbane corpus of work—unlike that of the current crop of legal critics. The Realists argued that law should rest on a rational basis, such as the emerging discipline of social science, not on abstractions. Accordingly, they urged judges to sweep away archaic common-law rules that no longer made sense. Their criticisms were unimpeachable—many of the traditional distinctions determining when someone was liable for an injury, for example, were wholly artificial. But the skeptical judicial housecleaner often turns into the sorcerer's apprentice. "Gradually, every limitation [on legal liability] begins to seem arbitrary," warns Philip E. Johnson, a law professor at the University of California at Berkeley. Once a precedent has been established for ignoring existing case law, decisions that follow the law require justification just as much as decisions that depart from it, says Johnson.

Legal Realism lost much of its glamour after World War II. But in the 1970s, leftist law professors dusted off the Realists' critique and dressed it up in German and French literary and critical theories. Their favorite phrase to describe their work—"trashing"—reflects their nostalgia for the anti-establishment 1960s. The result of their efforts was Critical Legal Studies (CLS), a diverse, sometimes impenetrable mix of Marxist analysis, postmodern literary criticism, and American legal skepticism. CLS dominated the academic left for well over a decade, gaining widespread media attention in the 1980s for tearing up Harvard Law School. (Concurrently, "Law and Economics"—equally iconoclastic—moved in from the right, creating, together with CLS, a pincer offensive on traditional jurisprudence.)

Like many of the Realists, the Crits (as CLS practitioners called themselves) argued that law is just politics wearing robes. But the Crits' real gripe was not with law but with liberal society. They berated liberalism's emphasis on individual freedom and limited state power. Many called for a world without distinct public and private spheres, in which the individual would not be "alienated" from the collectivity. The Crits were particularly scornful of "illegitimate hierarchies," a phrase that included every possible type of ranking or distinction among individuals. Harvard's Duncan Kennedy, the original bad boy of CLS, infamously called for breaking down law school hierarchies by rotating all law school jobs—from dean to janitor—on a regular basis and paying all employees the same salary.

According to the Crits, the real purpose of law is to make an oppressive capitalist system appear inevitable. Law does this by duping people into believing that the rules that govern the distribution of property, the performance of obligations, and the relation between the state and civil society are "natural" and necessary. We forget, say the Crits, that law is man-made and could as easily be constructed quite differently—property need not be private, for example; or an employer could have no right to control his employees' behavior; or responsibility for deviant behavior could be assigned not to the individual but to social forces.

Unlike the Realists, the Crits seldom ventured into the practical world of law reform, preferring instead to generate anti-bourgeois theory in academic comfort. To the extent they did make practical proposals, these consisted of familiar Old Left prescriptions: public ownership of banks and insurance companies, rent control, union control of business, and vigorous housing-code enforcement.

Ironically, one of CLS's most utopian aspects led to its demise as the left's regnant theory. Some CLS theorists called for the abolition of rights. Rights, they argued, merely reinforce the classical liberal view of individuals as autonomous and potentially antagonistic. They prevent individuals from fusing into the truly mutual community that the Crits seek.

Not so fast, objected minority scholars in the late eighties. We *need* rights. We have seen enough truly mutual communities, from Birmingham, Alabama, to Little Rock, Arkansas, to know that we mustn't eviscerate government protection of individuals. By shattering the Crits' claim to speak for the oppressed, this minority critique nearly stopped the movement dead in its tracks. The Crits looked in the mirror and saw faces that were white, heterosexual, and, usually, male—badges of shame in the multicultural eighties. Their bravura evaporated.

Alan Freeman, a Crit at SUNY/Buffalo, was particularly vulnerable to the new minority challenges, for he had argued that antidiscrimination law merely masks institutional discrimination. He struck the new tone of self-abasement in responding: "I regard this essay as the most difficult one I have ever tried to write. I am writing nervously. I do not want to be charged, at least unfairly, with insensitivity. I am not going to try to refute systematically the arguments made in the critique. I will begin with myself and the question whether, given my whiteness, I am at all qualified to write about racism." Similar apologies for whiteness, as well as for maleness, heterosexuality, and "middle class" status, now routinely preface the writings of CLS's most redoubtable warriors.

At that point, the critical movement splintered into warring factions defined by race, gender, and sexual orientation. Inevitably, minority and female scholars emerged triumphant. Yet having dethroned the Crits, the critical race theorists took up almost all their rhetorical ploys. They attacked liberalism as mystifying and oppressive. They even adopted the Crits' argument against rights and antidiscrimination law, though some race theorists have added a black nationalist twist: since minorities can never hope for justice from whites, they argue, they should form their own schools, communities, and business organizations. Integration, according to these race theorists, is an unworthy ideal, for it ignores the distinctness—and superiority—of African-American culture.

The ascendancy of critical race theory and feminist jurisprudence almost makes one yearn for the good old days of CLS, which at least had analytic content and sometimes dealt with actual legal cases. Not so, much of the newest scholarship. Picking up the Crits' assumption that legal reasoning is a sham, the new race and gender theorists have given it a final postmodern twist that carries it beyond the domain of law entirely. Law, they assert, is just a "story" told by white males.

Pronouncing something a story has powerful consequences in the academy these days. It absolves the speaker from having either to affirm or to deny the truth of the so-called story, since, according to the "deconstructionist" movement in literary criticism, "there is nothing outside the text." Calling legal opinions stories allows professors to approach judicial decisions as if they were literature and frees them from the need to analyze an opinion's reasoning and use of precedent.

What, then, *do* they do? An article by Jack Balkin, a "deconstructionist" law professor at Yale, typifies the new style of legal analysis. Balkin discusses a Supreme Court decision denying parental rights to a man who fathered a child born to another man's wife. Rather than analyzing whether the decision was correct (beyond accusing Justice Antonin Scalia of "establishing the hegemony of Ozzie and Harriet" in the Constitution), Balkin engages in the fatuous word games deconstructive literary critics play.

He purports to find great significance in the etymological connection between "tradition" and "betrayal." He lambastes 1950s and '60s sitcoms. He discovers parallels in soap-opera plots to the adulterous conception in the case.

To these games, race and feminist legal theorists add a less playful element. The problem with white male legal stories, these theorists say, is that they "silence" the voices of women and minorities. Law does this, some feminists argue, through the bogus patina of reason in judicial opinions, which masks self-interest and political manipulation. Other feminist critics seem to grant the reality of rationality, only to dismiss it as a perversely male way of approaching experience. Lucinda Finley, for example, a feminist professor at SUNY/Buffalo, argues that "rationality, abstraction, [and] a preference for statistical and empirical proofs over experiential or anecdotal evidence" reflect the "life experiences typical to empowered white males." (Women who adopt "male" ways of thinking have been co-opted, according to Finley.) Triumphantly, Finley enumerates what male legal stories silence: "Rage, pain, elation, the aching, thirsting, hungering for freedom on one's own terms, love and its joys and terror, fear, utter frustration at being contained and constrained by legal language all are diffused by legal language." (And a good thing, too, since dispassionate legal reasoning is meant to *correct* the distortion of "rage" and other emotions.)

Feminists and race theorists are unanimous about the antidote to male legal stories: "counter-stories" by women and minorities. Robin West, an influential feminist at Georgetown Law Center, urges her colleagues to "flood the market with our own stories until we get one simple point across: men's narrative story and phenomenological description of the law are not women's story and phenomenology of the law."

The result: a new genre of legal scholarship—first-person narrative. The most-cited law review articles today have dispensed with the conventions of legal scholarship—case analysis, statement of a legal problem followed by suggestions for its resolution—in favor of personal anecdotes telling of the author's oppression.

There are no limits on what constitutes a relevant story. Paulette Caldwell, Linda P.'s professor at NYU, began the article that won her tenure: "I want to know my hair again, to own it, to delight in it again, to recall my earliest mirrored reflection when there was no beginning and I first knew that the person who laughed at me and cried with me and stuck out her tongue at me was me." The hair theme is picked up again by Margaret E. Montoya, professor of law at the University of New Mexico, in *"Mascaras, Trenzas, y Grenzas* [Masks, braids, and messy hair]: Un/masking the Self While Un/braiding Latina Stories and Legal Discourse." She begins: "One of the earliest memories from my school years is of my mother braiding my hair, making my *trenzas.*" Not since the Age of Aquarius has hair possessed such political significance.

Even more personal subjects are also favored. In an article widely viewed as a model of the narrative genre, Marie Ashe of Suffolk Law School presents graphic descriptions of her reproductive life, including the birth of her children.

Legal storytelling has redefined the goal of legal scholarship and, with it, standards of evaluation. The purpose of stories is to "build community"—defined in racial and gender terms. Good scholarship strengthens community; bad scholarship threatens it. The implicit corollary is that only those within that community can contribute to the scholarly effort. Critical race theorists are virtually all minorities; feminist theory is almost exclusively the domain of women. Anyone who suggests applying traditional meritocratic standards to critical race scholarship (or to hiring decisions regarding those who produce it) is branded a racist. A central contention of race theorists is that meritocratic standards are a front for white supremacy.

A favorite theme of the new writing is the author's oppression at elite law schools, often Harvard. For example, Montoya's article on braids and messy hair, while rambling across a bewildering terrain of topics, including "Latina Mothertalk" and "Daughtertalk," makes the obligatory visit to (racist) Harvard, where Montoya was a student. Critical race superstar Patricia Williams has generated much attention by windily recounting her courageous battles against racist faculties and administrations in the various elite schools where she has taught.

In this new scholarship, factual accuracy is no longer important. Writes Stuart Alan Clarke in the *Yale Journal of Law and the Humanities:* "It is naive, if not disingenuous, to suggest that all that matters is the promotion of the truth." Patricia Williams's portrayal *à clef* of her teaching stint at Stanford Law School is deeply distorted, according to former colleagues there—leftists all. Williams fittingly takes refuge against such charges in the shadow of Tawana Brawley: "When students . . . believed and then claimed that I had made . . . up [another of her personal victimization stories], they put me in a position like that of Tawana Brawley." Indeed, Brawley, whom Williams beatifies as the patron saint of victimized black women, is the perfect symbol of the movement: as Brawley's supporters on the radical left would have it, it didn't matter if her story of racial brutalization wasn't actually true, because it *could* have happened that way.

The legal storytelling movement rests on the premise that all women share a single, distinct voice, as do all minorities. Establishing the precise origin of that separate voice can be tricky, however. Duke law professor Jerome McCristal Culp, Jr., a black, invokes his coal-miner father to educate his students about the differences between black and white law professors though it turns out that two of his white colleagues at Duke also had coal-miner fathers. As for women's distinctive voice, Ann C. Scales of the University of New Mexico Law School suggests that it derives from the injury done to women by the imposition of a male solar calendar on their lunar biological cycles.

Still newer versions of "different voice" theory are already enshrined in law school catalogs.

Harvard Law offers two courses in gay and lesbian theory: one of them, "Law, Sex and Identity," "explore[s] sexual identification (Bi?, Straight?, Gay?, Other?), outness and the closet, violence (domestic, gay bashing, gay/lesbian battery, S/M), art/erotica/pornography, community intersectional identities, regulations of sexuality, sexuality and disease, deviance and sexual outcasts, families and children and others." Yale Law School also offers two courses in gay (or "Queer") theory. More multicultural legal specialties are sure to follow.

Although not all critical race and feminist scholarship uses the first-person voice, all of it aims to overthrow settled expectations of law and society. University of Pennsylvania law professor Regina Austin, for example, specializes in promoting black deviance. In a widely republished article, Austin argues that the black community should embrace the criminals within its midst as a form of resistance to white oppression. "Reliance on the traditional values of hard work, respectable living, and conformity to law," may, under certain circumstances, be "a perfectly progressive maneuver for 'the community' to make," she grudgingly concedes. But "on the downside, [traditional values] intensif[y] divisions within the black community." Austin is more persuaded by the downside. She urges the community to discard the distinction between lawful and criminal activity. People of color should view "hustling" as a "good middle ground between straightness and more extreme forms of lawbreaking." Examples of hustling include "clerks in stores [who] cut their friends a break on merchandise, anti-pilfering employees [who] spread their contraband around the neighborhood." (It apparently never occurs to Austin that the hustlers' employers may be black.)

Austin has also argued in favor of teen pregnancy, which she irresponsibly claims has a positive effect on teens' schooling and commitment to the workforce. Like lawbreaking, teen pregnancy has a political dimension as well: it represents an "attempt to break out of the rigid economic, social, and political categories that a racist, sexist, and class-stratified society would impose" on poor black girls. Austin has also characterized prostitution as an "exciting job in a public sphere" and has warned against assuming that black streetwalkers "have nothing to teach us, such as how to identify and deal with pimps."

How could Harvard resist so innovative a thinker? In the late 1980s it hired Austin as a visiting professor. (It did not offer her tenure, however, prompting then-professor Derrick Bell to storm off in one of his signature protests.)

The proposals of feminist legal theorists can be equally dramatic. Martha Fineman, a professor at Columbia Law School, argues in her book *The Neutered Mother, the Sexual Family, and Other Twentieth-Century Tragedies* for the abolition of marriage—a bold new response to the incontrovertible evidence that divorce harms children. According to Fineman, it is only the unnecessary "moral baggage" currently associated with divorce, and not parental separation itself, that hurts children. Therefore, Fineman would replace the concept of spouse with "sexual affiliates." If sexual affiliates want to separate (assuming they have decided to cohabit at all), there would be no moral consequences and so the children would emerge unscathed.

Fineman dismisses children's need for a male role model in the house: "A role model who beats them? Who abuses their mother?" she asks sarcastically. In Fineman's view, domestic abuse is "fairly common"; indeed, if you include emotional abuse, it is "extremely common." This contempt for the male contribution to child rearing is a standard feature of feminist legal scholarship. Accordingly, radical scholars are working hard to cleanse illegitimacy of whatever deviant status still adheres to it and establish single motherhood as the norm for child rearing. They have targeted "familialism" for particular scorn.

Classroom assignments in many feminist and critical race classrooms follow the fashion of starting from the self. Students write "reflection papers" that either relate their reading to their personal experience and emotions or sometimes even dispense with outside sources entirely. At Rutgers, for example, Charles Jones asks his students to describe and rank in importance their various identities: "Is the fact that you're gay more important than that you're Jewish?" he prompts the class.

The message that objectivity is a sham and that law should be a forum for self-expression hits a chord with many students. Those who feel overwhelmed by law school—a common experience—now have a ready explanation: their voice has been silenced. Writing in NYU Law School's student paper, Karen L. Myers, a first-year student, reflects the influence of the new scholarship: "I have been searching for myself and my experiences in the law books and I have not been able to locate either. [How] could I possibly be expected to sit in a contracts class and swallow [the idea] that formal reasoning is anything more than a smokescreen for keeping the white male perspective as the interpretive elite?"

The evolving persecution complex in many female students can make teaching difficult. Says Fordham law professor Marc Arkin: "If you call on them, you're imposing hierarchy; if you don't call on them, you're overlooking them. Either way, they're upset." To help professors navigate this dilemma, Fordham gave its faculty sensitivity training in classroom gender relations.

Feminine self-pity received a wonderful boost this February when Lani Guinier, a University of Pennsylvania law professor and President Clinton's failed nominee for assistant attorney general, published a study showing that women do worse in law school than men. Guinier and her co-authors attributed the gap to "insidious" sexism in legal education. The article was an immediate hit. Law schools across the country convened conferences to discuss how to improve the "hostile learning environment" for women and minorities; increasing the number of feminist and critical race theory courses usually headed the list of suggested reforms.

Not just female students have absorbed the doctrine that law should reflect their individual "voice." In 1990, participants in NYU's annual moot court competition refused to argue one side of the chosen case: a father's custody petition against his estranged lesbian wife. The father's position was indefensible, the students claimed; dignifying it with an argument would be "hurtful" to themselves, to homosexuals, and to the NYU community. Such a protest would have been unthinkable even twenty years ago, but when law becomes a vehicle for telling one's own "story," it becomes difficult to ask students to take positions contrary to their own beliefs.

Yet for every student who finds his or her calling as a victim in the new legal scholarship, many more reject the heavy-handed politicization of the classroom. "It was the worst learning experience of my life," says Richard B., a first-year law student at Columbia, about his course with Patricia Williams. "If [Williams's] goal is racial equality, she does more to impede it. She breeds racism. I'm embarrassed that she's here." Linda P., the scapegoat of Paulette Caldwell's class at NYU, says that the course inadvertently taught her "how *not* to deal with people. I was known as a super-liberal feminist in the firm I worked in over the summer. I would tell people: 'You can't say that because you're a privileged white male.' Now I feel like calling up and apologizing."

Such student skeptics have a hard time getting heard, however. Though administrations take students' oppression as minorities and women for granted, they pay more attention to maintaining faculty "diversity" than to students' problems as just students. Columbia's Patricia Williams is a case in point. Williams's own book chronicles the anguish she has caused students, who complain that she is "in over her head," incoherent, and given to personal tirades. How could she commit such a response to the page? Because it demonstrates her students' racism, she claims. Despite a history of devastating student evaluations and a corpus of writing that makes Captain Queeg look well-adjusted, she has traveled from one prestigious law school to another, finally landing tenure at Columbia. This year a delegation of her first-year students went to the dean of students requesting placement in a different section. Though Columbia had set up an alternative class for students unhappy with a conservative professor, it told Williams's students to stay put. Given Columbia's presumed determination to hold on to a minority professor in an age of scarcity, the school's apparent unwillingness to ruffle her feathers is unsurprising. Williams's predilection for chronicling the abuses she has suffered from a racist world may also exert a chilling effect on an administration's willingness to respond to student complaints.

The response of the law school professoriate to the burgeoning of critical race theory and feminist jurisprudence has been as meek as that of school administrators. Unlike CLS, which provoked a firestorm of protest at Harvard and enormous debate in the law reviews, race and feminist theory have achieved their position of dominance with little argument: their practitioners wear the impregnable mantle of victimhood. Few professors are willing to question publicly the worth of the first-person narrative movement, though some of its sharpest unpublished critics are the Crits themselves, who call the first-person movement an intellectual dead-end lacking all analytic content. When Randall Kennedy, a mainstream black scholar at Harvard, criticized the "different voice" theory of race scholarship in the *Harvard Law Review*, he found himself nearly frozen out of conferences.

These new fashions in legal education have changed law schools in fundamental ways. The schools are under enormous pressure from student caucuses and leftist faculty to hire race theorists and feminists. But because of the paucity of highly qualified minority law graduates, hiring standards are dropping. John McGinnis, a professor at Cardozo Law School, one of the more conservative schools, says: "We interview people who would not be given a second thought if they were white, for the applicant pool for minority scholars is far, far weaker."

Critical race and feminist theories also have affected how traditional courses are taught. For example, teaching rape doctrine in criminal law has become a minefield. Moreover, students now seem to assume as a matter of course that the law has a color: the president of the *Harvard Law Review*, David Friedman, explained to me that "you can't study criminal law and not have race come up a lot. The mere fact that so many defendants are black means that the law treats blacks differently."

Similarly, many students have absorbed the doctrine that law is purely discretionary on the part of judges. A student in a constitutional law course at Columbia recently argued that it didn't matter whether a law was constitutional, as long as a judge was enforcing it. Such a view undermines the very premise of a constitutional law course—that laws violating the Constitution are void and unenforceable. Yet the professor—a critical race theorist—accepted the student's remarks approvingly and moved on without further comment to a different topic.

The speech code movement in academia owes its theoretical scaffolding to the critical race scholars. From its onset, critical race theory has singled out the First Amendment for particular scorn: free speech, the theory argues, is nothing more than a tool of the powerful to oppress the weak. The marketplace of ideas will never correct racist views, the theorists claim, because racism silences its victims. Therefore, censorship is needed. "We should not let a spurious motto that speech be 'everywhere free' stand in the way of outlawing speech that is demonstrably harmful," argue Richard Delgado and Jean Stefancic of the Colorado Law School. "Overextending [the First Amendment] provokes the anger of oppressed groups."

But the most striking impact to date of race and feminist theory has been on the law reviews, where critical race theory and feminist jurisprudence now reign supreme. It's hard to find a top law review that will publish a conventional contract or tax article anymore, according to Fred Schapiro, a Yale law librarian who is conducting a study of legal scholarship over the last decade. Moreover, the proper race and gender are becoming a de facto prerequisite for writing on certain subjects. Richard Delgado, a leader of the critical race studies movement, has strongly implied that whites who write on civil rights issues should quietly retire. Indeed, if the logic of hiring minorities and women is that they bring a unique perspective of oppression to the law, why do we need white males to write about "minority" and "women's" subjects at all?

Outside the academy, much of critical race and feminist legal scholarship is unlikely to influence policy. Proposals such as promoting black deviance or abolishing marriage are wildly out of step with the national mood regarding values. Critical race theory and feminist jurisprudence thrive in the academic hothouse where they need never confront practical reality. The concept of law as story, for example, is utterly useless in either practicing or reforming law. Unlike a story-teller, a judge *has* to decide between competing claims in reference to a given set of rules.

The feminists' attack on objectivity as destructive of female connectedness is equally naive. Robin West of Georgetown Law Center urges that judges abandon their pretense of objectivity and openly empathize with litigants. West's proposal overlooks a basic fact of human nature: empathy flows most naturally to someone who is *like* the empathizer. To ask judges for empathy is to ask them for partiality.

Indeed, for all their sophisticated skepticism about the rule of law, contemporary leftist legal theorists are remarkably credulous about the ability of their communitarian utopia to treat everyone fairly. The Crits and their progeny vaguely gesture toward a system of informal communal justice, seemingly oblivious to the fact that such discretionary systems have produced the guillotine in France and Mao's People's Courts in China, to cite just two examples. As for their wholesale rejection of all hierarchy as "illegitimate," historian Eugene Genovese has remarked that the "Crits appeal to no history whatsoever to support their contention that civilized life is possible without some form of hierarchy. History shows that were men left wholly free to express themselves they would eat each other alive."

But though most of feminist jurisprudence and critical race theory is both useless in the practical realm and antithetical to the very concept of law, the movement's primary political message—that American society remains ineradicably racist and sexist—has found an eager audience outside the academy. Extraordinary to say, it has affected practice in courtrooms across the nation.

Radical feminist law professor Catherine MacKinnon, for example, has revolutionized sex discrimination law through hundreds of federal lawsuits. In 1977 she persuaded a court for the first time to recognize sexual harassment as a form of illegal sex discrimination. In 1986 the Supreme Court accepted her argument that a "hostile work environment" can constitute sexual harassment. In Canada she has had even greater success with legislators and judges. The Canadian Supreme Court has adopted her definition of pornography as any material that subordinates, degrades, or dehumanizes women. In addition, MacKinnon and local feminists engineered a Canadian law requiring men to take "reasonable steps" to ensure consent before engaging in any sexual activity. (MacKinnon has also implied that *all* sexual intercourse is rape, which of course would make consent irrelevant.) In the United States, pressure from feminist theorists has forced changes in rape law. Some of the pressure has been salutary, but some of it aims, MacKinnon-style, to make sexual intercourse per se suspect.

Individual judges and court bureaucracies have responded to the message that racism and sexism pervade American law and society. Jack B. Weinstein, senior district judge for the Eastern District of New York, quoted feminist legal scholars, including Columbia's Martha Fineman, in a speech to the New York City Bar Association last March. Weinstein criticized the federal sentencing guidelines for excluding the consideration of sex—along with race, national origin, and other factors—in sentencing. Echoing feminist theorists, Weinstein said that many women who commit crimes are "oppressed and driven by the males in their lives . . . [and are suffering from] the long-term psychological effects of socialized dependence and abuse." Needless to say, to portray women as lacking responsibility for their actions resurrects an ancient stereotype of feminine helplessness. No matter —contemporary feminist theory has so far had it both ways: arguing bias *and* seeking special treatment.

Prodded by feminist and critical race law professors, as well as by political activists, state and federal courts have undertaken a feverish search for internal sexism and racism. Eight of the eleven U.S. circuit courts of appeals, numerous district courts, and at least thirty-four states have created task forces to study gender and race bias in judicial administration, at enormous taxpayer expense. "I have never seen such fear among judges all over the country," says Laurence Silberman, a judge on the D.C. Circuit Court of Appeals. "All are agreeing to task forces; women judges are under particular pressure." The failure to uncover concrete evidence of bias stops no one. In the words of one task force report: "Gender bias is alive and well. It has just gone underground."

No court has taken the anti-bias campaign further than the Ninth Circuit Court of Appeals on the West Coast. Inspired by a four-hundred-page task-force report alleging widespread gender bias, it adopted a resolution in 1994 urging all courts within the circuit to prohibit "comment or behavior that can reasonably be interpreted as manifesting prejudice or bias toward another on the basis of gender, race, ethnicity, or national origin, citizenship, pregnancy, religion, disability, age, or sexual orientation." Incredibly, in a circuit with no shortage of conservative jurists, only one judge—the ultra-liberal Stephen Reinhardt—objected to the resolution as a violation of free speech. "The Ninth Circuit has gone insane," argues Judge Silberman.

"A lot has been stirred up by the gender study," says Ninth Circuit Judge Alex Kozinski, a little ruefully. A fellow judge accused him in a dissent of sexism and misogyny for using the phrase "the iron maiden of bankruptcy law" in an opinion.

The only bias task-force effort to have received close scrutiny has been the D.C. Circuit's five-hundred-page document. The results were devastating. Stephan Thernstrom of Harvard analyzed the report's statistical methods and found that, far from supporting its claim of widespread discrimination, the report's own evidence proved the opposite. Minorities are *over*represented on the nation's judiciary, Thernstrom found; the chance of being appointed a judge if you are a black or Hispanic lawyer is twice that of a white lawyer. Likewise, minority law graduates—at least black graduates—are almost certainly overrepresented as judicial law clerks, since students at the top of the class in all the major law schools are disproportionately white, and those at the bottom are disproportionately black. "The report implicitly views meritocratic claims as a smokescreen for bias," writes

Thernstrom, "but if clerks were selected purely on merit, there would be no minority law clerks." In a rare show of courage, the D.C. Circuit voted no confidence in the report.

The final tally on the impact of critical race theory and feminist jurisprudence is not yet in. Some conservative law professors, such as Yale's Robert Ellickson, argue that the impact of various multicultural movements in the academy has been overstated. It is true that, for all the ferment in law schools, most students graduate pursuing that lucrative job in a law firm just as ardently as when they matriculated. The majority of students regard legal theory as a sideshow; they chafe when they think even traditional courses are not preparing them to pass the bar. Even those who are persuaded that law is wholly indeterminate have to forget their skepticism pretty quickly when asked for their first client opinion letter.

Yet the prominence of race and feminist legal theory should be cause for concern. Grant Gilmore of Yale once wrote: "What is taught in the law schools in one generation will be widely believed by the bar in the following generation." And when law schools award mediocre scholars with jobs and tenure simply for espousing the fashionable view that American society is pathologically racist and sexist, they provide an authoritative stamp of legitimacy to that view. A student of Patricia Williams, who was otherwise deeply critical of her teaching, told me: "If Williams thinks racism is *everywhere*, then it must be more prevalent than I think it is." The race card, played so skillfully by defense lawyer Johnnie Cochran in the O. J. Simpson trial, may become more frequent and more respectable as young attorneys, fed on critical race doctrine, join the bar.

Moreover, exotic courses in victimology come with an opportunity cost. The problem isn't limited to radical theories: a variety of interdisciplinary studies like "Law and Literature" or "Law and Psychology" are crowding out traditional courses in commercial law, bankruptcy, and jurisdiction, so that students come out of school with less legal knowledge than did students three decades ago. Andrew Kleinfeld, a judge on the Ninth Circuit Court of Appeals, argues in the journal *Academic Questions* that top students from the best schools know less law, and far less history and government, than they used to. The consequence, Kleinfeld says, may be inadequate legal craftsmanship, ironically—and ominously—making a reality of the theory that law is nothing more than the arbitrary imposition of judicial power.

Student efforts to return the curriculum to the mainstream can be unavailing. Students at Rutgers-Newark, a hotbed of critical race theory, recently petitioned the administration for more business law courses. Many minority students signed the petition. Charles Jones, one of the many critical race theorists there, suggests where the battle lines will be drawn: "It's fine to have more business courses, assuming they don't come at the cost of more recent innovations." But given the limited resources of most schools, simply adding more traditional courses is rarely an option.

Few professors today, on either the right or the left, share Judge Kleinfeld's view that law school should focus on teaching students legal doctrine. They view their role as more exalted—as paid thinkers about the law. Teaching legal rules, they say, is stultifying and often futile, since laws change. But the value of traditional courses is not only that students absorb a fixed body of law but that they teach students to think like lawyers: to analyze facts and reason from principles.

Race and gender studies take legal training further away from that analytic ideal than any previous critical theory. The Crits were at least interested in doctrine; many were excellent teachers. But the proper response to the oppression stories favored by race and feminist theory is not analysis but empathy. Indeed, warn Daniel Farber and Suzanna Sherry of the University of Minnesota Law School, "some advocates of storytelling come close to suggesting that silence is the only permissible response to stories. Whites who sympathetically attempt to analyze or even recount stories told by people of color are said to be guilty of misappropriating the storyteller's pain." This antagonism to critical thought is antithetical to everything law school once stood for. It is particularly ironic in theorists who denounce the "silencing" of "voices."

Needless to say, critical skepticism has a vital role in legal education. Many legal doctrines cry out for revision, and law schools should encourage students to think critically about the role of legal institutions in society, including their impact on women and minorities. But to cross the line from skepticism to nihilism is a risky business. Were the view that law is *only* the judge's politics ever to be widely held, citizens would have no reason to grant judges legitimacy, and the basis of the legal order would crumble.

In fact, the Crits and their multicultural progeny are fighting a straw man. Few citizens are so "mystified" by the law that they believe that it is handed down on tablets of stone, untouched by human hands. People are well aware that legal rules and the concomitant distribution of property are human constructs; questioning the current legal regime is the very stuff of political debate. Nor are people blind to the role of discretion in judicial decision making. We are all Legal Realists now. Contemporary judicial confirmation battles reflect the Realist view that a judge's politics matter as much as his legal training.

Yet the current crop of critical thinkers overestimates the uncertainty of legal reasoning. The majority of potential disputes never reach a court because the legal outcome is already clear. And even when legal rules do not literally dictate the decision in a case, they influence it by channeling the judge's discretion in a predetermined direction. Over sixty years ago, John Dickinson rightly identified legal skeptics as "disappointed absolutists": "Holding an impossibly exalted view of [legal] certainty, they insist on all or none."

Race and much feminist theory represent a dangerous flight from reason and logic. A legal system that aspires to objectivity is one of culture's greatest accomplishments. The fact that, like other human institutions, law does not always live up to its goals is no argument against its trying to do so. The current effort to give law a color and gender or to dismantle it entirely in the name of racial and sexual solidarity would be a giant step toward unreason.

[1995]

Why Johnny's Teacher
Can't Teach

AMERICANS' nearly last-place finish in the Third International Mathematics and Sciences Study of student achievement caused widespread consternation this February, except in the one place it should have mattered most: the nation's teacher education schools. Those schools have far more important things to do than worrying about test scores—things like stamping out racism in aspiring teachers. "Let's be honest," darkly commanded Professor Valerie Henning-Piedmont to a lecture hall of education students at Columbia University's Teachers College last February. "What labels do you place on young people based on your biases?" It would be difficult to imagine a less likely group of bigots than these idealistic young people, happily toting around their handbooks of multicultural education and their exposés of sexism in the classroom. But Teachers College knows better. It knows that most of its students, by virtue of being white, are complicitous in an unjust power structure.

The crusade against racism is just the latest irrelevancy to seize the nation's teacher education schools. For over eighty years, teacher education in America has been in the grip of an immutable dogma, responsible for endless educational nonsense. That dogma may be summed up in the phrase: Anything But Knowledge. Schools are about many things, teacher educators say (depending on the decade)—self-actualization, following one's joy, social adjustment, or multicultural sensitivity—but the one thing they are not about is knowledge. Oh sure, educators will occasionally allow the word to pass their lips, but it is always in a compromised position, as in "constructing one's own knowledge," or "contextualized knowledge." Plain old knowledge, the kind passed down in books, the kind for which Faust sold his soul, *that* is out.

The education profession currently stands ready to tighten its already viselike grip on teacher credentialing, persuading both the federal government and the states to "professionalize" teaching further. In New York, as elsewhere, that means closing off any routes to the classroom that do not pass through an education school. But before caving in to the educrats' pressure, we had better take a hard look at what education schools actually teach.

The course in "Curriculum and Teaching in Elementary Education" that Professor Anne Nelson (a pseudonym) teaches at the City College of New York is a good place to start. Dressed in a tailored brown suit with close-cropped hair, Nelson is a charismatic teacher, with a commanding repertoire of voices and personae. And yet, for all her obvious experience and common sense, her course is a remarkable exercise in vacuousness.

As with most education classes, the title of Professor Nelson's course doesn't give a clear sense of what it is about. Unfortunately, Professor Nelson doesn't, either. The semester began, she said in a pre-class interview, by "building a community, rich of talk, in which students look at what they themselves are doing by in-class writing." On this, the third meeting of the semester, Professor Nelson said that she would be "getting the students to develop the subtext of what they're doing." I would soon discover why Professor Nelson was so vague.

"Developing the subtext" turns out to involve a chain reaction of solipsistic moments. After taking attendance and—most admirably—quickly checking the students' weekly handwriting practice, Professor Nelson begins the main work of the day: generating feather-light "texts," both written and oral, for immediate group analysis. She asks the students to write for seven minutes on each of three questions:

"What excites me about teaching?" "What concerns me about teaching?" and then, the moment that brands this class as hopelessly steeped in the Anything But Knowledge credo: "What was it like to do this writing?"

This last question triggers a quickening volley of self-reflexive turns. After the students read aloud their predictable reflections on teaching, Professor Nelson asks: "What are you hearing?" A young man states the obvious: "Everyone seems to be reflecting on what their anxieties are." This is too straightforward an answer. Professor Nelson translates into ed-speak: "So writing gave you permission to think on paper about what's there." Ed-speak dresses up the most mundane processes in dramatic terminology—one doesn't just write, one is "given permission to think on the paper"; one doesn't converse, one "negotiates meaning." Then, like a champion tennis player finishing off a set, Nelson reaches for the ultimate level of self-reflexivity and drives it home: "What was it like to listen to each other's responses?"

The self-reflection isn't over yet, however. The class next moves into small groups—along with in-class writing, the most pervasive gimmick in progressive classrooms today—to discuss a set of student-teaching guidelines. After ten minutes, Nelson interrupts the by-now lively and largely off-topic conversations, and says: "Let's talk about how you felt in these small groups." The students are picking up ed-speak. "It shifted the comfort zone," reveals one. "It was just acceptance; I felt the vibe going through the group." Another adds: "I felt really comfortable; I had trust there." Nelson senses a "teachable moment." "Let's talk about that," she interjects. "We are building trust in this class; we are learning how to work with each other."

Now, let us note what this class was not: it was not about how to keep the attention of eight-year-olds or plan a lesson or make the Pilgrims real to first-graders. It did not, in other words, contain any material (with the exception of the student-teacher guidelines) from the outside world. Instead, it continuously spun its own subject matter out of itself. Like a relationship that consists of obsessively analyzing the relationship, the only content of the course was the course itself.

How did such navel gazing come to be central to teacher education? It is the almost inevitable consequence of the Anything But Knowledge doctrine, born in a burst of quintessentially American anti-intellectual fervor in the wake of World War I. Educators within the federal government and at Columbia's Teachers College issued a clarion call to schools: cast off the traditional academic curriculum and start preparing young people for the demands of modern life. America is a forward-looking country, they boasted; what need have we for such impractical disciplines as Greek, Latin, and higher math? Instead, let the students then flooding the schools take such useful courses as family membership, hygiene, and the worthy use of leisure time. "Life adjustment," not wisdom or learning, was to be the goal of education.

The early decades of this century forged the central educational fallacy of our time: that one can think without having anything to think about. Knowledge is changing too fast to be transmitted usefully to students, argued William Heard Kilpatrick of Teachers College, the most influential American educator of the century; instead of teaching children dead facts and figures, schools should teach them "critical thinking," he wrote in 1925. What matters is not what you know, but whether you know how to look it up, so that you can be a "lifelong learner."

Two final doctrines rounded out the indelible legacy of progressivism. First, Harold Rugg's *The Child-Centered School* (1928) shifted the locus of power in the classroom from the teacher to the student. In a child-centered class, the child determines what he wants to learn. Forcing children into an existing curriculum inhibits their self-actualization, Rugg argued, just as forcing them into neat rows of chairs and desks inhibits their creativity. The teacher becomes an enabler, an advisor; not, heaven forbid, the transmitter of a pre-existing body of ideas, texts, or, worst of all, facts. In today's jargon, the child should "construct" his own knowledge rather than passively receive it. By the late 1920s, students were moving their chairs around to form groups of "active learners" pursuing their own individual interests, and, instead of a curriculum, the student-centered classroom followed just one principle: "activity leading to further activity without bad-ness," in Kilpatrick's words. Today's educators still present these seven-decade-old practices as cutting-edge.

As E. D. Hirsch observes, the child-centered doctrine grew out of the romantic idealization of children. If the child was, in Wordsworth's words, a "Mighty Prophet! Seer Blest!" then who needs teachers? But the Mighty Prophet emerged from student-centered schools ever more ignorant and incurious as the schools became more vacuous. By the 1940s and 1950s, schools were offering classes in how to put on nail polish and how to act on a date. The notion that learn-ing should push students out of their narrow world had been lost.

The final cornerstone of progressive theory was the disdain for report cards and objective tests of knowledge. These inhibit authentic learning, Kilpatrick argued; and he carried the day, to the eternal joy of students everywhere.

The foregoing doctrines are complete bunk, but bunk that has survived virtually unchanged to the present. The notion that one can teach "metacognitive" thinking in the abstract is senseless. Students need to learn *something* to learn how to learn at all. The claim that prior knowledge is superfluous because one can always look it up, preferably on the Internet, is equally senseless. Effective research de-pends on pre-existing knowledge. Moreover, if you don't know in what century the atomic bomb was dropped without rushing to an encyclo-pedia, you cannot fully participate in society. Lastly, Kilpatrick's influ-ential assertion that knowledge was changing too fast to be taught presupposes a blinkered definition of knowledge that excludes the great works and enterprises of the past.

The rejection of testing rests on premises as flawed as the push for "critical thinking skills." Progressives argue that if tests exist, then teachers will "teach to the test"—a bad thing, in their view. But why would "teaching to a test" that asked for, say, the causes of the Civil War be bad for students? Additionally, progressives complain that testing provokes rote memorization—again, a bad thing. One of the most tragically influential education professors today, Columbia's Linda Darling-Hammond, director of the National Commission on

Teaching and America's Future, an advocacy group for increased teacher "professionalization," gives a telling example of what she considers a criminally bad test in her hackneyed 1997 brief for progressive education, *The Right to Learn*. She points disdainfully to the following question from the 1995 New York State Regents Exam in biology (required for high school graduation) as "a rote recall of isolated facts and vocabulary terms": "The tissue which conducts organic food through a vascular plant is composed of: (1) Cambium cells; (2) Xylem cells; (3) Phloem cells; (4) Epidermal cells."

Only a know-nothing could be offended by so innocent a question. It never occurs to Darling-Hammond that there may be a joy in mastering the parts of a plant or the organelles of a cell, and that such memorization constitutes learning. Moreover, when, in the progressives' view, will a student ever be held accountable for such knowledge? Does Darling-Hammond believe that a student can pursue a career in, say, molecular biology or in medicine without it? And how else will that learning be demonstrated, if not in a test? But of course such testing will produce unequal results, and that is the real target of Darling-Hammond's animus.

Once you dismiss real knowledge as the goal of education, you have to find something else to do. That's why the Anything But Knowledge doctrine leads directly to Professor Nelson's odd course. In thousands of education schools across the country, teachers are generating little moments of meaning, which they then subject to instant replay. Educators call this "constructing knowledge," a fatuous label for something that is neither construction nor knowledge but mere game playing. Teacher educators, though, possess a primitive relationship to words. They believe that if they just label something "critical thinking" or "community-building," these activities will magically occur.

For all the ed school talk of freedom from the past, teacher education in this century has been more unchanging than Miss Havisham. Like aging vestal virgins, today's schools lovingly guard the ancient flame of progressivism. Since the 1920s they have not had a single new idea; they have merely gussied up old concepts in new rhetoric, most recently in the jargon of minority empowerment. To enter an education classroom, therefore, is to witness a timeless ritual, embedded in an authority structure of unions and state education departments as rigid as the Vatican.

It is a didactic ritual as well. The education professor's credo is: As I do unto you, so shall you do unto your students. The education professor "models" how she wants her students to teach by her own classroom methods. Such a practice is based on a glaring fallacy—that methods that work passably well with committed twenty-two-year-olds, paying $1,800 a course for your wisdom, will translate seamlessly to a class of seven- or twelve-year-olds.

The Anything But Knowledge credo leaves education professors and their acolytes free to concentrate on far more pressing matters than how to teach the facts of history or the rules of sentence construction. "Community-building" is one of their most urgent concerns. Teacher educators conceive of their classes as sites of profound political engagement, out of which the new egalitarian order will emerge. A case in point is Columbia's required class, "Teaching English in Diverse Social and Cultural Contexts," taught by Professor Barbara Tenney (a pseudonym). "I want to work at a very conscious level with you to build community in this class," Tenney tells her attentive students on the first day of the semester this spring. "You can do it consciously, and you ought to do it in your own classes." Community-building starts by making nameplates for our desks. Then we all find a partner to interview about each other's "identity." Over the course of the semester, each student will conduct two more "identity" interviews with different partners. After the interview, the inevitable self-reflexive moment arrives, when Tenney asks: "How did it work?" This is a sign that we are on our way to "constructing knowledge."

A hallmark of community-building is its overheated rhetoric. The education professor acts as if she were facing a pack of snarling Serbs and Croats, rather than a bunch of well-mannered young ladies (the vast majority of education students), hoping for a good grade. So the community-building assignments attack nonexistent problems of conflict. Tenney, sporting a black leather miniskirt and a cascade of blond curls, hands out a sheet of paper and asks us to respond to the questions: "What climate would allow you to do your best work? How should a class act to encourage open and honest and critical dialogue?" We write for a while, then read our response to our interview partner.

Now is this question really necessary, especially for a group of college graduates? Good classroom etiquette is hardly a mystery. In the evil traditional classroom, and probably also at Teachers College, if a student calls another a fathead, thus discouraging "open and honest and critical dialogue," the teacher would simply reprimand him, and everyone would understand perfectly well what just happened and why. Consensus already exists on civil behavior. But the education classroom, lacking a pressing agenda in concrete knowledge, has to "problematize" the most automatic social routines.

Of course, no amount of writing about the conditions for "open dialogue" can change the fact that discussion is not open on many issues at Teachers College and other progressive bastions. "If you don't demonstrate the correct point of view," says a student, "people are hostile. There's a herd mentality here." A former student of Tenney's describes the difficulties of dissent from the party line on racism: "There's nothing to be gained from challenging it. If you deny that the system inherently privileges whites, you're 'not taking responsibility for your position in racism.'" Doubtless, it would never occur to Professor Tenney that the problem this student describes impedes community-building.

All this artificial "community-building," however gratifying to the professors, has nothing to do with learning. Learning is ultimately a solitary activity: we have only one brain, and at some point we must exercise it in private. One could learn an immense amount about Schubert's *lieder* or calculus without ever knowing the name of one's seatmate. Such a view is heresy to the education establishment, determined, as Rita Kramer has noted, to eradicate any opportunity for individual accomplishment, with its sinister risk of superior achievement. For the educrats, the group is the irreducible unit of learning.

Fueling this principle is the gap in achievement between whites and Asians, on the one hand, and other minorities on the other. Unwilling to adopt the discipline and teaching practices that would help reduce that gap, the education establishment tries to conceal it under group projects.

And so the ultimate community-building mechanism is the ubiquitous "collaborative group." No activity is too solitary to escape assignment to a group: writing, reading, researching, thinking—all are better done with many partners, according to educational dogma. If you see an ed school class sitting up in straight rows, call a doctor, because it means the professor has had a heart attack and couldn't arrange the class into groups.

For all their "progressive" sympathies, not all ed students like this regime. "I'm a socialist at heart," says one of Tenney's students, establishing her bona fides, "but some tasks, like writing, are not collaborative. It's hard when someone loses their voice." Another Columbia student in the Education Administration program complains that "teachers here let the group projects run wild." At $1,800 a course, it's frustrating "when the last four sessions of a class are group projects that are all garbage." Lastly, small group discussions have a habit of careening off the assigned topic. The professors rarely intervene, however, says a Teachers College student, "because they don't want to interfere with the interaction."

The elevation of the group entails the demotion of teachers—yet another plank in the Anything But Knowledge platform. To accord teachers any superior role in the classroom would be to acknowledge an elite hierarchy of knowledge, possessed by some but not all, at least without effort. Teachers traditionally represent elitism, learning, authority—everything that progressivism scorns—and so they must be relegated to the role of mere facilitators for the all-important group.

Linda Darling-Hammond's description of collaborative learning perfectly captures how inextricable the political is from the educational in progressive theory. "Whereas traditional classrooms tend to be still but for the sound of teacher talking, learning-centered classrooms feature student talk and collective action." (The "learning-centered classroom" is Darling-Hammond's jargon for a student-centered classroom.) "Collective action"—how exciting! But though lots of undirected "student talk" hardly seems conducive to learning, progressives abhor quiet. David Schaafsma, one of Columbia's more politicized teachers, told his English Methods class of visiting a quiet third-grade class in the Bronx, explaining: "It terrifies me when kids are really really still. They've got to move." It never occurs to these apostles of the Free Self that for many inner-city children, reaching a state of calm attention is a wonderful achievement.

Collaborative learning leads naturally to another tic of the progressive classroom: "brainstorming." Rather than lecture to a class, the teacher asks the class its opinion about something and lists the responses on the blackboard. Nothing much happens after that; brainstorming, like various forms of community-building, appears to be an end in itself. Hunter College professor Faith DiCaprio (a pseudonym) recently used two levels of brainstorming—whole group and small group—with her "Language and Literacy in Early Childhood" class. The class had just read *Wally's Stories* by Vivian Paley, essentially a transcript of freewheeling discussions among kindergartners in a progressive classroom. First, DiCaprio asked her students what they liked about the book. As students called out their responses—"I liked how she didn't correct the students," "She reminded us why a child-centered room is so necessary: she didn't intrude on their conversation"—DiCaprio writes their responses in abbreviated ed-speak on big posted sheets of paper: "Tolerance: they negotiated meaning" and "Created safe arena."

After DiCaprio fills up the posted pages, nothing happens. Nothing needs to happen, for the lists of responses are visible proof of how much the class already knows. We have just "constructed knowledge." On to the next brainstorming exercise. This time, it's a twofer—brainstorming plus collaborative learning. DiCaprio breaks the class into small groups. Their assignment: list and categorize the topics discussed by the kindergartners in *Wally's Stories.* So the students dutifully make lists of fairies, food, plants, witches, and other meaty matters. One outspoken girl enthuses to her group: "And the kids were smart, they were like, 'The turnips push up with the roots,' and I was like, 'How'd they know that?'" After the groups complete their lists, they read them to the rest of the class. Learning tally? Almost zero.

The consequences of the Anything But Knowledge credo for intellectual standards have been dire. Education professors are remarkably casual when it comes to determining whether their students actually know anything, rarely asking them, for example, what can you tell us about the American Revolution? The ed schools incorrectly presume that the students will have learned everything they need to know in their other or previous college courses, and that the teacher certification exams will screen out people who didn't.

Even if college education were reliably rigorous and comprehensive, education majors aren't the students most likely to profit from it. Nationally, undergraduate education majors have lower SAT and ACT scores than students in any other program of study. Only 16 percent of education majors scored in the top quartile of 1992–93 graduates, compared with 33 percent of humanities majors. Education majors were overrepresented in the bottom quartile, at 30 percent. In New York City, many education majors have an uncertain command of English—I saw one education student at City College repeatedly write "choce" for "choice"—and appear altogether ill at ease in a classroom. To presume *anything* about this population without a rigorous content exit exam is unwarranted.

The laissez-faire attitude toward student knowledge rests on "principled" grounds, as well as on see-no-evil inertia. Many education professors embrace the facile post-structuralist view that knowledge is always political. "An education program can't have content [knowledge] specifics," explains Migdalia Romero, chair of Hunter College's Department of Curriculum and Teaching, "because then you have a point of view. Once you define exactly what finite knowledge is, it becomes a perspective." The notion that a culture could possess a pre-political common store of texts and ideas is anathema to the modern academic.

The most powerful dodge regurgitates William Heard Kilpatrick's classic "critical thinking" scam. Asked whether a future teacher should know the date of the 1812 war, Professor Romero replied: "Teaching and learning is not about dates, facts, and figures, but about developing critical thinking." When pressed if there were not *some* core facts that a teacher or student should know, she valiantly held her ground. "There are two ways of looking at teaching and learning," she replied. "Either you are imparting knowledge, giving an absolute knowledge base, or teaching and learning is about dialogue, a dialogue that helps to internalize and to raise questions." Though she offered the disclaimer "of course you need both," Romero added that teachers don't have to know everything, because they can always look things up.

Romero's tolerance of potential teacher ignorance perfectly reflects New York State's official policy on learning, a sellout to progressivism in its preference for "concepts" and "critical thinking" over measurable knowledge. The Regents' much-vaunted 1996 "student learning standards" are vacuous evasions of facts and knowledge, containing not a single book or document or historical fact that students should know. Literature? The word isn't mentioned. Instead, proclaim the standards in classic educationese, "students will listen, speak, read, and write for literary response and expression"—literally a meaningless statement, matched in its meaninglessness only by the next "English Language Arts" standard: "Students will listen, speak, read, and write for social interaction." Teachers need to get hold of the third level of documentation accompanying the standards to find any specific historical figures or events or books, but there, excessive detail and gaseous generalization will overwhelm them.

But what New York State expects of its students is a model of rigor compared to what it formally expects of its teachers. The State Teacher Certification Exams are a complete abdication of the state's responsibility for ensuring an educated teaching force. If any teachers in the state know anything about American history, English literature, or chemistry, it is a complete accident, for the state's highest education authorities have not the slightest interest in finding out. The Liberal Arts and Sciences Test, the ticket to a teacher's first five years in a classroom, contains absolutely no substance; at most, it tests reading skills. The test preparation booklet is a classic of educationese. The exam section on "Historical and Social Scientific Awareness" (note: not "knowledge"), for example, tests teachers' "understanding [of] the interrelatedness of historical, geographic, cultural, economic, political and social issues and factors."

Now, by loading on the different types of "issues and factors" that prospective teachers are supposed to understand, the exam ensures that they need know nothing in particular. The only thing that test takers do have to know is the multicultural dogma that there is no history, only "multiple perspectives" on history. The certification exam asks prospective teachers to "analyze multiple perspectives within U.S. society regarding major historical and contemporary issues"—*not* history, but "historical *issues*," and not even "historical issues," but "multiple perspectives" on "historical issues." Such a demand is ripe for spouting off, say, on the "Native American perspective" on the Western expansion, without having the slightest idea what fueled that expansion, when and where it occurred, who peopled it, and what its consequences were. In fairness, the Content Specialty Tests teachers must take for permanent certification are much more substantive, especially in science and math, but only one-third of the teachers seeking provisional certification ever make it that far.

The pedagogy portion of the Liberal Arts and Sciences certification exam resembles a catechism more than an exam. "Multiple perspectives" are clearly not acceptable in answering such loaded questions as: "Analyze how classroom environments that respect diversity foster positive student experiences," or, "Analyze how schoolwide structures (i.e., tracking) and classroom factors (e.g., homogeneous versus heterogeneous grouping [presumably by ability], student-teacher interactions) may affect students' self-concepts and learning." Will a would-be teacher who answers that classrooms should stress a common culture or that ability-grouping promotes excellence remain just a would-be teacher? One hopes not.

The exams echo with characteristic ed school verbiage. The student doesn't learn, he achieves "learning processes and outcomes";

the teacher doesn't teach, she "applies strategies for facilitating learning in instructional situations." Disregard for language runs deep in the teacher education profession, so much so that ed school professors tolerate glaring language deficiencies in schoolchildren. Last January, Manhattan's Park West High School shut down for a day, so that its faculty could bone up on progressive pedagogy. One of the more popular staff development seminars was "Using Journals and Learning Logs." The presenters—two Park West teachers and a representative from the New York City Writing Project, an anti-grammar initiative run by Lehman College's Education School—proudly passed around their students' journal writing, including the following representative entry on "Matriarchys v. pratiarchys [*sic*]": "The different between Matriarchys and patriarchys is that when the mother is in charge of the house. sometime the children do whatever they want. But sometimes the mother can do both roll as a mother and as a father too and they can do it very good." A more personal entry described how the author met her boyfriend: "He said you are so kind I said you noticed and then he hit me on my head. I made-believe I was crying and when he came naire me I slaped him right in his head and than I ran . . . to my grandparients home and he was right behind me. Thats when he asked did I have a boyfriend."

The ubiquitous journal-writing cult holds that such writing should go uncorrected. Fortunately, some Park West teachers bridled at the notion. "At some point, the students go into the job market, and they're not being judged 'holistically,'" protested a black teacher, responding to the invocation of the state's "holistic" model for grading writing. Another teacher bemoaned the Board of Ed's failure to provide guidance on teaching grammar. "My kids are graduating without skills," he lamented.

Such views, however, were decidedly in the minority. "Grammar is related to purpose," soothed the Lehman College representative, educrat code for the proposition that asking students to write grammatically on topics they are not personally "invested in" is unrealistic. A Park West presenter burst out with a more direct explanation for his chilling indifference to student incompetence: "I'm not going to spend my life doing error diagnosis! I'm not going to spend my weekend on that!" Correcting papers used to be part of the necessary drudgery of a teacher's job. No more, with the advent of enlightened views about "self-expression" and "writing with intentionality."

However easygoing the education establishment is regarding future teachers' knowledge of history, literature, and science, there is one topic that it assiduously monitors: their awareness of racism. To many teacher educators, such an awareness is the most important tool a young teacher can bring to the classroom. It cannot be developed too early. Rosa, a bouncy and enthusiastic junior at Hunter College, has completed only her first semester of education courses, but already she has mastered the most important lesson: America is a racist, imperialist country, most like, say, Nazi Germany. "We are lied to by the very institutions we have come to trust," she recalls from her first-semester reading. "It's all government that's inventing these lies, such as Western heritage."

The source of Rosa's newfound wisdom, Donaldo Macedo's *Literacies of Power: What Americans Are Not Allowed to Know*, is an execrable book by any measure. But given its target audience—impressionable education students—it comes close to being a crime. Widely assigned at Hunter, and in use in approximately 150 education schools nationally, it is an illiterate, barbarically ignorant Marxist-inspired screed against America. Macedo opens his first chapter, "Literacy for Stupidification: The Pedagogy of Big Lies," with a quote from Hitler and quickly segues to Ronald Reagan: "While busily calling out slogans from their patriotic vocabulary memory warehouse, these same Americans dutifully vote . . . for Ronald Reagan, giving him a landslide victory. . . . These same voters ascended [sic] to Bush's morally high-minded call to apply international laws against Saddam Hussein's tyranny and his invasion of Kuwait." Standing against this wave of ignorance and imperialism is a lone twelve-year-old from Boston, whom Macedo celebrates for his courageous refusal to recite the Pledge of Allegiance.

What does any of this have to do with teaching? Everything, it turns out. In the 1960s, educational progressivism took on an explicitly political cast: schools were to fight institutional racism and redis-tribute power. Today, Columbia's Teachers College holds workshops on cultural and political "oppression," in which students role-play ways to "usurp the existing power structure," and the New York State Regents happily call teachers the "ultimate change agents." To be a change agent, one must first learn to "critique" the existing social structure. Hence, the assignment of such propaganda as Macedo's book.

But however bad the influence of Macedo's puerile politics on future teachers, it pales compared to the model set by his writing style. A typical sentence: "This inability to link the reading of the word with the world, if not combated, will further exacerbate already fee-ble democratic institutions [*sic*] and the unjust, asymmetrical power relations that characterize the hypocritical nature of contemporary democracies." Anyone who dares criticize Macedo for his prose is merely trying to "suffocate discourses," he says, with the "blind and facile call for clarity." That Hunter College could assign this gross be-trayal of the English language to future teachers is a sufficient reason for closing its education program down. Rosa's control of English is shaky enough as it is; to fill her ears with such subliterate writing rep-resents professional malpractice.

But Macedo is just one of the political tracts that Hunter force-fed the innocent Rosa in her first semester. She also learned about the evils of traditional children's stories from education radical Herbert Kohl. In *Should We Burn Babar?* Kohl weighs the case for and against the dearly beloved children's classic *Babar the Elephant*, noting in passing that it prevented him from "question[ing] the patriarchy ear-lier." He decides—but let Rosa expound the message of Kohl's book: "[*Babar*]'s like a children's book, right? [But] there's an underlying meaning about colonialism, about like colonialism, and is it OK, it's really like it's OK, but it's like really offensive to these people." Better burn *Babar* now!

In New York, as in almost every state, the focus on diversity and anti-racism indoctrination comes with the highest imprimatur. The State Board of Regents requires all prospective teachers to have at least one course in "diversity"; many local ed schools pride themselves on weaving "diversity" into all their courses. The nation's most influential education school, Teachers College, promotes the most extreme race consciousness in its mandated diversity program. In her large lecture course, Professor Valerie Henning-Piedmont sneered at "liberal correctness," which she defined as "I don't see the color of my students." Such misguided color blindness, she said, equals: "I don't see the students."

Expect the folly only to grow worse. A draft report from the Regents Task Force on Teaching, grousing that future teachers lack sufficient grounding in diversity, calls for special training in such challenges as "teaching both sexes," thus further legitimizing the ludicrous proposition that schools mistreat girls. The Regents also make recruiting a more "diverse" teaching force a top priority, based on the assumption that minority students learn best from minority teachers. Currently, 34 percent of teachers in New York City, and 15 percent statewide, are minorities, compared to a student population that is 83 percent minority in New York City and 43 percent statewide. Asked what evidence the Regents have for the proposition that the color of the teaching force correlates with achievement, Doris T. Garner, staff coordinator for the Task Force, admitted, "I don't think hard evidence exists that would say that." If black students should be taught by black teachers, should white students be taught by white teachers? "I would not recommend that," replied Garner, fearless of illogic.

Since the Regents are making teacher diversity a top priority, something is going to have to give. Currently, blacks fail the content-free Liberal Arts and Sciences Test of provisional certification at a rate five times that of whites. But that's just a temporary obstacle, because the test-bias hounds may be already closing in for the kill: the discovery that the exam discriminates against minorities. The Regents' most recent paper on teacher training warned that the certification exam "must exclude language that would jeopardize candidates, and include language and content that reflects diversity." Now, the only candidates who would be jeopardized by the exam's language are those, of any color, who are deeply troubled by hot air. As for "cultural bias," at present the exam is a rainbow of multicultural examples and propaganda—one sample question, for example, features a fawning review of a "multicultural dance work that is truly representative of the diversity of New York." Don't be surprised if the complete absence of any "bias" in the exam, however, fails to prevent a concerted, taxpayer-funded effort to redraft it so as to guarantee an equal pass rate among all groups of takers.

Though the current diversity battle cry is "All students can learn," the educationists continually lower expectations of what they should learn. No longer are students expected to learn all their multiplication tables in the third grade, as has been traditional. But while American educators come up with various theories about fixed cognitive phases to explain why our children should go slow, other nationalities trounce us. Sometimes, we're trounced in our own backyards, causing cognitive dissonance in local teachers.

A young student at Teachers College named Susan describes incredulously a Korean-run preschool in Queens. To her horror, the school, the Holy Mountain School, violates every progressive tenet: rather than being "student-centered" and allowing each child to do whatever he chooses, the school imposes a curriculum on the children based on the alphabet. "Each week, the children got a different letter," Susan recalls grimly. Such an approach violates "whole language" doctrine, which holds that students can't "grasp the [alphabetic] symbols without the whole word or the meaning or any context in their lives," in Susan's words. Holy Mountain's further infractions include teaching its wildly international students only in English and failing to provide an "anti-bias multicultural curriculum." The result? By the end of preschool the students learn English and are writing words. Here is true belief in the ability of all children to learn, for it is backed up by action.

Across the city, young teachers are dumping progressive theories faster than Indonesian currency. For all the unctuous talk of diversity, many progressive tenets are dangerously ill-adapted to inner-city classrooms. "They don't say 'boo' about this population," scoffs Samantha, a recent Hunter graduate now teaching in Brooklyn's

Bedford-Stuyvesant section. "My course in multiculturalism had zero to do with the classroom."

A former dancer, Samantha was an open receptacle for progressive ideas. But her early efforts to follow the model have left her stranded. Her fourth-grade class is out of control. "I didn't set it up in a strict manner at the beginning," she laments. "I gave them too many choices; I did a lot of things wrong." Collaborative learning? Forget about it. "My kids resort to fighting immediately if I put them in groups." Samantha tried to use groups to make a poster on electricity. "It was mayhem; they couldn't stay quiet," she recalls.

The student-centered classroom is equally a fraud. "You can't give them choices," Samantha asserts flatly. Next year, with a new class, she will do things differently. "I will have everything set up to the last detail—their names on the desks, which notebooks to buy, how to label them. They need to know what hook to hang their coat on and where to go from there. Every minute of the day has to be scripted. You can't just say: 'Line up!' because they'll fight. Instead, you have to say: 'Boys, stand up, push in your chairs, and here are your line spots.'"

As for "metacognition," that is out as well. "My kids need the rote; they can't do half of six or four divided by two." Samantha is using the most unholy of unholies to teach her children to read—a basal reader, derided by the education establishment as spirit-killing. But the reader gives her specific skill sets to work on—above all, phonics and grammar. "My kids don't hear the correct sound of words at home, such as 'th' or the ending of words, so teaching reading is harder."

Journals, whole language, and "portfolio assessment" became more casualties of the real world at the Holy Cross School in the Bronx. The school recently hired a Teachers College graduate who arrived fired up with those student-centered methods. No more. Now she is working very hard on grammar, according to assistant principal William Kurtz. "Those [progressive] tools don't necessarily work for kids who can't read or tell you what a noun or a verb is," he says. In his own history class, Kurtz has discovered that he needs to be as explicit about study habits and research methods as Samantha is about classroom behavior. "When I give an essay question, I have to be very structured about going to the library and what resources to use. If you don't do that, they look up nothing."

The education establishment would be unfazed by these stories. Samantha and William, it would say, are still prisoners of the "deficit model." All these two benighted teachers can see is what their kids don't know, instead of building on their strengths. If those strengths are hip-hop music, for example, focus on that. But for heaven's sake, don't deny the children the benefits of a child-centered classroom.

In fact, the strict environment that Samantha plans is the best thing that could happen to her pupils. It is perhaps the only place they will meet order and civility. Samantha's children are "surrounded by violence," she says. Many are not interested in learning, because at home, "everyone is dissing everybody, or staying up late to get high. My kids are so emotionally beat up, they don't even know when they're out of their seats." A structured classroom is their only hope to learn the rules that the rest of society lives by. To eliminate structure for kids who have none in their lives is to guarantee failure.

Given progressive education's dismal record, all New Yorkers should tremble at what the Regents have in store for the state. The state's teacher education establishment, led by Columbia's Linda Darling-Hammond, has persuaded the Regents to make its monopoly on teacher-credentialing total. Starting in 2003, according to a Regents plan steaming inexorably toward adoption, all teacher candidates must pass through an education school to be admitted to a classroom. We know, alas, what will happen to them there.

This power grab will be a disaster for children. By making ed school inescapable, the Regents will drive away every last educated adult who may not be willing to sit still for its foolishness but who could bring to the classroom unusual knowledge or experience. The nation's elite private schools are full of such people, and parents eagerly proffer tens of thousands of dollars to give their children the benefit of such skill and wisdom.

Amazingly, even the Regents, among the nation's most addled

education bodies, sporadically acknowledge what works in the classroom. A Task Force on Teaching paper cites some of the factors that allow other countries to wallop us routinely in international tests: a high amount of lesson content (in other words, teacher-centered, not student-centered, learning), individual tracking of students, and a coherent curriculum. The state should cling steadfastly to its momentary insight, at odds with its usual policies, and discard its foolhardy plan to enshrine Anything But Knowledge as its sole education dogma. Instead of permanently establishing the teacher education status quo, it should search tirelessly for alternatives and for potential teachers with a firm grasp of subject matter and basic skills. Otherwise ed school claptrap will continue to stunt the intellectual growth of the Empire State's children.

[1998]

An F for Hip-Hop 101

AS THE M TRAIN crawls toward Brooklyn over the Williamsburg Bridge, it traverses a gauntlet of graffiti. Scrawls cover every surface of the bridge—from the aging wooden trestles all the way up to the central towers, so impasted with spray paint that they appear made of lace. The cupola of a church, visible from the train, wears a graffiti crown of thorns. So it is sadly fitting that below, directly in the shadow of the bridge, students at a Brooklyn public high school are learning how to write graffiti for academic credit.

"I don't know what happened with this piece," instructor Edgar Miranda says impatiently, as he scrutinizes a student's design for "bombing" a subway car, or covering it head-to-toe in graffiti. The scribbles don't hang together as an artistic whole, Miranda frets. Another student fares much better. "This piece is dope," Miranda enthuses in up-to-the-minute street slang, praising a design of a smoking man on one side of a subway car with a whale-like bubble on the other. "You've actually used 'characters'"—graffiti terminology for human figures.

Welcome to Hip-Hop 101, at El Puente Academy for Peace and Justice, a course that teaches students not only how to write graffiti but also how to deejay at parties, break dance (a once popular form of street gymnastics), and emcee or rap. These four activities make up the ghetto-born movement known as "hip-hop culture." Hip-Hop 101 students carry around the traditional graffiti vandal's "black book" in which to perfect their personal graffiti "tag." Do they transfer their learning to the real world? "I have no knowledge of it, nor do I care to find out," instructor Miranda laughs. But of course, the answer is both predictable and easily within reach.

A quick glance around El Puente Academy for Peace and Justice would suggest that a course in hip-hop culture is about as needed as Viagra at the high school prom. El Puente is a small, very friendly, emphatically non-traditional alternative public high school, crammed into every cranny of an abandoned church in the Hasidic and Hispanic neighborhood of Williamsburg. The billowing denim, the beepers, and the designer logos on the school's mostly Hispanic student body suggest a keen awareness of every nuance of ghetto culture.

But El Puente is not about to let mere redundancy stand in the way of a class as trendy as Hip-Hop 101, for the academy is the very embodiment of progressive education, and Hip-Hop 101 is progressivism made flesh. El Puente calls its teachers "facilitators," considers the collaborative student group the foundation of learning, and organizes its curriculum around large, politically correct themes, like sweatshops or the connection between sugar and slavery. Also quintessentially progressive is the central role political activism plays in the school's mission. El Puente evaluates students on their commitment to "social and economic justice." The students have demonstrated such commitment by protesting a local incinerator as "environmental racism"; as part of El Puente's after-school program, they will soon staff a center intended to help the garment workers' union, UNITE, organize workers. Executive director Luis Garden Acosta summed up the school's philosophy to *Newsday* in 1992: the school is "not just about reading and writing and math," he said, "but it's also about wellness, career development, housing, racial justice, and peace."

This may seem a large agenda for a small school, but Acosta is used to thinking big. After serving in the administration of New York mayor John Lindsay in the late 1960s, Acosta joined the Young Lords, a militant Puerto Rican gang whose thirteen-point platform included such demands as the abolition of capitalism, "liberation for all Third World peoples," and "armed self-defense and armed struggle [as] the only means to revolution." Acosta has become more Establishment since then, but his rhetoric, with its talk of "education for liberation," contains much of the old fire.

For progressive idiocy, nothing beats Hip-Hop 101. The course is a classic example of student-centered learning. Rather than imposing a fixed, traditional curriculum, student-centered learning argues for letting students pursue their own intellectual interests (though assuming they reliably have any is, of course, the first mistake). In the 1960s, this doctrine picked up a new catchword: students and teachers alike began demanding education that was "relevant" to youth, especially urban youth. The result? Courses in ghetto culture—of which Hip-Hop 101 is an extreme example—that reinforce the parochialism of inner-city kids rather than open their minds to broader intellectual worlds.

Hip-Hop 101 epitomizes ed school progressive claptrap in a second respect: its implicit lack of concern toward El Puente students' glaring educational deficiencies. These students have a very tenuous command of basic skills. The school's average SAT scores in 1997—385 in verbal, 363 in math (out of a possible 800 in each)—lagged far behind the city's already abysmal average of 443 in verbal and 464 in math. During a non-traditional mathematics class, the students were stumped by the concept "at least." The phrase "There are at least as many adult men as adult women on a wagon train" means, they agreed, that there could be fewer men than women. The phrase "There is at least one child per family" means "There is no more than one child per family," explained one girl with brown lipstick and long tendrils of hair.

Any school administrator not blinded by the folly of progressivism would put such pupils on a strict regimen of real language study, filling their ears with the best examples of English prose, as well as drilling them on basic math. To spend any class time studying and writing rap lyrics, with their street slang and obscenities—not to mention studying graffiti and deejaying—is an unconscionable diversion from the students' real educational needs.

Unfortunately, Hip-Hop 101 is no aberration. Desperate for "relevance," teachers across the country swamp rap groups such as Run-

DMC with requests for lyrics. In New York, many teachers use rap lyrics as a way of "relating to where [the students] are," in the words of a teacher at Park West High School. Graffiti instruction is not yet as widespread, but it's a worrisome portent that Columbia University's Teachers College, the fountainhead of progressive-education gospel for the city and the nation, invited Edgar Miranda to give a presentation on Hip-Hop 101 last December. And El Puente's foundation support—the school has received thousands of dollars from the Annenberg Foundation—gives it the stamp of Establishment approval. Hip-Hop 101, then, provides a troubling benchmark for how far the trivialization of contemporary education can go.

How could a school so lose its moral bearings that it cheerfully teaches illegal activity? Hip-Hop 101's pedigree includes not just progressive pieties but also the 1960s' widespread belief that crime was a quasi-political protest of the oppressed. In the late 1960s and early 1970s, graffiti started metastasizing across New York City, quickly evolving from runic "tags" scrawled on mailboxes and walls to huge multicolored murals covering every inch of the city's subways. And just as quickly, the elites began romanticizing it. *New Yorker* cartoonist Saul Steinberg declared the commission of graffiti a "necessity for entering the art scene." Norman Mailer, America's premier guru of adolescent rebellion, brayed that with each graffiti "hit," "something in the whole scheme of the system gives a death rattle." A *New York* magazine cover story in 1973, called "The Handwriting on the Walls: Should We Love It and Leave It?" cheered the "first genuine teenage street culture since the 1950s" and sneered at the "executive in his camel's hair coat," who cringes in subway cars with windows and interiors wholly blackened by paint. Did graffiti make the working stiff and office clerk feel besieged? So much the better, the elites gloated; they're faceless conformists anyway, whereas graffiti "artists"—they're authentic! Naturally, all the fawning media attention merely increased the incentive to "tag."

Soon enough, the media discovered that graffiti was part of a bigger, more exciting movement: hip-hop. In the seventies, many of the kids who were spraying subway cars were also staging open-air discos in Bronx parks. They would plug their sound systems into light poles and compete at deejaying—not just playing albums but also producing odd sounds by scraping the record with the stereo stylus. Eventually, they started talking over the instrumental breaks in songs, a practice known as emceeing or rapping.

Competition was fierce. "If the crowd didn't like you, you might get shot at," rapper Grand Master Flash recalled in 1983. Early raps celebrated partying and sexual prowess or railed at ghetto conditions. To accompany the rapping, kids spun and twirled like dervishes in a form of street dance called break dancing or B-boying. Here, too, the line between artistic competition and ordinary street violence was sometimes thin. "A [dance] battle would get you into a fight," former break-dancer Steve ("Mr. Wiggles") Clemente told the *Washington Post* in 1995. "[Crazy Legs, another break-dancer] got his jaw broken. He got jumped, I got jumped. Now we're more mature."

The graffiti vandals, rappers, and B-boys organized themselves into "crews," somewhat less criminal forms of association than gangs. Some ended up break dancing and spraying graffiti murals at Lincoln Center and the Kennedy Center; most turned out less glamorously. Almost half of all fifteen-year-old graffiti writers apprehended in 1974 had been arrested three years later for burglary and robbery. Says one survivor of the late 1970s graffiti and break-dancing scene: "[A lot of us] were stickup kids, things like that. We all did our foul stuff also."

In the early 1980s, film crews and reporters descended on Washington Heights and the South Bronx to capture this movement. Sure, graffiti was colorful and break dancing energetic, but what really attracted the media was hip-hop's attitude and style. As rap impresario Bill Adler has explained: "The meaning of [rapper] LL Cool J, whatever his explicit message is, is 'I'm young, I'm black, I don't sing, I don't smile for the camera, I don't wear a tuxedo, and I'm still making stupid dollars.'"

The elites ate up such contempt. Hip-hop, *Time* magazine enthused breathlessly in early 1983, was "black, young, and ineffably, unflappably cool, . . . like spray-painted murals down the side of a New York City subway, or a ghetto blaster carried on a shoulder broadcasting 130 beats a minute all over a Bronx street." *Time* swooned over "rapper flash . . . the jeans, the leathers, the heavy personalized belt buckles, even the jewelry," and tittered knowingly at ski cap "legends like I'D RATHER BE SKIING [that] refer not to snowy slopes but to white mounds of a certain illicit inhalable substance."

Today, rap music has overwhelmed all other aspects of hip-hop culture. Defeated in the subways, spray-painted graffiti has slunk back to walls and telephone booths, its glamour dulled. Break dancing may as well be a minuet, for all its current attraction to teens. Yet hip-hop, defined now almost exclusively as rap and attitude, is stronger than ever. Not only does it generate billions of dollars annually in record, video, and clothing sales, but it puts food on the table of many a professorial home, whose owners reciprocate by conferring on hip-hop the impenetrable jargon of the academy. Sample, courtesy of the University of Pennsylvania's Houston A. Baker, Jr., former president of the Modern Language Association: "We meditate the legal 'X' of erasure not in an effort to assume the role of latter-day phenomenologists—but to consider the inversive and brilliant powers of symbolic transformation possessed by African-Americans."

Progressive-education theory, then, may have put Hip-Hop 101's "facilitator," Edgar Miranda, in the classroom, but three decades of graffiti glorification and ghetto romanticization have given him his lines. Miranda is a wiry and articulate twenty-seven-year-old, with a narrow face and dark eyes framed by heavy glasses, goatee, and ponytail. His vintage graffiti cant is untouched by the broken-windows thesis or insight into the seriousness of quality-of-life crimes or any of the other advances in our understanding of public misbehavior. Miranda has a personal stake in graffiti glorification. "When I did graffiti," he recalls nostalgically, "I was making a statement. I was poor and small and grew up on public assistance."

In promoting graffiti, Miranda uses the favored strategies of academic apologists everywhere: false analogy (graffiti is like "hieroglyphics or petroglyphs in Caribbean caves"; "my students are learning an arts discipline, like if I asked them to draw a still life");

romanticization (graffiti is a "cry for notice: 'I'm still here!' "); and changing the subject.

Changing the subject—or the "root cause" strategy—is the most useful ploy. "To talk about graffiti," Miranda says, "you must critically look at the socioeconomic resources of the community." Or: Youths do graffiti because they "don't see themselves in a positive light on the news." (How defacing property will improve youths' image, Miranda doesn't explain.) Some "root causes," however, are taboo. In laying out the deficient "resources" of the community, Miranda observes: "If you give yourself a tour of a New York City housing project, you would find table-hockey tables in the community centers missing the plastic parts." Well, aren't the deprived youths themselves the "root cause" of those missing parts? "You can't solve the problems in one week," Miranda responds philosophically.

Invoking root causes allows Miranda to evade the biggest blind spot in graffiti glorification: the impact on the property owner. Why, I asked him, should a small property owner bear the costs of cleaning up graffiti? "You're missing the larger question," Miranda shot back. "Why are young people painting on this building?" Miranda never answered the smaller question.

Actually, Miranda does have a solution for the small property owner—reach out to youth. Artists are starting to gentrify the area around El Puente. Remember that, according to Miranda and every other graffiti glorifier, graffiti is, above all, artistic expression. And yet, oddly, Williamsburg's new residents don't recognize graffiti vandals as fellow artists. In fact, according to Miranda, they're downright offended when their doors get tagged. One friend of Miranda's, however, "trips out" his fellow artists, Miranda says, because he has the only untagged door on his block. The reason? He has "reached out" to youth. "Young people see these [new residents] as invaders," Miranda explains. Their response: "'What are you doing here?' Ta! Ta! Ta!," Miranda cries, mimicking the blasts from a can of aerosol paint.

But why should the burden be on the property owner to "reach out to youth" as a precondition of unmolested property? Small business owners, in particular, find New York's hostile business climate overwhelming enough; to demand that they also engage in youth outreach to ensure a graffiti-free storefront is extortion. I asked Miranda if his graffiti students would be allowed to tag El Puente Academy. No, he replied, "how we look at it is, they don't tag their own home," and El Puente is like their home. It turns out that graffiti is rich artistic expression as long as it's on someone else's property.

Miranda may get the opportunity to test his convictions soon, for he is planning to buy a house in Williamsburg. I ask him: If someone tags your house, does that make you an oppressor? "I don't want to get down on the person," he says, beneficently. It would be interesting to know how long his open-mindedness will continue, if local teens decide to "resist the economic conditions of youth" on his front door. For now, however, his graffiti and hip-hop gospel is unsullied by conflicting loyalties.

One day last April, Hip-Hop 101 met in a bright classroom at the top of a narrow staircase. The students sat in a large semicircle, pressed up against the far walls of the room; Miranda, wearing a black Young Lords T-shirt inscribed with the slogan EVERY GENERATION CARRIES THE STRUGGLE FORWARD, lectured in front. Ironically, Miranda is a neat, organized teacher with terrific graphic skills and a fairly strict classroom manner. Rather than putting the students in collaborative groups, he uses a question-and-answer format. Students take exams and write research papers. But there, any similarity with traditional education ends.

Take the exams, for example. These tested the students' knowledge not of history or literature but of graffiti principles. In one, the students had a mere ten minutes to execute a sketch for "roasting" a subway car—a clever simulation, no doubt, of real-world conditions. In another, the students had to produce a more elaborate full-color mural on an 11-by-17-inch stencil of a subway car—like target practice on a human outline. "Points were taken off if they did fill-ins" or violated other graffiti conventions, Miranda explains. That day in April, Miranda individually examined those few students who had actually completed their graffiti assignments ("What are the style, elements, and theme of this piece?"). The students were supposed to write a short essay addressing these questions; few, if any, had done so.

Such academic conventions add up to a "fine arts" course, rather like studying the Renaissance, Miranda claims. Just for the record, it does not. Leaving aside for the moment the all-important question of illegality, graffiti remains, with few exceptions, a crude (if energetic) form of visual expression.

During Miranda's one-on-one student conferences, the rest of the class, directed to practice their individual graffiti tags in their black books, just sat passively, waiting for the next part of the class. That came quickly, since there were so few graffiti murals to examine. Before closing out the section on graffiti, Miranda once again quizzed the class: "When we talked about hip-hop, we talked about its four elements—graffiti, emceeing, B-boying, and deejaying. Who can describe what graffiti is?" "The expression of selves," answered one student. "Artistic expression," chimed in another. Good, they've got it. Time to move on to break dancing.

Either out of good pedagogy or because there is so little substance to Hip-Hop 101, Miranda frequently reviews material from previous classes; evidently, classroom drill, anathema to progressive educators, is permissible for subjects dear to facilitators' hearts. After drawing a lovely freehand map of the Western Hemisphere on the blackboard, Miranda recaps a lecture on the transmission of African culture to the Americas. The students remain a bit confused over geography. Asked why a dance, the *capoiera*, began in Brazil, one student answers that the slaves were going north in the underground railroad. So crammed are today's students with the by-now iconic figures and institutions of the abolitionist era—the only historical figures they've reliably encountered—that these keep popping up in inappropriate places. When Miranda asks for manifestations of African culture in the United States, the students volunteer, correctly enough, songs and spirituals. But then they keep going with the underground railroad, Harriet Tubman, and the code name "Moses"—all only distantly related, if at all, to Africa. Such free associations suggest that what these kids need most is history, not hip-hop, but that is not the agenda here.

From his thumbnail sketch of early African-American culture, Miranda jumps to the present. "How is hip-hop similar to or different from these elements?" he asks. To get the class thinking, he writes "Gangs, Crews and Family" on the board and asks them to respond. Except for the mention of "drugs," "cops," and "fighting," the image of gangs that emerges bears more resemblance to the Elks than to the perpetrators of drive-by shootings. Family, however, receives the highest marks. As one student explains: "Family is like something you should keep real with. Your gang can only go so far with you; your crew and your family can go all the way with you." Not the ideal endorsement, perhaps, but an endorsement nonetheless.

Next, Miranda quickly traces the emergence of break-dancing crews from street gangs, mentioning in passing the noble, communitarian origins of the Black Panthers and the Young Lords. Then, it's time for that staple of modern education: watching videos. Miranda recycles even these, popping in for quick review two videos that the students have already watched. In the first, a 1983 PBS documentary on graffiti, the camera pans over massive graffiti murals as the cheerful narrator, who sounds as if he just stepped out of a 1960s educational film of the *Better Living Through Chemistry* ilk, extols the hip-hop state of mind he calls "rocking." "For graffiti artists," he explains admiringly, "it's rocking the city with your name on the train; for the B-boys, it's rocking the mike." The scene shifts to a dance floor on which two break-dancing teams compete by writhing and spinning. One boy moons the competition; another finishes his number by grabbing his crotch.

In the next video, a low-budget movie from 1984 called *Wild Style*, a terrified-looking white woman with platinum hair and a string of pearls wanders woodenly through a throbbing black club scene. As a rapper in a turtleneck chants: "I'm proud, I'm proud to be black, you know," the blonde tentatively starts smoking a joint and swaying to the beat. Bing Crosby in blackface could not have come up with a more stereotypical portrayal of blackness.

However devoid such videos are of intellectual content, nothing so fully conveys the educational vacuum that is Hip-Hop 101 as the students' "research" assignments. Miranda had brought into class heartbreakingly neat file folders, filled with carefully copied articles from such fan magazines as *Rap Pages* on such topics as the "neglected but not forgotten West Coast graffiti scene," deejays on the black-run New York radio station Hot 97, and up-and-coming Latino hip-hop. To write their "research paper"—on "pioneering artists in hip-hop"—the students had merely to pick out a few articles and summarize them.

Nothing in this assignment comes remotely close to offering the slightest shred of education. Miranda's students may sense, however remotely, that they are being shortchanged. I asked a student who was sitting slumped in his chair why he had not responded to Miranda's call to pick up some articles. "I got those magazines in my house, too," he answered, contemptuously.

Now what is the payoff from this craven capitulation to anti-intellectualism? Virtually nothing. Student-centered education promises to deliver excited, involved learners. None of those was in evidence at Hip-Hop 101. Students slouch in their chairs, eyes glazed, though at least they are not disruptive. No one bothers to open a notebook, much less take notes. Miranda might as well be translating Sallust, for all the "active learning" going on. And students still hand in assignments late and incomplete.

So the bargain has proved hollow. Progressive educators jettison the great body of Western learning in a desperate bid for students' attention, only to find the same blank looks and poor performance said to be the natural outcome of dead languages and white male Anglo-European authors. Debasing the classroom with the most superficial aspects of contemporary culture is no guarantee of student interest.

What Hip-Hop 101 has guaranteed, however, is a future supply of graffiti "artists" in the city. El Puente officially denies this. Alpha

Anderson, the school's courtly assistant principal, says quite sincerely: "I don't think anyone has the right to spray-paint your property; we don't advocate that." Miranda is far less straightforward: "I'm not telling them what to do and what not to do." Such calculated neutrality is hardly convincing. But even if Miranda had tried to discourage real-world application of his lessons, it is preposterous to think that a course lionizing graffiti vandals will have no effect on its students' graffiti production.

Miranda's refusal to intervene in his students' extracurricular activities has an unimpeachable source: progressive-education ideology. "Following [Marxist pedagogue Paolo] Freire, I don't have the power to tell a young person what to do and not to do," Miranda asserts. "I can give them the tools"—an unfortunate image—"and they find the path. If I tell a child, 'don't, don't, don't,' they'll say, 'Why always No?'" But the role of a teacher, despite progressive theory, is precisely to exercise intellectual and moral guidance; once that is abdicated, education is not possible.

Well, Miranda may not care to find out, but how are his students applying their knowledge of graffiti principles? I ask a tall boy in a big jacket, who has been sitting low in his seat, legs splayed, throughout the class, to show me his black book. It is filled with scribbles resembling tangled fishing wire. "I've been practicing my Gs," he explains. Like many of the class's budding graffiti "artists," "Jigga" (the boy's *nom de can*) is modest about his accomplishments. "I just started with graffiti—on phones," he says, "but I'm not a pro yet." Who decides if you're a pro? I ask him. "If you will look corny, [then you're not a pro]," he replies. But who judges? "Yourself and what people say about your pieces." Jigga knows what he needs to do to become more professional: "More style, more graphics. When you write bubble letters, it's wack, it's corny. You have to be [more] creative."

Like any downtown artist, Jigga seeks exposure. "You go writing everywhere, because the more you get around, the more famous you are." Are there any samples of his work in this neighborhood? I ask. He nods. Jigga obviously does not shrink from competition, since the area around El Puente is already tagged to saturation.

Another boy has not yet made his professional debut, but he intends to. "You take a plain wall and make it look so magnificent," he says dreamily. Like Jigga, this husky boy knows his artistic limits: "When I first started [practicing], it was kind of corny, but I'm getting better at it. I want feedback." Where will he debut? "Well, I live on Coney Island," he hints.

Not all Miranda's students share such artistic ambition; some, in fact, repudiate the message that graffiti is art. One baby-faced boy, who got 100 on his subway mural exam, says he doesn't like graffiti: "It's just messin' up other people's property." But many students are convinced that doing graffiti represents a career path. "These are established artists," a boy with a nascent mustache tells me. "If a kid wants to start developing himself, they do travel, if they make it big." Another adds: "People do get hired. Pepsi . . . Marvel . . . and a clothes line, PMB, was started by three graffiti artists."

Youth culture can be cruel, however. For all Miranda's street talk and cool demeanor, he is already obsolete. One student, asked what he thought of the class, responds witheringly: "I'm not going to comment. I expected to learn how to professionalize on the lettering, but I already knew everything." Another student agrees: "Most of the stuff in the class I already knew. It was more like a refresher." There is a lesson here for anyone who dares teach popular culture to teenagers: don't bother—you'll be behind before you even begin.

Hip-Hop 101 is on the same spectrum as other progressive-ed nostrums, not in a world of its own. That a school could embrace a practice both illegal and destructive of the city's spirit is a troubling indication of how far the educational system has lost its bearings. Desperate to show "sensitivity" to minority students and to create subjects in which they can unequivocally excel, schools have cast aside responsibility for academic and moral education. The decision to teach graffiti is also the natural outcome of the inclusion of contemporary popular culture in the curriculum. Once you shrink from distinguishing Montaigne from Madonna, it becomes indefensible to make distinctions within low culture and exclude aspects of it that some benighted segments of society deem illegal.

El Puente's teachers and administrators are clearly well-meaning, but they could not have designed a course more likely to keep their students down than Hip-Hop 101. Meretricious and evanescent, hip-hop "culture" is simply not something that schools should waste a single second on when facing children as ignorant of the wider world as El Puente's are. But cutting-edge educators are sleepwalking through the apocalypse, seemingly indifferent to the educational meltdown we face.

[1998]

Revisionist Lust:
The Smithsonian Today

RECENT VISITORS to the Smithsonian's Natural History Museum were greeted with some unpleasant news: the museum was contaminated. Not by asbestos or toxic chemicals, mind you, but by far more noxious substances: racism, sexism, and anthrocentrism. To protect the unwary, warning labels throughout the halls identified which of the museum's venerable dioramas were infected by which ideological error. "Female animals are being portrayed in ways that make them appear deviant or substandard to male animals," warned a label next to an exhibit of American hartebeests. A beloved family of lions at a watering hole was also branded for sexism, because the standing male and reclining female suggested to the museum's gender police a prefeminist division of labor. A leaping Bengalese tiger was dismissed as too predatory, a violation of the communitarian animal ethic.

The Natural History Museum is not the only Smithsonian institution to have rethought its mission in recent years. Next door at the National Museum of American History, visitors encounter an America characterized by rigid class barriers, ever-growing economic inequality, predatory capitalists, and oppressed minorities. Several blocks away, curators at the Smithsonian's American Art Museum are busy exposing art as just another "social text" masking illegitimate power relations. And across the Mall, Air and Space Museum curators, still fuming over the cancellation of the shameful Enola Gay exhibit, whine like grounded teenagers about the old military fogies now directing the museum who are inhibiting the curators' revisionist lust.

Anyone who still doubts that the madness currently possessing American universities matters to society at large should take a stroll through today's Smithsonian. The Institution has been transformed by a wholesale embrace of the worst elements of America's academic culture. The staples of cutting-edge academic "research"—smirking irony, cultural relativism, celebration of putative victims, facile attacks on science—are all thriving in America's premier museum and research complex, its showcase to itself and to the world. The changes at the Smithsonian are not unique to that institution. Museums across the country have rushed headlong into what may be called the "new museology," based on a mindless parroting of academic fads. But the Smithsonian's embrace of postmodern theory and identity politics is of greatest import, because of the Institution's contribution to America's public identity.

For most of its history, the Smithsonian has been driven by the thirst for knowledge. In 1835, the U.S. chargé d'affaires in London received news of a most unusual bequest. James Smithson, a British aristocrat and amateur scientist, had left his estate of a hundred thousand pounds to the "United States of America, to found at Washington, under the name of the Smithsonian Institution, an establishment for the increase and diffusion of knowledge among men." Smithson, a bastard of august lineage, had never been to America; his gift may have been revenge against his native society for snubbing him for his illegitimate birth, or it may have simply reflected his admiration for the democratic experiment under way across the Atlantic.

Smithson's bequest caused an enormous stir. After eight years of heated debate over its interpretation—suggestions included an agricultural college and an observatory—Congress finally defined the institution in 1846 as a national museum for government collections, a laboratory, an art gallery, and a library.

An explosion in scientific knowledge and America's passionate desire to discover what lay west drove the Smithsonian in the nineteenth century. Smithsonian naturalists accompanied westward expeditions, and returned to the Castle (the Smithsonian's first building) on the Mall with crates of mineral, animal, and vegetable specimens. Smithsonian geologists heroically mapped unknown territory, and Smithsonian ethnographers lovingly chronicled Indian cultures. For the next century and a half, this drive for knowledge would continue, until eventually, the Institution's collections would constitute a veritable library of the world.

In the late 1960s and 1970s, however, while the Smithsonian's scientific research continued apace, its historical and cultural identity subtly changed. As its current curators proudly describe it, the Institution became sensitive to the social and political currents swirling around it—ghetto riots, Vietnam War protests, and women's "liberation." Museums nationwide became terrified of the charge of "elitism," and adopted the media of popular culture to increase their "relevance."

The Smithsonian of the 1970s already looked to the academy for its inspiration, particularly to the new fields of social and cultural history. A 1976 show on immigration at the Museum of History and Technology (since renamed the National Museum of American History) reflected this influence in its acute attention to race and class. Also academically inspired was the Institution's newfound zest for exhibiting the detritus of popular culture, most famously, its Archie Bunker Chair.

But nothing in the 1970s matched the changes ushered in by anthropologist Robert McCormick Adams, who assumed the Smithsonian secretaryship in 1984. Adams had been sold to Congress as someone who would increase the scholarly standards at the Institution, illustrating yet again the utter cluelessness of politicians and ordinary people regarding the academically enfranchised cultural left. Described by the *Washington Post* as a "happily successful Establishment radical," Adams declared the purpose of museums to be "confrontation, experimentation, and debate"—a politically charged manifesto that pointedly ignored the Smithsonian's mandate to increase knowledge. Adams dictated an aggressive program to "diversify" the Institution, and set out to hire curators, mostly from the academy, that shared his commitment to "critical" scholarship.

The Adams regime (which ended in 1994) perfected the "new museology" at the Smithsonian. The most important principle of the new dogma is "honoring multiple ways of interpreting the world." Curatorial expertise and scientific knowledge are out; "multiple voices" and relativism in all its forms are in. (As we will see, however, only certain "voices" ever seem to get heard.) In furtherance of the "multiple interpretations" principle, the new museologist consults with "the community" in devising exhibits. Moreover, those exhibits must aim to enhance self-esteem: they are designed to increase the ethnic pride of minorities. Concomitant with this redressive principle, a new museological exhibit is grossly ahistorical: it exports contemporary standards of equity to the past in order to make its case against oppression and victimhood seem stronger.

The final two principles of the new museology are contempt for the public, and infatuation with high-tech wizardry. With the exception of these last two tenets, the new museology is directly imported from the academy. The Smithsonian's recent public relations fiascoes all embodied one or more of its principles.

A prototypical new hire of the Adams regime—and classic "new museologist"—was Robert Sullivan, responsible for the warning labels on the Natural History Museum's dioramas. Sullivan was brought to the museum in 1990 as director of public programs, and his existence there is particularly unfortunate, for no museum better embodies the Smithsonian's glorious past. To Sullivan, however, that past is cause for shame and criticism. Sullivan is nothing if not steeped in theory, and he can reel off Foucauldian riffs with the best of them. Natural history museums embody the concept of "Safe Terror," he explains; they were part of the "Victorian campaign of containing wildness." "While the etiquette books were talking of how to conceal, repress, and deny bodily functions of any sort," he says, "natural history museums were created as a place to exhibit such wildness from a safe distance." Among the practices that were being "repressed on the street" while being shown in museums, according to Sullivan, were scarification and tattooing—not heretofore recognized as important Anglo-American traditions. Sullivan's sinister interpretation of natural history museums clashes with their philanthropic origins. Such institutions, their advocates argued, would allow the urban poor, increasingly imprisoned by large industrial cities, to enjoy the "refreshment, humanism, and inspiration" of nature, as one nineteeth-century proponent wrote.

Sullivan shares Foucault's contempt for civilization, which he characterizes as "quote-unquote 'civilization.'" He also has fully imbibed the postmodern academy's skepticism about science (though of course he continues to enjoy its benefits daily). He announced breezily upon his arrival that the "Western-scientific-anthropological world view is merely one more alternative way of knowing and encoding the world, no more valuable or accurate, no less ideological or culture-bound, than any other."

A critic espousing such contempt for the achievements of Western civilization is poorly suited to help lead an institution so intimately related to the "Western-scientific-anthropological worldview." Indeed, Sullivan almost didn't accept the position. As he confided to Frank Talbot, the museum director at the time, "I was so frightened and discouraged by the overwhelming needs I see [at the museum] and the seeming indifference of the visitors." Those annoying visitors, he explained, "don't want to be engaged, empowered, or even educated, [but] just want to be distracted . . . from the dailiness, the tedium, the fear of their lives." But courageous and self-sacrificing fellow that he is, Sullivan manfully accepted the job at the largest research museum in the country, explaining grandiloquently: "We must affirm life, have the courage to name what is intolerable to us, and act against it."

Sullivan immediately set to work "erasing [the museum's] racist belief system." He assembled a gender-race bias task force to "critique exhibits and produce policy and practices manuals on Gender and Race Equity." Faced with budget limits, Sullivan was unable to tear down and replace everything he found offensive about the museum; his second-best solution was the so-called "dilemma labels" (since removed) placed next to the dioramas. "If you couldn't change the exhibits, can you make an exhibit out of the exhibit, and show the cultural values in science?" Sullivan explains, demonstrating his close familiarity with self-reflexive postmodern practice.

Ironically, many of the museum's naturalists had complained for years of *scientific* inaccuracies in some of the exhibition labels, but their complaints went ignored. Science has no constituency, however; politics does.

Sullivan also acted on his announced intention to grant to "minority cultures . . . access to collections and meaningful influence on interpretive points of view." Upon his arrival at the museum, he started a "dialogue" with a radically Afrocentric "community" group that had long complained of the museum's alleged racism. Sullivan invited the group Tu-Wa-Moja to advise the museum regarding planned revisions to its Africa Hall and Human Evolution exhibit.

The result was predictable. The group made life extremely difficult for the archaeologists and anthropologists who had been ordered to find common ground with it; but little else was accomplished. The museum tried to defuse Tu-Wa-Moja's objections to the Africa Hall by putting "dilemma labels" on the exhibits, but the group was not satisfied. In a remarkable symbol of the new museology, Sullivan simply shut down the hall. "Tearing down the hall was a way to build trust," he explains. Leaving it up while the new hall was in development would have damaged the Smithsonian's credibility, Sullivan concluded, because the "community had great mistrust about whether the Smithsonian would redo it in an inclusive way." As a final gesture of "trust," Sullivan allowed Tu-Wa-Moja to film the shuttered hall for its Afrocentric propaganda materials; Leonard Jeffries served as de facto master of ceremonies. The moral of the story is that in order to stoke an ethnic interest group's self-esteem, the new museology demands that everyone else be denied the opportunity to learn from the Smithsonian's collections.

To his credit, Sullivan has not pressured the museum's curators to accept Tu-Wa-Moja's views on the African origins of everything. But why was the group invited in the first place? What did this group of Washington residents know about evolution to justify their advising a team of physical anthropologists, with all the extra labor that that interaction cost the museum, or about Africa to justify their advising cultural anthropologists? The answer, of course, lies in skin color—more specifically, in the racial essentialism that holds that a young, black Washington male is an expert on all things African.

The "community consultation" imperative that brought Tu-Wa-Moja into the Natural History Museum has cast a wider net than just local Afrocentrics. Over one hundred people are advising the museum on its new Africa Hall, most of them black. Again, the process is extremely time-consuming. Mary Jo Arnoldi, an African curator at the museum, explained why the community consultations are necessary: "Museums are becoming aware that in a postmodern world, the people you're representing say: how come you're the expert? Sullivan's only echoing what the academy has been talking about for a long time."

The new Africa Hall will be impeccably postmodern. It will tell African "stories" with African "voices." Its theme is not Africa per se, but African identity: over half the hall will be devoted to the "African diaspora"—peoples of African origin living elsewhere. Geographical divisions of Africa will be minimally included as a grudging concession to visitors who expect it. The new museology has little use for the traditional organizing tools of natural history, such as geography or species classification, which are seen, no doubt, as relics of the "Western-scientific-anthropological worldview." But what is a natural history museum if not the record of the interaction of humans with a particular patch of the natural world? In an era when Americans' geographical and historical knowledge is shrinking into nothingness, a deemphasis on geography is dangerous.

The old Africa Hall was criticized in the press and the "community" as showing a timeless Africa of quaint or barbaric customs; curators of the new Africa Hall are determined to avoid such charges. "We have to make sure to let people know there are as many Africans in science labs as are working in the fields," says Mary Jo Arnoldi. The self-esteem imperative seems to have overridden truth here: given the backward state of Africa's still largely rural economy, it seems highly unlikely that Africa is producing as many scientists as subsistence farmers. Oddly, when identity groups seek to legitimate themselves, they draw on traditional Western criteria of accomplishment, such as science, despite the cultural left's disdain for such alienating forms of thought.

To date, Sullivan has been better at shutting things down than putting them up. Occasionally, his revisionist agenda has met with stiff internal opposition. He had tried to remove from the museum's rotunda its famous charging elephant, for example—as a hunting trophy, a symbol for Sullivan of white capitalist aggression. But a passionate protest by the museum's animal scientists shelved the plan. Anyone who cares for museum aesthetics can be glad for that, since Sullivan's suggestions for a replacement included a "large animated programmable globe," illustrating the cardinal truth that while the new museum bureaucrat may be chock full of political opinions, he is absolutely devoid of taste.

But there are large changes in the offing, and readers with a love of traditional natural history museums are advised to visit the Smithsonian soon, before it's too late. Eventually, all of the museum's enchanting human culture halls will be torn down, to make way for the new museological extravaganza "Changing Cultures in a Changing World." This overarching cultural anthropology exhibit will focus on three or four big ideas about "cultural change"—one of the watchwords, along with "global change," of the new thinking.

The ideology of "cultural change" is the antithesis of everything natural history museums once stood for. The naturalists and anthropologists who created those museums wanted to present the vast wonders of the earth in a logical, coherent fashion; they had an enormous respect for details and facts. The Smithsonian's glorious dioramas—the creation of scientists with obvious artistic flair—gave visitors a panoramic, but specific, view of the world's cultures. But museums no longer strive for comprehensiveness or specificity. Instead, the educator's favorite "idea" is paramount. "We have the space to tell four to five potent stories," says Sullivan. "All the dioramas will be gone, we're not worried about covering the same ground." There is considerable irony to this breezy indifference to coverage. Native American activists have attacked the museum for only showing *one* tribe of Eskimos; now, there will likely be none. (In the interim, to respond to Native American complaints, Sullivan will put a video next to the Eskimo diorama showing contemporary Aleut life—a gross and unconscionable violation of the aesthetics of the Americas Hall.)

If the theme of "cultural change" does not highlight specific places and peoples, what then is it all about? Like most everything in postmodern politics it is about "identity." But there is a twist. "Every visitor [to the new hall] should find something about themselves," says Sullivan. Future visitors should find that they are "the culmination of cultural change that makes them the same as every other visitor. They will not meet the exotic other here, they will meet themselves." The unspoken agenda here is that all cultures are equal, and influence each other equally.

The Natural History Museum provides one further contrast between the old and the new museology. The old museology created places of refuge, where visitors could contemplate nature in stillness. The new museology abhors stillness; the key word is "interactivity." The new museum halls are starting to resemble video arcades: recorded voices drone over and over from all corners, TV screens run the same video endlessly, and computers beep and blink before jamming up. For all Sullivan and his ilk's professed distaste for "rational-logical-technocratic society," they are absolutely besotted with gadgetry. An exhibit on marine ecosystems features several video screens embedded in fake rock and tacky plywood, as well as an LED display. On either side of the cluttered exhibit are the traditional bird and mammal halls, featuring such endearing vitrines as "Mammal Parachutes" and "Concealing Coloration." The brilliance and variety of the animals, many collected by Theodore Roosevelt, makes the point about "biodiversity" far more effectively than the beeping, whirring technologies next door. With so splendid a species collection, why would the curators opt for the simulacrum of video?

"Interactive" museum technologies are supposed to allow visitors to "create the meaning" of the exhibit, or, less pretentiously, learn at their own speed. But the new technology is about as interactive as a factory time clock. Typically, the viewer punches a few keys on a computer screen to access data, and the computer spews it out. The answer was predetermined; there is no reason the information could not have been presented in straight graphic format. But the new technology allows curators to feel up-to-date with the information age.

To be sure, there is only so much a new museologist at an old museum can do. Despite the best of revisionist intentions, not all the old exhibits can be junked immediately. To achieve a perfect embodiment of the new museology, one must start from a clean slate. What luck for Secretary Adams that such a slate existed—the last undeveloped piece of land on the Mall. On it, Adams decreed the erection of the National Museum of the American Indian, planned for completion in 2001. The project has sucked money out of existing parts of the Smithsonian, but from Adams's perspective, nothing was too good for the museum, for it would seal his reputation as protector of ethnic identity groups. The American Indian Museum provides an ominous harbinger of museums to come.

The museum was born in racial animus. Its administrator declared early on: "If we do not take responsibility for the work, the white people will win the day. . . . We cannot let some arrogant, racist, or stupid people defeat us." Questions. The museum is supposed to be not just *about* American Indians, but by them and for them as well. Museum planners describe American Indians as their "constituency," an overtly political concept. Naturally, a Native American is designing the building; he renews himself for further battles by retreating to his "sweat lodge" in Rock Creek Park.

Anyone eager for a foretaste of this pure new museological creation can get it in the Smithsonian's historic Arts and Industries Building. There, a preview exhibition, predictably called "Stories of the People," is installed. And what a preview it is! The first jolt comes from the wall labels, which use the first-person plural throughout: "As tribal people, . . . we are wonderfully diverse yet essentially similar";

"our Cherokee story is one of balance—men and women, animals and plants, complementing each other's lives." Had a white curator presumed to use the first-person plural, the postmodernists would be busy deploring the "construction" of the viewer as "the Other."

The second jolt from "Stories of the People" is the embarrassing vacuousness of the accompanying texts, many of which seem transcribed from Chinese fortune cookies. "Apache culture is adaptive and reflects the times," reads one. The conceit of "living in balance" with nature pervades the exhibition, though one does wonder about the buffalo run off cliffs by Indians: did they, too, feel in perfect harmony with nature? Even "men and women" lived in balance, as the Cherokee text quoted above claims. Let us recall that that balance consisted of the women doing hard labor domestically while the men hunted and went to war. If an eighteenth-century burgher had made a similar claim for his domestic arrangements, he would be impaled on the stake of false consciousness.

Finally, there is the overtly political nature of the show. The exhibition is a piece of advocacy from start to finish, arguing the validity of Indian legal claims against the U.S. government. The following statement is typical in its clumsy juxtaposition of folksy English translations and hard-nosed legal claims:

> Today, the environment is not as rich as it was before the House on the Water People came. Conflicts between our Tribe and the House on the Water People still exist. The harvest and management of fisheries is a contentious issue, despite court decisions affirming our right to half of the fish in our waters.

Although construction of its new multimillion-dollar taxpayer-financed building on the Mall proceeds apace, there may be little to fill it when it is completed. The museum is depleting its collections under the aegis of the Native American Graves Protection and Repatriation Act of 1990, which governs the return of native remains to tribes. In essence, the museum sent around a shopping list of goodies, asking tribes if they wanted to make a claim on its collections. The claims are becoming increasingly attenuated. Anthropologist Clement Meighan laments: "Adams sold us out. The institution is spending to destroy its collections."

Like the Natural History Museum, the National Museum of American History is firmly tied to the Smithsonian's past; and like the Natural History Museum, it has just as surely betrayed it. Repository for over a century of the nation's tangible heritage, the museum is conducting a fierce revisionist campaign. Like the other Smithsonian museums, it has taken its cue directly from the multicultural-mad, victim-celebrating universities.

The collections at American History originated when the U.S. Patent Office transferred the contents of its National Cabinet of Curiosities to the Smithsonian in 1858. Included were George Washington's tent and the Star-Spangled Banner. The collections got another boost in 1876, from the Centennial Exposition of 1876 in Philadelphia. The present museum, a windowless battlement possessing all the charm of an airplane terminal, opened in 1964 as the National Museum of History and Technology. Its ground floor, now featuring a noisy, high-tech exhibit about industrial materials, resembles a food court in a large suburban mall. The museum was ominously renamed the American History Museum in 1980, confirming a change of emphasis that was already taking place inside it. While some wonderful traditional exhibits of great hulking machines still stand, the social historical exhibits take an attitude toward technology that is typically ironic and skeptical.

Anyone looking for political history in the museum will be disappointed. It features nothing on the American Revolution or the constitutional conventions, nothing that embodies the ideals that animated the United States. America's presidents? You'll find their shadowy images sticking out from underneath the First Ladies' portraits arrayed across a wall. And tucked back in a tiny case behind an escalator are some presidential possessions, such as Woodrow Wilson's golf clubs and Lincoln's gold cane. Good luck finding the case, however.

Instead of political history, the museum focuses on a congeries of identity groups. Two themes emerge: America's ever-growing in-equalities, and the unpleasantness of white people. Take any point in time in the Smithsonian's America, and you will find shocking in-equalities that only get worse. After the Revolution: "The gulf be-tween rich and poor, powerful and powerless . . . did not vanish after 1776. . . . Whatever their race or gender, working Philadelphians found that the Revolution had not solved the problems of social and economic inequality." During the nineteenth-century industrial revo-lution: there was increasing "economic inequality." Turn of the cen-tury: "By the 1890s, . . . growing contrasts of wealth and poverty, and rigid racial barriers had created urgent social problems." Modern era: "It is much easier in the United States to be decently dressed than it is to be decently housed, fed or doctored" (quoting socialist Michael Harrington).

What is most striking about the Smithsonian's survey of Ameri-can inequality through the ages is its utter lack of historical awareness. The curators bring to the past no historical context; they observe and judge the past as if it were simultaneous with the present. The postrevolutionary period was characterized by "social and economic inequality," say the curators. Compared to what? Judged by contem-porary European standards, America was the least class-bound society in the world, and would remain so for two centuries. Titles, primo-geniture, feudal rights, strict distinction between the nobility and the merchant and servant classes—*those* were the indices of eighteenth-century inequality, and America had cast them off.

Similarly inapt is the observation that during the Progressive era, the "rigid structures of American society were difficult to overcome in building cross-class and interracial alliances." That is an agenda straight out of the 1990s multicultural campus, with its vacuous talk of class consciousness and rainbow coalitions; it has nothing to do with the Progressive agenda.

Nowhere is the Smithsonian curators' self-absorption more ap-parent than in their treatment of "women's issues." Barbara Clark Smith, a curator, notes scornfully that late eighteenth-century Philadelphians "continued to assume that women of both races would

and should be dependent on men." Well, of course they did—
"women's lib" was still 180 years away! A young student reading such
comments will nevertheless come away with the impression that the
American past was a shamefully inadequate place.

Even the language used to describe the past is self-absorbed. The
"settlement house" movement, wherein social workers helped immigrants assimilate, "enabled women to use gender concepts as a source
of empowerment," coos an exhibition on women's social movements.
The statement would have been absolutely incomprehensible to an
early twentieth-century citizen; it is still meaningless today, rendering
it a bona fide product of the academy.

The Smithsonian's assault on the American past doesn't end with
its obsessive harping on social and economic inequality. The museum
has a far more specific agenda to pursue, and that is against whites. An
exhibition on postcolonial society suggests that American history was
formed of equal parts white, black, and Indian influence, and a good
thing, too, because black and Indian cultures, according to the exhibit,
were superior in every way. The first generation of American citizens
were social-climbing, ruthless, obsessed with status and power, indifferent to equality, sexist, and, of course, viciously hypocritical in their
embrace of slavery. Their victory over Britain was due to the "labors
of the African-Americans they enslaved," not, apparently, to their zeal
to found a new, classless society.

A display of a Virginia planter's parlor says it all. Droning incessantly above the barren room is a recorded male voice that interprets
the space. "Every aspect [of the room] is designed for social advancement," the tape sneers. "The construction of the staircase was *fashionable*, [long pause], *expensive* [long pause], *showy*." The narrator
practically spits out the words: "This is more than just a *room*; this is
an elaborate proclamation of prosperity and ambition, the public face
of a *man*, [who is] part of a fiercely competitive social system." The
planter and his neighbors, the narrator sniffs, used "every occasion to
prove themselves *better* [pause], *richer* [pause], more *powerful* than
each other."

It is no surprise, then, when we learn later in the exhibit that the planter had murdered his wife. *This* is the family the Smithsonian chose to highlight as a typical early Southern family! Not only were the white citizens slavers and social-climbers, they were also domestic murderers. Now there undoubtedly was a pecking order in postcolonial society. But there is little reason to suppose that early Americans were more socially aggrandizing than potlatching "native peoples" or a king in a slave-trading African dynasty.

The Smithsonian's selection of a New England family is also telling. Did it choose one with a glorious revolutionary past? Not a chance. It selects an opponent of equality and possible Royalist. Merchant Samuel Cotton "disapproved of the notions of equality that were spreading in the northeast." Not only a reactionary, Cotton is also a greedy capitalist: an audiotape ceaselessly reenacts a court hearing that found him guilty of profiteering off the Revolution by overcharging for sugar, molasses, salt, and rum.

Fortunately, there is an escape from this backbiting, petty society: we can visit the Seneca Nation of the Iroquois Confederacy. And suddenly, we reencounter the curatorial "we": "Our ancestors considered it a great transgression to reject the council of their women." Apparently, the Indians deserve a "voice," and the whites do not. This carefully chosen female-centric aspect of Iroquois society contrasts sharply with eighteenth-century white society, wherein women, Clark notes, had more rights as widows than as wives. Whom is she kidding? Does Clark really believe that "gender roles" were less rigid among the bloody Iroquois than in England or America? The "rights of women," a concept even then being debated in England, would have been incomprehensible to the Indians.

There isn't a single myth about the nobility of the oppressed to which Clark doesn't subscribe. "Most African-Americans, Native Americans, and women white Americans . . . studied nature in order to work in harmony with it, not to control it," she declares breathlessly. If Native Americans and blacks did not "control nature," it is because they did not possess the technology and scientific knowledge to do so. African-Americans performed voodoo rituals with animals. Was that more "harmonious" than cultivating livestock?

But the Smithsonian knows no such ambiguity. It presents the so-called "systematic spirit—or deep faith in the power of reason and science" as white man's religion, no more efficacious or valid than the lore of illiterate peoples. Astoundingly, it puts the onus on *white Europeans* to understand native cultures, not vice versa: "Because of cultural bias, Europeans frequently were unable to comprehend the systems by which the knowledge passed from teacher to student in these traditional cultures, and the content of that knowledge." This is balderdash. First of all, if Europeans were "unable to comprehend" the "knowledge systems" of traditional cultures, it was undoubtedly because the high priests who presided over those "knowledge systems" kept them shrouded in mystery, not only to outsiders, but to members of the native culture itself. The notion of the public availability of knowledge and scientific research was a Western creation and a great tool of equality, to boot. It was utterly foreign to primitive cultures, who understood long before Foucault that knowledge (and even the appearance of knowledge) was power.

Second, if "cultural bias" prevented Europeans from understanding the occult mysteries of native "knowledge systems," fairness would require mentioning that illiteracy and scientific ignorance prevented native cultures from understanding Western "knowledge systems." But the Smithsonian sees the deficiency only on the whites' side.

The notion that native peoples lived in "harmony" while whites lived in conflict with the natural world pervades the exhibit. A label in a case on popular science announces darkly: "The air pump subjected nature to unnatural forces." There is no room in Clark's intellectual universe for the joy of experimentation; in her scheme, eighteenth-century popular interest in physics smacks of imperialism, aggression, and probably also racism and sexism. Eli Whitney's cotton gin, an ingenious invention, is simply labeled: "An Engine of Slavery."

The romanticization of native peoples continues in another American History exhibit: "New Mexico: An American Encounter," about the interaction of American Indians and Hispanics, and their fight against white imperialism. The exhibition states that Indian tribes take in tourists because of their "desire to share"; apparently the aggressive marketing of Indian artifacts springs from a similarly disinterested motive. A full-length mirror shaped as a human with a camera hanging from the neck (actually, the camera has been stolen, leaving just a plastic mount) silently accuses the museum visitor of "objectifying the Other." Again, no one is forcing the tourist industry on the Indians. The show glosses over the often brutal missionizing of the Indians by the Spaniards.

Smirking irony is a favorite conceit of academic demystifiers, and it pervades the Smithsonian. It entails liberal use of scare quotes, or implicit scare quotes, to debunk concepts that twenty years ago were quite unproblematic. Echoing Robert Sullivan's theme that middle-class manners are tools of power, the American History Museum questions the most basic mechanism of American history: assimilation. A section called "Social Service v. Social Control" in the women's reform movement exhibition argues that

> middle-class reformers . . . often imposed their concepts of the "American Way" on people. . . . Teaching immigrants and the less fortunate how to "better" themselves involved making judgments of moral and cultural "superiority."

For those immigrants who came over without a proper sense of hygiene, who beat their wives, who took their children out of school to work, that "bettering" process was essential to their social progress. But the adolescent sees all forms of authority as oppressive.

The cynical debunking of core American beliefs doesn't always use scare quotes. Another favorite ploy is the "Americans believed" construction, which introduces a note of irony into what are generally unobjectionable views. A show on the American industrial revolution from 1790 to 1860 subtly mocks Americans' enthusiasm for the new industrial inventions: Americans "believed that economic progress depended on technological advance." Why is this noteworthy, unless we are to understand it as a bizarre belief? But Americans saw daily the impact of technology on the economy. Nineteenth-century Americans' belief in the efficacy of gifted individuals is another howler to the Smithsonian: "Many Americans believed . . . that progress was the work of a few great inventors." One can almost hear curator Steve Lubar's guffaws as he wrote this. A sophisticated social historian such as Lubar understands that such concepts as "greatness" and even the "individual" are just political fictions designed to conceal oppressive power relations.

Curator Lubar also singles out for implicit scorn the "widespread [nineteenth-century] assumption that work was good for people." How repressive, we murmur sympathetically. Even worse, " 'houses of industry' helped to keep the poor busy and out of trouble." How much more humane are the ready welfare benefits that cultivate a huge class of non-working, dependent, and often criminal people!

No museum has better employed academically inspired scorn, however, than Air and Space, and nowhere is the effect more jarring. If ever there were a testament to the power of science, engineering, and mental mastery, it is the Air and Space Museum. Yet as the recent Enola Gay debacle revealed, the museum is now populated by curators and, until recently, a director who sought to debunk technology and military prowess. Pilots and former military men once dominated the museum; today, academic historians rule the place. Secretary Adams orchestrated this change, to bring the museum into line with the academy, which had long derided Air and Space for its allegedly celebratory attitude toward aeronautic technology.

The results of this academic incursion were in long before the Enola Gay controversy. A curator recalls the heady pre–Enola Gay days, when the public hadn't yet noticed the changes under way in the museum: "There was a sense of optimism in the 1980s and 1990s that we could stretch boundaries and do cultural history." A show on World War I fighter pilots argues that Americans have been hoodwinked into a naive romanticization of air war. Displays of commercial detritus with pilot themes drive home the point that Americans can't tell the difference, say, between Snoopy in his Red Baron flying gear or a Red Baron pizza box and the realities of war. This dour "deconstruction" of popular culture comes right from the academy. A previous exhibit—a wildly popular show on *Star Trek*—also drew on academic fads to reveal the searing social critique in the TV series. The important point about the exhibit devoted to *Star Trek* is not that it represented a crass pandering to popular culture (although it did), but that it found in the series a criticism of racism, sexism, militarism, and, in an earlier draft of the exhibition's script, the Vietnam War.

But nothing, obviously, can match the enormity of the Enola Gay disaster. The true outrage of the project was not that it used spurious analyses to second-guess the military necessity of the atomic bomb, or that its authors chose the fiftieth anniversary of the end of World War II to propound their revisionist views, or even that it portrayed the Japanese as quasi-victims during the war they started with a surprise attack on Pearl Harbor. The true outrage lies in the disgusting condescension and contempt shown to the public and to the war's veterans by the Smithsonian personnel, from Adams on down.

The abortive exhibition presented Hiroshima not as the conclusion of World War II, but as the start of the arms race. To Martin Harwit, director of the Air and Space Museum, the conjunction of the atom bombing of Hiroshima and Nagasaki and the end of the war was purely coincidental. This perspective on the bomb set the stage for the follies to come, guaranteeing that the veterans and the curators would be talking past each other.

From the start, Smithsonian officials held themselves out as the only people sensitive enough to understand the horrors of nuclear war and the anxieties of the nuclear age. Responding to one of the many World War II veterans campaigning tirelessly for the restoration and exhibition of the Enola Gay, Secretary Adams intoned piously: "'Decent respect for the opinions of mankind' requires us also to touch on the demonstrated horror and yawning future risk of the age that the Enola Gay helped to inaugurate." Adams's condescension was not lost on the vet, who shot back that Adams was a "Washington satrap."

Harwit easily matched Adams for self-righteousness. Handpicked by Adams to bring a critical perspective on strategic bombing to the museum, Harwit, an astrophysicist, was the first director of the museum without a flying or military background. Writing to Japan's ambassador in Washington, Harwit revealed his deep contempt for the public: "Unless the public is willing to understand the events that led to the bombings, and the terrible destruction they wrought, the most valuable lessons that can be learned from history will be lost." The gall of this message is nearly unfathomable. Harwit posits the public as his quasi-adversary, determined to hold on to its blind ignorance in the face of his proffered enlightenment. It is the height of arrogance for Harwit to present himself and his curators, none of whom served in the war, as the repositories of wisdom regarding the "events that led to the bombings."

Even more offensive than the museum's condescension toward the public was its contempt for the veterans. In statement after statement, the museum's personnel caricatured the vets as an annoying, insignificant, self-engrossed interest group in conflict with the public good. In one of the most explosive statements during the public controversy, a curator named Tom Crouch wrote to Harwit: "Do you want an exhibit to make veterans feel good, or do you want an exhibition that will lead our visitors to think about the consequences of the atomic bombing of Japan? Frankly, I don't think we can do both." In his self-exculpatory book, Harwit adopts the same stance, alleging that the vets merely sought to "satisfy their nostalgia" or to be celebrated.

Only someone who had never served in a war could characterize the vets' desire for a public history as "nostalgia" or "feel-good" therapy. Harwit and his curators exemplify the offensive self-righteousness most often found in academia—that of a generation that has lived without sacrifice and that sneers at tradition. Contrary to the Smithsonian's dismissive rhetoric, the vets showed themselves throughout the battle as extraordinarily eloquent, informed, and morally wise.

But few at the Smithsonian seem to have learned anything from the episode (except the current secretary, Michael Heyman, who, upon succeeding Adams in 1994, canceled the original exhibition and fired Harwit). Throughout the Institution, curators and historians stew about the grievous injury done to their intellectual freedom by the cancellation of the show, and complain darkly about continuing censorship. The resentment is strongest, naturally, at Air and Space, which is still licking its wounds. "The outlook in this place is bleak; we can't do anything that's critical of anything, we're so constrained by the political right wing," one curator fumed to me. Note his assumption: his primary goal is to be "critical," not to share knowledge or edify. But even more remarkable is the curator's shocking lack of respect for experience and seniority. "A bunch of seventy-five-year-olds—two World War II vets—are running this place now," he complained, who "bring the mindset of that generation."

Next up at Air and Space: a show on the *Star Wars* trilogy, one of the last Harwit projects still on the books. A bid for popular appeal, to be sure, but don't be surprised to find trenchant social criticism served up as well—perhaps a paean to diversity and sensitivity. In line with the redressive mission of the Smithsonian, Air and Space is also planning an exhibit on the black experience in aviation, following the precedent of a 1994 show on a female aerial acrobat that demonstrated that young girls really *can* triumph against the sexist odds!

If many of the Air and Space curators seek to debunk the alleged myths of flight technology, many curators at the American Art Museum, housed in the splendid neoclassical Old Patent Office Building, are determined to debunk art itself. Ideally, some believe, there would cease to be any distinction between art—what one curator snidely calls "so-called paintings"—and ephemera such as political cartoons. All would be marshaled to the great project of tearing down America's ideals.

Mention of the sublime to some curators provokes a recoil of distaste. In a recent essay on art curating, curator William Truettner scoffs: Museum visitors used to believe that works of art "disregard everyday life in favor of expressing what was profound and lasting about the human spirit." Such aesthetic idealism is repugnant to Truettner; he wants to "bring art museum visitors back to earth [and] make them believe that works have more-limited [sic] meanings."

Truettner brought the public thuddingly to earth in his much-criticized "The West as America" exhibit of 1991. The show argued that the great heroic canvases of the Western expansion were really about Eastern capitalism, ethnic strife, and greed. Truettner, who has read his Derrida, finds exploitation and despair in the most peaceful of canvases, for the very absence of social strife and oppression from a canvas "has the ironic effect of calling them back to life," he argues.

Truettner's heavy-handed decoding of art violates the interpretive code he professes to follow. Mouthing platitudes about the open-ended nature of meaning, Truettner's interpretations admit of no variation over time; they are presented as the definitive decoding of the canvas. Though he invokes a populist philosophy—everyone can understand art—his bizarre allegorical readings of paintings must appear far more arcane to an average viewer than a formal or moral analysis. Like his colleagues in the academy, he approaches canvases with a checklist of politically correct "issues": if a painting contains a woman, that's a "gender issue." If it contains a black person, that's a "race issue." If it contains a woman *and* a black person, it's time to cash in. Analyzing an 1861 historical allegory called "The Founding of Maryland," Truettner fills out his scorecard: "The demure colonial wife, her head covered by a blue shawl, looks askance at the three bare-breasted Indian women, raising not only racial but gender issues." If the painting had been half as skilled, presumably the analysis would be identical: the "issues" would be duly noted, and not a word said about the aesthetic qualities of the work.

In the odd world of the museum, curators regard shows as failures if the public innocently enjoys them. A recent show on the nineteenth-century landscape painter Thomas Cole sought to portray the paintings as a reactionary critique of Jacksonian democracy. "We got nowhere with the show," laments one curator. "Visitors just didn't get it." The visitor comment books contained such responses as "Great show! Wonderful paintings!" "Do more shows like this!"—a source of curatorial embarrassment.

A forthcoming exhibition scheduled for March 1999 continues the museum's project of debunking American history and culture. A companion to "The West as America," it will focus on late-nineteenth-century images of New England. Such images, often idyllic, the curators will argue, represent a desperate attempt of whites to hold on to an ideal Anglo-Protestant America, in a time of black migration from the South and ethnic migration from Europe. What else is new?

If aesthetic values are meaningless and transitory, the museum finds enormous value in identity politics. A spate of recent contemporary art shows focused on ethnicity and "political orientation." Serving up the worst atrocities from SoHo, the museum has displayed repulsive installations and tasteless postmodern junk art, such as Pepon Osorro's tacky chandeliers constructed from plastic beads, tiny soccer balls, and cheap knickknacks. As Osorro explains: "My work is socially relevant because that is the need I see in the community." How about the need for a good grammar-school education in using the English language? Isn't that socially relevant?

The museum's acquisitions policy is just as bad, causing some traditional curators to despair that the Smithsonian is selling off its heritage to buy politically correct junk. The Institution's race- and ethnicity-based acquisitions policy is part of a much broader diversity drive. Adams made diversity the centerpiece of his tenure, ordering museum directors to bring in a staff that was more "representative" of the country. "Sometimes these hires worked out, others were dead on their feet," recalls a curator at Natural History. The deadwood is the most likely to have survived, given the difficulties of firing federal employees. The only practical recourse available to a manager of an incompetent employee is to find an unwitting supervisor in another museum and try to palm the employee off on him.

Adams also encouraged the formation of identity-based employee advocacy groups. These have increasingly flexed their muscles regarding the content of exhibitions. The Hispanic lobby seems to be in the ascendancy today. In 1993, Secretary Adams authorized the formation of a Task Force on Latino Issues, charged, in essence, to prove that the Smithsonian is guilty of discrimination. The Task Force was chaired by Raul Yzaguirre, president of the National Council of La Raza, one of the most radical Hispanic advocacy groups in the country.

The Task Force performed exactly as expected. A year after its formation, it published "Willful Neglect," an extraordinarily dishonest report charging the Smithsonian with deliberately excluding Latinos from its collections and staff. Count one of the indictment was the absence of a separate museum dedicated to Latinos—ethnically coded museums have now become the primary litmus test of the Smithsonian's ethnic good faith. Like all arguments for Hispanic power, "Willful Neglect" cast a wide net in its definition of Hispanic, including Mexican-, Puerto Rican–, Cuban-, Dominican-, Central American–, South American–, and Spanish-Americans, despite the wide cultural differences between those groups. When I asked the Smithsonian's new counsel for Latino affairs, Miguel Bretos, if these groups really constituted a single identity, he responded with an amazing reinterpretation of American history. A common Hispanic identity was "emerging rapidly," Bretos said: "The American tradition of E Pluribus Unum is taking root in the Hispanic community; there is an increasing sense of a common fund of culture that cuts across tribes." That, in a nutshell, describes American ideals today—assimilation no longer means assimilation to a common American identity, but to a heightened ethnic identity.

"Willful Neglect" worked its anticipated magic. The Smithsonian created an entire office dedicated to Hispanic advocacy within the Institution, headed by Bretos. "Basically, Bretos wants a gallery in every museum devoted to Hispanics," says a curator of natural history who has had repeated dealings with him. In a particularly cowardly move, the Smithsonian changed the name of Bretos's office from Latino Affairs to Community Affairs, trying to cover up its partisan nature, though no one within the Institution is fooled.

But the bureaucratic spawn of "Willful Neglect" spilled over beyond the Community Affairs office. Secretary Heyman, in a continuing token of his ethnic good faith, empowered two high-level panels to study employment and affirmative action policy, on the one hand, and programming and acquisitions, on the other. Their reports will undoubtedly find grievous gaps in the Smithsonian's efforts to achieve a "diverse" museum.

All this is pretty impressive fallout from a report based on misrepresentation and virtual falsehood. Even its authors backpedal wildly when confronted with its misstatements. "Willful Neglect" charges the Smithsonian with deliberately failing to hire an ethnically proportionate Hispanic workforce. A chart grimly documents the absence of Hispanic curators. Such a charge makes sense only if there is a pool of Hispanic qualified museologists upon which the Smithsonian should have been drawing. I asked Bretos if such a pool exists. He responded: "It's relatively small, which is part of the difficulty of making sure that all the voices are represented." More accurately, the number of Hispanic art history or archaeology or aerospace Ph.D.s is probably close to zero, given the continuing problem of low academic achievement among Hispanics. What about lower-level staff, also a target of scathing criticism in the report? "The Smithsonian is at a disadvantage in Washington in attracting Latinos," admitted Bretos, "because it's a first-generation immigrant community." In other words, few qualified Hispanics for clerical work either.

How, then, can you charge the Smithsonian with *willful* neglect, I asked Bretos. He dodged the query. "The question is one of focus: how do you present the narrative of America?" he replied. He laughed: "I wrote poisonous pages regarding the Smithsonian Institution." No wonder he's laughing: these days, there is no better way to end up in a sinecure than to blast an institution with false charges of racism.

The report's allegation that the Institution's collections ignore Hispanic material is just as spurious. Smithsonian archaeologists have been lovingly collecting and documenting culture in the Southwest almost since the Institution's founding; a curator at American History has specialized in Hispanic-American material since 1965. And again, the report's authors now take a far different line. "The collections from Latin America are incredible," says Bretos. "We are one of the largest Latin American collections in botany and zoology."

The precedent set by "Willful Neglect" is ominous. If the Smithsonian capitulates so spinelessly to ethnic extortion, a parade of other ethnic lobbies will be sure to follow the model of the Hispanics, splintering the Institution further into just so many grievance groups.

Ironically, the only place one can consistently find traditional curating in the Smithsonian these days is in the non-Western art museums—the Sackler and Freer galleries of Asian art and the National Museum of African Art. All three are elegant and understated, displaying art and even ritual artifacts as aesthetic objects, rather than as social texts. Apparently, the concepts of beauty and the sublime are still appropriate for non-Western cultures, while the West is busily deconstructing itself.

The Smithsonian's future is not auspicious. On the positive side, Secretary Heyman, a former chancellor of the University of California at Berkeley, is far more sensitive to the commemorative, celebratory function of a national museum than Robert McCormick Adams ever was, and he has openly questioned the advocacy curating favored by the Smithsonian's academically inspired professionals. His cancellation of the Enola Gay exhibit was welcome. Yet there remain many reasons for apprehension. Heyman vehemently promoted racial quotas at Berkeley; he is continuing race-conscious policies at the Smithsonian, putting further out of reach the ideal of a national museum that transcends race and ethnic differences.

Moreover, Heyman's proposed solution to the controversies that have scorched the Institution recently misdiagnoses the problem. In a speech last year at Georgetown Law Center, Heyman argued that issue-oriented curators should follow the model of the legal system and present both sides of a political debate: "Presenting at least two sides of an important issue, and letting the visitors know exactly what is evidence and what is interpretation, can only enhance broader public understanding."

But the problem with the politicized exhibitions at the Smithsonian is not that they present only one side of an issue; the problem is the manufacture of such specious "issues" in the first place. When William Truettner is spotting his race and gender issues, what possible "other side" could be presented? When the American History Museum sets out to multiculturalize and relativize Anglo-American culture, when it deliberately selects unsympathetic white families to contrast with the virtuous natives, no counterargument is even possible, because the ground of debate is already so skewed. To accept the terms of debate is already to have lost.

Short of a total housecleaning of staff, there is little that can save the Smithsonian from being further engulfed by the poisonous trends of identity politics and postmodern theory. These chic academic assumptions are by now thoroughly ingrained in the Smithsonian's bureaucracy. Ultimately, only a change in the powerful culture of universities can restore America's public culture.

[1997]

Homeless Advocates in
Outer Space

IN EIGHTEENTH-CENTURY LONDON, aristocratic elites visited the mad in Bedlam Hospital and called it entertainment. In twentieth-century New York, professional elites visit the mad in the streets and call it homeless outreach. The results in both cases are the same: the objects of attention are left to rot in their own filth, perhaps to lose a limb or two to gangrene, or to die. The intention, however, could not be more different: in modern times, such hands-off treatment shows "sensitivity" and "respect."

Only by entering the realm of political myth can one understand how such deliberate neglect could constitute professional treatment. Contemporary homeless policy is one of the odder expressions of utopian political fantasy since Rousseau famously denounced society as oppressive and corrupting. For their advocates, the homeless are potent symbols of heroic alienation, concrete embodiments of the advocates' own adolescent longing for rebellion and nonconformity. The plight of the homeless, in the advocates' view, is a searing indictment of American culture. Should the left ever lose interest in dramatizing the Rousseauian myth—an unlikely event—the homeless will disappear, removed to safer abodes.

A recent homelessness conference in New York City perfectly demonstrated how fanatically the advocates hold on to their myths. Called to discuss the failure of a model outreach program, the conference unwittingly showed instead why the homeless are still on the streets.

The Times Square Business Improvement District (BID), a coalition of business owners dedicated to the revival of New York's famed crossroads, has long prided itself on its generous homeless programs, aimed at getting derelicts off the district's streets. From 1992 to 1994, the BID funded an outreach program designed to coax the local homeless into temporary and permanent housing. The payoff was meager: some two hundred long-term homeless, according to program estimates, remained on the streets around Times Square, impervious to the efforts of the outreach workers.

So in 1994 the BID decided to up the ante. It procured over $2.5 million in state and federal money to create what it and its government funders touted as a highly innovative homeless program. Under the plan, a brigade of gentle, well-meaning professionals from six local social-service agencies would roam the streets sixteen hours a day, spending an unlimited amount of time with their "clients" in their natural habitat. The outreach workers would try ever so delicately to persuade the homeless to visit the BID's renovated "respite center," located in the basement of a Times Square church, where they could get overnight shelter, showers, healthy meals, clothing, and medical attention—with no strings attached. For example, if a client wanted to booze on the streets during the day, that was fine, at least for his initial visits. Or if he wanted just to hang out and watch television, that was fine, too. On-site social workers would ensure that he was in receipt of every welfare benefit to which he was entitled, with nothing demanded in return.

If a client ultimately entered and completed detox, the center would require him to refrain from using drugs or alcohol and to attend group therapy sessions run by on-site psychiatrists and social workers. Ultimately, the BID hoped, the center's longer-term clients would deign to accept government-subsidized housing, lined up by the center's staff.

What was supposedly innovative in this utterly conventional program? The same people in the outreach teams would also work in the respite center, allegedly providing continuity and building trust with the homeless. In the hermetic world of homeless practice, such minor tinkering passes for radical rethinking.

One year and $700,000 later, only two people had accepted housing. The rest had staunchly balked. This remarkable result was certainly not for lack of trying. Over the year, the outreach workers had made 1,511 "contacts" with 206 individuals (only a handful of whom, it turned out, actually called Times Square home; the advocates and outreach workers' original estimate of the local homeless population had proved, as usual, to be wildly excessive). Those 1,511 contacts were seemingly more meaningful to the outreach workers than to the homeless: only 37 of the 206 contacted individuals agreed even to visit the BID's respite center, while a mere 15 condescended to stay overnight. The homeless, it appeared, did not really want housing, housing, housing.

To its enormous credit, the BID decided to publish a report on the year's efforts. This document, "To Reach the Homeless," written by Columbia journalism professor Bruce Porter, is a jaw-dropping account of state-of-the-art homeless rehabilitation techniques. Unprecedented in its honesty, it provides a rare window into the mad futility of the homelessness outreach profession. In the battle of wits between the wily homeless and guileless outreach workers, it's no contest, for the outreach workers will not infringe on the "autonomy" of the homeless, while the homeless feel no corresponding scruple.

As recounted in "To Reach the Homeless," a typical day of outreach resembles a Dantean pilgrimage through the underworld. One day, for example, outreach workers stop by a coffin-sized box across from the *New York Times* building. "We know it's a person," reports Porter, "because we can discern a hand moving underneath some rags." The workers knock on the box and say hello but get no response. Because the hand is still moving, though, the team concludes that whatever it is attached to must be okay, so they move on.

They next come across "Shoeshine Bill," "an old man with a shoeshine kit and markedly swollen ankles who is sitting in a puddle of his urine." Shoeshine Bill assures the workers that he is doing "fine," so they move on. An old black woman is raving unintelligibly about drugs in Harlem. She's "not very open to help," says an outreach worker. A young white couple lying on the street banter off a suggestion that they visit the respite center; they'll go, jokes the gaunt male, "only if they could get a private room for an hour with a bed." The woman has deteriorated markedly from alcoholism over the previous months. The outreach worker drops a few condoms on their blanket and moves on.

Some of the homeless demonstrate admirable energy and persistence in avoiding the outreach workers' ministrations. "Heavy," a large black man who reigns, according to the report, as the "undisputed king" of Times Square, is one such vagrant. Heavy is highly visible: "[H]e is invariably dressed in a dark green jump suit, two or three canvas Post Office mail carts nearby heaped six feet high with his stuff—filthy quilts, dirty towels and plastic bags packed with plastic bottles, broken broom handles presumably used for defense, a half-dozen milk crates filled with wastepaper and tied on with bits of nylon rope, gallon ketchup bottles, some of the sauce still sloshing around the bottom. Sprouting up out of the pile is an eight-foot-tall iron pipe that is tied with long orange streamers fluttering in the wind."

Fortunately for Heavy, the outreach workers are also highly visible. Whenever he spots their bright red jackets approaching, he wedges himself behind a fence or other barricade, "prepared to resist the service providers at all costs." One time, the team tried to capture him with a pincer movement, but he dashed into traffic and nearly got hit. "After that, we seriously had to ask ourselves what exactly we were accomplishing by this," recalls the director of the program. Sadly, the workers' doubts were fleeting.

Other street residents avoid the outreach workers out of embarrassment. As an outreach team chats with three vagrants sharing a jumbo bottle of beer in a hotel garage, a sixty-three-year-old man named Charlie hides nearby in back of a refrigerator. The workers have taken him to detox four times, and now he's ashamed to face them. The team leader is philosophical: "[H]e's smelling pretty bad these days, so we'll probably be hearing from Charlie soon. He usually comes in to take a shower when he gets that way."

Such repeated efforts are the norm. A lost soul from Rochester named Toni relies on the seemingly inexhaustible trust of the workers to avoid going to alcohol detox. The workers have given her subway fare to the treatment center, as well as fare home, many times, but each time she either never gets on the subway or gets off a few stops down and returns to her haunts. Toni's reception upon her return is not always gracious. "Last night I got the shit beat out of me, right here," she tells the workers. "Dutch did it. He's crazy. He hit me for no reason, just popped me in the face, no reason." The workers try to draw a moral from the situation: "You realize if you got out of detox and went home, this might not have happened?" they ask her. Toni halfheartedly assents to this proposition, so the workers once again give her fare to a detox center on Staten Island and see her on to the train. As usual, their homily vanished into thin air: one stop down the line, she got off and went straight back to Times Square.

Nothing, however, compares to the difficulty of enticing the homeless into housing. Time after time, a client deemed "housing-ready" will balk at the threshold of his new abode and plunge back into the most squalid street life. Only a few vagrants even get that close; most keep themselves safely removed from the housing process. The respite center's staff, faced with their meager record of accomplishment, have defined success down, to adapt Senator Moynihan's resonant phrase. The fact that the homeless sometimes return to the outreach center to "reveal how screwed up they've become" shows that the "staff has affected them in some positive way," the report concludes wanly.

The charity our society showers upon people living on the street makes possible this hardy resistance to seeking help. In true New York fashion, even vagrants can get home-delivered food: a do-gooder group from Dobbs Ferry called Midnight Run makes regular deliveries of sandwiches and juice, along with toiletries and blankets, right to people's cardboard boxes. The homeless know the hours and locations of every local soup kitchen, and the more enterprising work out deals for other personal needs. One older alcoholic would throw away a new pair of underwear every couple of days, secure in the knowledge that Midnight Run would soon bring another pair. Other homeless use more unorthodox approaches to street survival. When it gets cold, re-counts a scraggly vagrant, "I smash a window with a brick and go to jail. I get along fine in jail."

Yet though no one is going hungry on the streets, vagrants' bod-ies often are disintegrating from a host of untreated maladies. Alco-holics lose toes, feet, and legs to infections they haven't even noticed. Workers at the BID's respite center work heroically to secure treat-ment for their clients, but the clients often disappear right before a scheduled operation. No one, of course, has the right to make them stay.

The costs of this charade to the larger society are enormous, too. To take only one example, Amtrak loses $11 million a year at Penn Station, just south of Times Square, because the homeless drive po-tential passengers away, according to Richard Rubel, community rela-tions officer at Amtrak. And the repeated trips the homeless make to hospital emergency rooms for thoroughly avoidable medical crises also ring up a hefty public tab, as do their resultant disability benefits.

"To Reach the Homeless" proves beyond a shadow of a doubt that the homeless are not on the street because they can't find hous-ing: desperate to give away subsidized apartments, the BID found al-most no takers. Clearly, most vagrants prefer the streets to the responsibilities of a housed existence. Some may simply refuse to play by society's rules, like many hoboes of old; for others, speculates the respite center's director, housing may represent a scary reencounter with whatever psychological demons drove them to the streets in the first place.

But although the homeless may prefer the streets, that is not why they are still there. They are there because the advocates need them to be there. Should society finally decide to end street vagrancy, it could go far in that direction by facilitating commitment to mental hospitals and enforcing existing laws against street living. Though the average householder would surely welcome such a change, the aver-age householder has no say in these matters; a vocal minority pur-porting to represent the interests of the homeless governs homeless policy. And those advocates, who range from single-issue advocacy groups to the ACLU to left-wing churches, fiercely resist any measure that would restrict the "rights" of the homeless to live on the streets.

They do so not just out of material interests—though many of them make a comfortable living off of homelessness—but out of a spiritual need. Homelessness confirms for the advocates their dearest beliefs: that American capitalism is corrupt and cruel, that the American Dream is a delusion, that American society deals harshly with its rebels and nonconformists. Remove the homeless from the streets, and Exhibit A in the advocates' brief against America also disappears. Even the outreach workers on the front lines, who would say that their fondest wish is to house the homeless, nevertheless reflexively take for granted a definition of autonomy suffused with left-wing romanticism and at odds with the best interests of the homeless.

The advocates' ideology has rarely been as visible as at a conference on homelessness that the Times Square BID organized last April. Provoked by the sorry results of its outreach program, the BID brought together some of the country's leading self-styled homeless experts for a good-faith discussion of the question, "What Do We Do When Homeless People Say 'No'?" What it got instead was an amazing and instructive display of deliberate duplicity and invincible self-righteousness. The advocates simply chose to ignore the BID's outreach program; wholly impervious to the facts, they brought with them instead their stock stories about housing shortages, a heartless society, and noble, helpless suffering. Their performance demonstrated why homeless policy has been so counterproductive.

Jack Coleman, former president of Haverford College and of the left-leaning Edna McConnell Clark Foundation, immediately set the tone of maudlin virtue. Coleman won acclaim in 1983 for living as a "street person" in New York City for ten days, an experience he wrote up as a cover story for *New York* magazine. The adventure was certainly a sociological "first": Coleman was undoubtedly the first "homeless" person to take a professional photographer on his rounds through soup kitchens and shelters to capture his every moment of despair—Coleman sitting next to a steam grate with forehead resting on fist, eyes closed, and face grimacing from fatigue and cold; Coleman gazing off pensively at a cheap diner; Coleman wolfing down his food in a shelter, surrounded by derelicts; Coleman staring hopelessly at the job listings in a minimum-wage employment agency (undoubtedly none called for his unique talents as a progressive foundation executive).

Now he once again put himself on display. He recounted his first moment back home after his "homeless" experience: he drew a hot tub, lay down in it, and started to cry. And lo! the tears began again, for everyone in the audience to behold. How many times Coleman had told this story to similar effect was anyone's guess, but it would prove a harbinger: if his tears spread Rousseauian "sentiment" throughout the conference, the subsequent speakers would suffuse it with Rousseauian self-righteousness. Before he left the podium, Coleman shared one further confession with us: he couldn't *really* lay claim to the full homeless experience, because he had always had change in his pocket with which to call his editor at *New York*! We the privileged can never really bridge the unfathomable gulf between ourselves and the homeless!

After Coleman's four-handkerchief histrionics, the next piece of drivel hit all the more painfully. It is our society's "intolerance of weakness and of the inability to compete in a free market" that causes homelessness, announced Mary Ann Gleason, an ex-nun who now heads the Washington-based National Coalition for the Homeless. If we were a gentler, more communal society, the implication seemed to be, the homeless would embrace our free housing. Yet the problem, in Gleason's view, transcends economics. It is spiritual. The reason the homeless don't come in off the streets, Gleason averred, is that "they don't have meaning in their lives." Translation: *we* don't have meaning in our lives, and until we get some, the homeless will maintain their lonely outpost on the streets, "the only community they can find." (The fact that this "community" sometimes beats up its own members, as the detox-avoiding Toni discovered, did not seem to detract from its soul-enriching value, in Gleason's eyes.) Gleason especially admired the Europeans for having labeled the homeless the "socially excluded"—though she never explained why, given this progressive diagnosis, the Europeans haven't solved the problem by "including" the homeless.

With the homeless thus transmuted into Romantic critics of soulless modern life, the remaining speakers had their theme. Dr. William Vicic, a "community medicine" specialist at St. Vincent's Hospital and author of a book entitled *Memory of a Homeless Man*, turned the title of the conference, "What Do We Do When Homeless People Say 'No'?" upon itself. "Is 'No' from the homeless an answer," he asked dramatically, "or an echo of us and the society we maintain?" In truth, he implied, it is we who say "No" to the homeless, not they to us. That we may have some rational grounds for saying "No" to substance abuse, criminal behavior, chronic irresponsibility, and inability to follow rules did not register with Vicic; through his Rousseauian spectacles, he seems to see only enslavement and oppression in society's rules.

Like Gleason, Vicic identified the roots of homelessness not in the dysfunctions of the homeless but in the closed-mindedness of the housed: "Separatism causes a lot of our problems," he said darkly. As a response to the events that precipitated the conference, Vicic's diagnosis seemed all the sillier. It's hard to imagine a *less* "separatist" program than the Times Square outreach and housing project: it sought to include the homeless on their own terms, without imposing conventional social rules on them. Yet even such unconditional inclusiveness could not overcome the determination of the homeless to stay homeless.

The most vacuous variation on the "Homeless Saying 'No'" theme came from the Reverend James A. Forbes, Jr., pastor at the nation's premier left-wing house of worship, Manhattan's Riverside Church. "We should value the one gift the homeless bring," Forbes admonished the audience—"the ability to say 'No.'" Forbes provided no clue as to how one "values" such a gift; he just reiterated his motif. The "ability to say 'No' is a strength," he said, adding that the burden was on us to figure out what the homeless are saying "No" to. One couldn't help wondering, if saying "No" is a strength, why the homeless are so beset by illness and fear. One wondered, too, if Forbes also celebrates as a gift the big "No" that criminals say to the law.

With excruciating predictability, Forbes went on to accuse society of a lack of compassion. This note rang particularly false in the most generous welfare city in the country, especially in the wake of a $2.5 million effort to house a handful of homeless people. Though money is a dubious measure of compassion, to be sure, it is the measure Forbes clearly had in mind.

Another speaker, Tena Frank, director of homeless services at Lenox Hill Neighborhood House, seemed to float far above the earth on a cloud of moral relativism. Our mainstream value systems regarding work and discipline, she explained, are just the way "*we* get *our* needs met"—exactly as the homeless get their needs met by using drugs. Our failure to see the similarity "allows us to blame the homeless," she concluded.

The only advocate to avoid romanticizing the homeless chose instead a bald-faced lie. Maria Foscarinis, director of the National Law Center on Homelessness and Poverty, is one of the shrillest advocates around. She lobbied tirelessly for the 1987 Stewart B. McKinney Homeless Assistance Act, a federal cash spigot that falsely identifies homelessness as a housing problem, and she wages a regular campaign in court and in the press on behalf of homeless "rights." At the conference, Foscarinis demonstrated the rhetorical techniques that have made her so successful. Cities have no right to enforce laws outlawing camping or urinating in public, she asserted, because the homeless are "people who literally have no place left to go." This was, without doubt, the most outrageous claim of the day. The very impetus for the conference was the fact that the Times Square homeless *did* have someplace to go but spurned the offer. Foscarinis, however, simply ignored that fact. Equally beneath her notice were the millions of public dollars dedicated solely to the small colony befouling Times Square. "The resources are not there," she announced grimly, "to provide an alternative place to sleep or eat." Again, a lie.

Such duplicity should disqualify its practitioners forevermore from having the slightest voice in determining policy. It hardly needs saying that the homeless are not lonely beacons of courage, taking their stand against a hypocritical world, but demoralized or broken creatures, fearful of the demands of adult life. Enslaved by their inner demons or the substances they abuse, they are the least likely to benefit from the sphere of absolute license their advocates have carved out for them. Yet self-serving fictions like those rampant at the Times Square conference have guided homelessness policy from the start, because few are willing to challenge the moral bullying of the advocates. The consequences for the purported beneficiaries have been dire.

A sane homeless policy would acknowledge two basic realities. First, many people on the streets need treatment, not housing. For the sickest, legislators need to change rules against involuntary confinement, and states need to recommission mental hospitals emptied by deinstitutionalization. Second, for the rest of the homeless the best medicine is the expectation of responsible behavior—the expectation of work and of civil and lawful conduct in public spaces. Accordingly, opinion leaders, from politicians to ministers, should decry all types of no-strings-attached handouts, such as no-demand soup kitchens and indiscriminate alms-giving to beggars, which simply subsidize self-destructive behavior. They should oppose allowing the homeless to turn public spaces into hobo encampments. Effective charity asks for reciprocity from the recipient, building patterns of work and discipline; to exempt the homeless from the rules that everyone else lives by infantilizes them permanently.

The advocates, clouded by ideology, may see the homeless as martyrs to American injustice or as free spirits marching to a different drummer, but by now most of the rest of us see them as disordered or confused souls who, for more than a decade, thanks to advocate-designed policies, have been marching to disaster.

[1997]

Compassion Gone Mad

IN 1984 the New York Legislature passed the Teenage Services Act (TASA), targeted at teen mothers on welfare. It is the perfect expression of New York City and State's failed war against social disintegration.

The city and state already spend millions on pregnancy prevention, pre- and neonatal care, day care, welfare, parenting classes, and drug-abuse prevention and treatment—none of which has had the slightest impact on spiraling teen pregnancy and its accompanying social pathologies. So who needs another program? But TASA is cleverly premised on that very glut of services. It creates a new category of social worker, whose sole purpose is to shepherd teen mothers through the maze of existing social workers and services.

TASA, one might say, is a rational response to an irrational situation. Over the last thirty years, New York City and State have devoted an increasing share of their revenues to the most dysfunctional members of society, and now social service spending constitutes the largest share of both city and state budgets. Yet as spending grew, so did the social problems that spending was supposed to solve. The government responded by adding more programs. The result is a tangle of entitlements and services so complex as to require a guide service like TASA and many similar programs.

All you need is the evidence of your senses to know that New York City's enormous commitment to social welfare spending has not stemmed social breakdown. The question is: has it made things worse? The answer is yes—on two counts. Social service spending has sucked out of the private economy capital that could have been used to create jobs, the best mechanism for ending poverty. But in response to inner-city poverty, welfare advocates call for *further* social service spending, thereby accelerating the flight of business from the city. This vicious circle characterizes welfare's impact on the family as well. The two-parent family is all but extinct in some neighborhoods, rendered superfluous by welfare's subsidy for illegitimacy. The resulting increase in juvenile delinquency, truancy, and teen pregnancy brings in more social services, which in turn further erode the incentives for personal responsibility.

The message social service programs convey is all too often the polar opposite of what the inner-city poor need. Typically, such programs reward dysfunctional behavior and subordinate the well-being of children to dubious ideology—such as the belief that even a flamboyantly neglectful single-parent household, riven by drugs, possesses basic strength and goodness. Above all, the basic purpose of these services—to provide the spiritual and material benefits of a stable two-parent family—is largely futile. Families create sound individuals by imposing discipline and moral values on children. Even if a government program *could* do this, these programs don't: for years, imposing values has been anathema to social workers, who studiously avoid making judgments about the "life-style choices" of their clients.

The best way to see the social service apparatus whole is to trace the life cycle of a family moving through it. Each stage has its appropriate service; the city even envisions "transitional services" in one program to ease a child's passage from children's to adult services.

Start with a woman below the poverty line, pregnant with an illegitimate child. Aid to Families with Dependent Children (AFDC) benefits begin in her sixth month of pregnancy. She can also get free or low-cost medical care from the city's clinics, as well as a host of "preventive" services, such as Healthy Start, a nationwide effort to reduce infant mortality.

In Healthy Start, which pumps $8 million of additional federal aid a year into nonprofit social service agencies in Mott Haven,

Bedford-Stuyvesant, and Central Harlem, we can see the outlines of many services to come. Like TASA, it is a "case management" program, a hot social service trend. Case management takes a "case"— that is, an individual who has made some very bad decisions—and "manages" it by directing the individual to *other* services, above all to various entitlements for which the client may have failed to apply. Healthy Start directs clients to pre- and neonatal medical care, for example, and to such welfare benefits as Medicaid and the Women, Infants and Children food program. "Case management is a real scam," judges University of Massachusetts sociologist Peter Rossi. It's a "marvelous way to keep social workers from dealing with clients. All they do is deal with the 'case' and talk to each other as to how to manage it."

Healthy Start employs an extremely fuzzy definition of infant-mortality prevention. It funds programs that train tenant organizers, that encourage teens to pursue careers in health and social services (thus perpetuating the life of the social service establishment, if not of infants), and that deliver "life skills" and self-esteem training for teens. The link between any of these services and the prevention of infant mortality is remote.

But in today's social service programs, nearly any service can count as "prevention" of nearly any social pathology. The same non-profit agencies, such as the ubiquitous Puerto Rican Family Institute or Victim Services, Inc., are under contract with a variety of government agencies, including juvenile justice, child welfare, youth services, and mental health, to provide the identical set of services, appropriately repackaged as "pregnancy prevention," "delinquency prevention," "truancy prevention," or "child-abuse prevention." While the logic of prevention may sound convincing—it's cheaper to intervene early to prevent social problems than to respond after the fact— there is little evidence that prevention programs make a difference.

Imagine the baby who's had this supposed "healthy start" a few years later. Assume his mother's parenting class didn't take, as parenting classes so often don't. The child, or children by now, start asking neighbors for food and appear unwashed and ill-clothed. A neighbor calls the Child Welfare Agency (CWA) to report neglect. A CWA case-worker investigates the home and finds the children sleeping on the floor, no food in the refrigerator, and a filthy kitchen and bathroom. Just as the birth of illegitimate children provided the mother with an income, so will deplorable child-rearing bring her a benefit. The CWA worker might conclude that the mother is overwhelmed with being a parent and assign her a homemaker to help with her chores. The caseworker might also order still more parenting classes. Meanwhile, the neighbors next door, a poor working couple struggling to provide a decent home for their child, are left to scrub their own floors.

If the maltreatment is serious enough to warrant placing a child into foster care—the temporary custody arrangement for victims of parental abuse or neglect—the CWA may decide to provide the mother with "family preservation" instead. A relatively late arrival on the social service scene, dating from the 1980s, family preservation is its current queen. It is prototypical in its confusion of moral deficit with material need.

Family preservation works as follows: for six to eight weeks, an abusive or neglectful parent gets several visits a week from a social worker, who is on call twenty-four hours a day. The social worker provides home-based therapy to the family on such topics as "anger management" and "rational-emotive control." Equally important, the social worker provides a host of material services: she may buy groceries for the family, pay any outstanding rent arrears, drive the mother to medical or other appointments, help with home repair, or buy furniture, all at taxpayer expense. Meanwhile, the working couple next door, who also could use new furniture, is again out of luck.

Family preservation presupposes that many families "at risk" of losing a child to foster care are in a short-term crisis. Give them the psychological skills and financial assistance to weather the storm, the theory goes, and the risk of foster-care placement will recede. But many target parents suffer from problems too deep for a short-term fix. A drug-addicted teen dropout who happens to have gotten pregnant in all likelihood lacks the maturity to raise children; propping her "family" up with an array of services will never make it whole.

The animating philosophy of family preservation—that all "families," however dysfunctional or fragmentary, deserve respect—epitomizes contemporary social work's refusal to make moral judgments. To family preservationists, a single mother on crack who neglects her children is equal to a family of two working parents who can't afford day care. This ideology has profoundly affected child-welfare agencies nationwide, making them see their dominant mission as "keeping families together" rather than protecting children.

Even in those cases when the city must conclude that preventive services haven't worked, that doesn't dampen social workers' zeal for keeping deeply troubled families together. Under an arrangement known as kinship foster care, the city pays relatives—usually grandmothers—to care for their kin's children. It's a lucrative arrangement: the monthly foster care payment ranges from $400 to $1,000 a head, depending on the children's "special needs"—far more than they are worth living with their mother.

Not only parents are eligible for family preservation. The practice has spawned several clones directed at the children of troubled families, with the same aim of preserving the often toxic family trait. Imagine a twelve-year-old boy—"Johnnie" (a composite based on interviews with dozens of social service providers)—whose drug-addicted mother has already received various "preventive" services, maybe even full-blown family preservation. His chaotic home life starts erupting at school. He fights with fellow students and falls ever further behind in reading. The system will start prescribing services. His school is likely to conclude that he suffers from a "behavioral disorder" and a learning disability. It will put him in the special-education program and give him his own social worker as part of his special-education School-Based Support Team.

Nevertheless, Johnnie grows increasingly unruly and agitated. One day he threatens his teacher with a box cutter. His school psychologist recommends that he be temporarily hospitalized. But the emergency-room doctor feels that hospitalization can be averted by providing the family with—no surprise—social services. He refers Johnnie to the Home-Based Crisis Intervention Program, overseen by the state's Office of Mental Health but run by community-based non-profits. A social worker from a nonprofit, on call twenty-four hours a day, will provide six to eight weeks of intensive "anger management" and "problem solving" training for the family in its home. The case-worker might teach Johnnie's mother how to budget or how to help her children with their homework. The worker will also meet with Johnnie's teachers and develop a "service plan" with them.

Sound familiar? It should. Home-Based Crisis Intervention is the brainchild of the same Washington-based organization—the Behavioral Sciences Institute—that developed family preservation. The program models are identical.

The families in Home-Based Crisis Intervention are, with few exceptions, from the most dysfunctional subset of the welfare population. This subset consumes a disproportionate share of service spending and has become so embedded in various service systems that "caseworkers [from different agencies] are tripping over each other," says Anita Appel, who oversees Crisis Intervention. Such families' entry into the social service universe is a foregone conclusion; the only mystery is the exact point of entry. "The typical scenario is a mother on crack who has lost custody of her mentally disabled child to CWA," explains Denise Arieli of the city's Department of Mental Health. "If the child's point of entry is mental retardation, and in the mental program he sets a fire, he becomes a mental health child. If he happens to set the fire first, however, he will be a juvenile-justice child. The kids touch multiple systems, and the larger system struggles hard with where they should go."

The system is certain, however, that kids should *not* go to an institution. The clumsy dance of social workers serving the same family grows out of the social service system's commitment to "community care," closely linked with the philosophy of "keeping families together." Rather than taking children or adults away from destructive environments, the reigning service ethic dictates that they remain "in the community" and "in the family" for treatment. This ethic, born in the 1960s, when "community" was a code word for minority "empowerment," is based on a romanticized view of both underclass communities and the troubled families they produce. "We don't listen to families enough," says Anita Appel of the Office of Mental Health, in defense of her agency's various community-based programs.

The greatest fallacy of community-based treatment is that usually there is no real community to go back to. Treating a juvenile delinquent in the war-torn environment that produced him does not look like a recipe for success. Some observers also question the worth of the community-based organizations. "The staff is usually one baby step above their clients in pathology," observes a teacher who works with disturbed children. "They're from the same population, without education."

As a child placed in special education or in the Home-Based Crisis Intervention program progresses deeper into the social service world, one pattern will become dominant: the transfer of parental functions to his social workers, themselves often very ill-qualified to be parental surrogates. For example, in the Intensive Case Management program, which often follows the Crisis Intervention program, "the intensive case manager is just like family," explains Jeffrey Holliman of the city's Department of Mental Health. The manager will sit in on planning sessions at the child's school to develop a service plan for him and will try to line up yet more services for the family to ensure that the child stays at home, rather than in an institution such as foster care, a psychiatric hospital, or a juvenile detention center.

The children in any of the city's social services could just as easily have landed in its criminal system. Many ultimately do. Family Court, which adjudicates juvenile crime along with foster-care proceedings, is the very vortex of the social service system. All social problems that haven't been solved by other agencies end up there—only to meet the usual services.

Imagine that Johnnie, at age fifteen, pulls a gun on a grocery clerk but runs away when he sees a guard coming. At his arraignment for attempted robbery and assault, the judge may order him into the

Probation Department's Alternative to Detention (ATD) program, a pre-trial probation program for chronically truant kids. It is the most desperate of the city's social services: faced with the obvious failure of every other institution in a child's life, it tries to do everything that those other institutions did not. "Because we have a captive population, once we're monitoring a child, we want to address as much as we can for the time we have them—reading, writing, literacy, math issues, drug counseling," explains Michael P. Jacobson, commissioner of probation. ATD places kids in a small school-like setting during the day and offers them schooling, individual and group therapy, and field trips. If a child does not show up one day, a social worker will try to find him.

After three months in ATD, Johnnie's case comes to trial; Johnnie admits to the attempted robbery. But rather than sending him upstate to prison, the judge orders him into Family Ties, the most remarkable offshoot of family preservation yet. Run out of the city's Department of Juvenile Justice, Family Ties gives convicted juvenile delinquents and their families eight weeks of the usual litany: cognitive restructuring, behavioral modification, anger management, and rational-emotive therapy. Then the Family Ties worker recommends a sentence—usually probation—to the judge. If the original idea of family preservation—that six to eight weeks of intensive counseling and material aid could cure child abuse and neglect—seems fanciful at best, the claim that short-term therapy can overcome the thirteen-odd years of lack of socialization that produces juvenile delinquency seems preposterous.

From this point, Johnnie's future is hazy. He may go straight, finish school, and stay out of trouble. But if he doesn't—if he ends up homeless or on drugs or HIV-positive or in and out of prison—the city will have social services for him at every stage.

Many social programs treat as short-term crises what are in fact unsustainable ways of life. The city's huge "homelessness prevention" efforts are typical. Consider a family living in an apartment that costs nearly twice as much as its welfare housing grant. The rent is far in arrears and the landlord is threatening eviction. The mother's social worker advises a trip to the Homeless Prevention Unit in her local welfare office.

The obvious thing to do would be to talk to the mother about finding a cheaper apartment. But the city's welfare agencies seldom do the obvious. "The overriding policy in the Human Resources Administration [HRA] is to prevent the loss of accommodations at all costs," explains HRA spokesman David Ortiz. After paying the back rent to forestall eviction, the homelessness-prevention worker decides to go for the gold: a "Jiggetts" supplement.

Named after a lawsuit filed by homeless advocates, Jiggetts supplements pay the difference between a client's monthly welfare shelter allowance and her actual rent—forever. The monthly shelter allowance for a three-person family is $286 a month; Jiggetts will double that to $572. Brokers and landlords frequently game the system, striking agreements to rent welfare clients apartments well beyond their means, and to forgo a few months' rent, with the understanding that the client will apply for a Jiggetts grant once she faces eviction.

The Jiggetts program exudes misguided beneficence. While the average rent in New York City is, in fact, well above the welfare shelter grant, Jiggetts money anchors indigents to a locale they can't afford, instead of leaving them to migrate to places with lower costs of living or better job prospects, as the poor have traditionally done. Further, tenants often face eviction because of personal irresponsibility, such as a drug habit that consumes the rent money. Propping them up only abets their underlying problem.

If homelessness prevention fails, more social services beckon. Thanks to court cases that gave the homeless the unconditional right to emergency shelter on demand, the city now operates the nation's largest, most expensive shelter system. All told, the city's expenditures on the homeless amount to an estimated $790 million a year, exclusive of medical costs, or $39,500 per homeless person, which includes transportation to visit renovated apartments, moving expenses, furniture allowances, and payments to landlords for renting to homeless families.

Homeless families, as distinct from homeless single individuals, get the most elaborate services. Visit, for example, the Westside Intergenerational Residence, a clean, orderly family shelter in an apartment building on Manhattan's staid West End Avenue. The shelter assigns each resident, almost always a single mother with one child, a social worker and a preventive services worker, who provide entitlement advocacy, counseling, referrals, and parenting-skills training. The residence requires enrollment in an educational program—though self-esteem and parenting-skills classes will sometimes suffice—and it provides two on-site day-care programs for its mothers. According to administrators, the residence's GED program uses an "unconventional" approach to teaching, emphasizing such activities as journal writing, along with academic subjects. "Our ladies won't come in just for reading and writing; getting up to go to math is very boring," explains director Linda Sergeant. And if a mother's attendance record is spotty, her social workers, instead of asking her to change, will create a less structured and less demanding program for her.

The residence has an informal program to help its mothers write to their political representatives in support of welfare, Medicaid, and child care. The residence's program isn't unique: students in a city high school for teen mothers recently traveled to Washington, at taxpayer expense, to lobby against welfare cuts. Such a program sends precisely the wrong message to homeless mothers: that more government spending can rebuild their lives. What that spending *can* do, of course, is preserve the jobs of the social service workers who assist their clients' lobbying efforts.

The social service imperative not to make moral judgments has a corollary: a social worker's job is to shield clients from the consequences of self-destructive behavior. This philosophy ends up normalizing bad behavior, nowhere more than in the city's response to teen pregnancy. The Board of Education has five high schools for pregnant and "parenting" teens, which supplement the regular curriculum with parenting classes. That's not all: the school system's Living for the Young Family in Education (LYFE) program operates highly enriched day-care centers in thirty-five regular schools and in several homeless shelters, at an annual cost of $7.6 million, or $12,666 per teen mother. Its purpose is to increase the chances that a teen mother will graduate from school by removing the burden of travel to an off-site day-care center. And LYFE is just one leg of the city's day-care empire, which cost $557 million in fiscal 1995.

The LYFE program epitomizes the way social services can feed the very problems they're supposed to cure. The program responds to the argument of necessity: ignoring the baby won't make it go away, so now we have to make the best of a bad situation. This argument is a powerful one. It motivates program after program intended to sop up the mess caused by socially destructive behavior. But the inevitable result is to legitimate that behavior. Day-care centers in schools cannot avoid sending the pernicious message that society not only tolerates but *expects* teens to have babies. By removing the pain from very bad decisions, such programs simply enable further bad behavior.

The LYFE program goes out of its way to insulate teens from the consequences of bearing illegitimate children. Teen mothers don't even have to visit the day-care center to feed their babies during the lunch period. "Lunch is the only time they get to hang out with their friends," explains Joan Davis, assistant principal of the program. "The hardest thing about being a teen mom is not being able to be a teen."

This is "compassion" gone mad. The last thing a child needs is a parent who acts like an adolescent. Yet with an unfailing instinct for doing the wrong thing, the social service establishment has made preserving adolescence a goal of the statewide Teenage Services Act for teen mothers on welfare. Director Harriet Nieves explains the TASA philosophy: "We try to give them support so that they can have some of the immaturity and giddiness of being a teen, yet still say to them: 'You have a child.'" TASA nurtures adolescent "giddiness," Nieves explains, by helping teens to "negotiate the school system and the dating scene," and to develop such crucial life skills as "how to budget and go to fashion stores."

The numbers show how dismally the whole social service effort has flopped. While city and state spending to fight poverty in New York City totaled between $100 billion and $150 billion between 1970 and 1990, the city's poverty rate increased from 15 to 19 percent in the same period. In 1970, 15 percent of poor households in the city were single-parent families; in 1990, 25 percent. The dependency rate in the city—defined as the percentage of the total population receiving means-tested public assistance, medical assistance, or Supplemental Security Income—is 19 percent. In Brooklyn it is 22 percent, in Manhattan close to 30 percent, and in the Bronx 30 percent.

The city's vast array of "preventive" services hasn't prevented much. Despite widespread sex education and pregnancy-prevention programs, teen birthrates rose 15 percent between 1986 and 1989. Drug-abuse prevention programs notwithstanding, 62 percent of preschool children in foster care in 1991 were at risk of serious health problems because of prenatal drug exposure, more than double the rate in 1986. And countless violence-prevention initiatives haven't made inner-city life more civil.

The cost of all this is mind-boggling. New York City spends over one-fifth of all local social service dollars *in the nation*. Local governments—cities and counties—spend an average of $6.74 on social services for every $1,000 of personal income within their jurisdictions; New York City spends nearly $40, though $11 of that pays for the New York City Medicaid contribution, a mandate on localities nearly unique to New York State. Largely because of its huge social service commitment, the city collected twice as much in taxes in 1992 per $1,000 of personal income as the national local government average and had a total budget that in 1994 was larger than forty-six *state* budgets.

Profoundly undemocratic, New York's social service industry consumes billions of tax dollars but is largely unaccountable to taxpayers. No one even knows exactly how much, in total, government spends on social services in New York City. All existing estimates are incomplete, since they don't include the vast social service operations tucked away in a host of city agencies, from the Board of Education to the Health Department to the Parks Department. The city comptroller's Comprehensive Annual Financial Report for fiscal year 1994, for example, put social service spending at $8 billion, or 26 percent of the city's budget—the largest share of city spending. The Board of Education was the next-largest share, consuming $7.15 billion, or 25 percent of the budget—but that includes school-based social services and massive spending on special education. The comptroller's estimate of social service spending includes only four agencies and excludes state and federal Medicaid spending.

No budget anywhere in the city lays out every social service program and its costs. Though the nine-volume city budget breaks down costs in infinitesimal detail, it doesn't link them to recognizable programs. The comptroller's annual financial report, considered the city's most accessible budget document, divides agency spending into two vast, murky categories: personnel spending and "other than personnel spending." Again, it doesn't break down spending by particular programs.

At the state level, the budget consists of five separate documents, once again lacking complete programmatic analysis. "People have worked hard for many years to make sure the budget is difficult to understand," explains Tim Murphy, director of fiscal research in the state comptroller's office. "It means nothing to say that an agency spent $21 billion. The question is, on what?"

The best rough estimate of spending in the city is the state Department of Social Services total expenditures within the five boroughs—$19.5 billion in 1993. This represents the total federal, state, and city spending on the anti-poverty programs DSS administers, though it excludes spending by city agencies such as the Board of Education and the Department of Homeless Services.

On the basis of the 1993 DSS figures, one can make certain broad observations about the city's social service spending. The lion's share goes to Medicaid ($11.4 billion, of which the city contributed $2.2 billion), followed by welfare "income maintenance" programs ($2.7 million total; city share, $924 million). The city's almost unique jurisdictional structure explains part of this huge cost. Unlike most cities, New York has no county government to share the burden of local welfare spending. Moreover, New York State requires localities to pay a greater share of non-federal welfare spending than any other state. New York is one of only two states—the other is North Carolina—that require a full fifty-fifty split for the non-federal share of AFDC. California, by contrast, picks up 90 percent of the non-federal share; New Jersey, 75 percent; forty-three states require no local matching at all. Even fewer states require local matching of Medicaid spending.

The city has no direct control over most of its welfare spending, concentrated in programs for which Albany sets the benefit levels and eligibility criteria. Whenever the state increases spending, the city must pay. Rudolph Giuliani seems to be the first mayor to have understood this: he made history in 1995 by asking the state to *decrease* its welfare budget. The city's social service establishment, however, has considerable muscle in the state legislature, which ultimately determines such matters.

But don't conclude that New York City bears little responsibility for the making of this vast municipal welfare state. Though recent mayors have chafed under the burden of state social service mandates, the city was an enthusiastic co-conspirator in the creation of the welfare establishment. During the New Deal, the city, regarding itself as more progressive than the state, seized control over new federally established welfare programs by volunteering to assume fiscal responsibility for them. Albany happily gave the city, much richer than the rest of the state, free rein in developing programs.

The other turning point came in 1966, the year John Lindsay was elected mayor. Lindsay came into office criticizing his predecessor, Robert Wagner, for his lukewarm embrace of the War on Poverty, which the new mayor, red-hot, had helped plan as a congressman. Convinced that social welfare programs would bring blacks and Puerto Ricans into the mainstream, Lindsay took the mandate in federal poverty initiatives for the "maximum feasible participation" of the poor quite literally. He devolved all authority for anti-poverty programs onto community groups, so that within a few years no one knew what programs or groups were out there or what their spiraling budgets were.

Just then, too, the welfare-rights movement, led by Frances Fox

Piven and Richard Cloward of Columbia University, sought to sign up every eligible person for welfare, to hike grant levels sharply, and to remove "demeaning" conditions on the receipt of aid. In an influential 1966 article in *The Nation*, Piven and Cloward had advocated mass protest and the disruption of welfare offices as a means of forcing these changes. Welfare clients obediently stormed the city's welfare centers, terrifying workers.

In response, the city boosted welfare grants and made procedural changes that proved costly. No longer would social workers visit applicants at home to confirm eligibility; the system would be based on trust. Welfare-rights attorneys won the right to a hearing before the termination of welfare eligibility; the U.S. Supreme Court would later adopt the ruling.

The movement's impact on New York City was jolting: welfare caseloads, already climbing 12 percent a year in the early sixties, rose by 50 percent during Lindsay's first two years; spending doubled. By the end of Lindsay's first term, welfare costs had reached $1 billion; the new Medicaid program cost another $1 billion.

The welfare-rights movement failed in its ultimate goal of overwhelming the welfare system and forcing a national guaranteed minimum income to take its place. But it succeeded in greatly weakening the stigma attached to welfare, in teaching the poor to view welfare as a right, and consequently in vastly increasing the rolls. The city had 150,000 welfare cases in 1960; a decade later it had 1.5 million.

The procedural changes of the 1960s, meanwhile, turned welfare into a check-writing system and took social workers out of the business of influencing their clients' behavior. Ironically, that suited the once-radical welfare workers just fine. Though many had entered the profession in the 1960s out of sympathy for the poor, years of harassment had taken their toll. By 1970 the caseworkers "were thoroughly in terror of the clients: they didn't want to go near them," says Charles Morris, who became Lindsay's welfare chief in 1971.

For Lindsay, too, the bloom had come off the welfare clientele. By his second term, he "hated welfare recipients," says Morris. "He had done all these good things for them, and they had fucked him. My job was to cut them." The public, once almost universally pro-welfare in the 1960s, was growing wary as well; good intentions seemed to have created a monster. Even liberal Governor Nelson Rockefeller warned in 1971 that, without reform, "the welfare system will eventually overload and break down our society."

Modest reform did come a few years later. In 1975, New York City—with the highest AFDC grant and the highest Medicaid costs per recipient in the country, the largest drug-addiction and methadone programs in the world—was bankrupt, and the state nearly so. Hugh Carey, the new governor, introduced anti-fraud measures in welfare and started to reform Medicaid. He slowed the rate of new program creation and kept spending growth below inflation.

But with the 1980s economic boom and the administration of Mario Cuomo, the growth of the welfare state barreled full speed ahead once more. New initiatives rolled out of Albany, designed to capture ever more federal matching dollars. State government spending rose at twice the rate of inflation; welfare rolls increased 24.5 percent statewide during Cuomo's three terms. In the city the same spirit of profligacy reigned. "The attitude was," says former city human resources chief William Grinker, "'We have the money; let's spend it.'"

Today, with the city's fiscal condition parlous and its economic growth anemic, with the federal government shifting responsibility for welfare spending back to the states, Governor Pataki and Mayor Giuliani have wisely begun to challenge the welfare establishment. Both leaders stress personal accountability. Giuliani has implemented the nation's most comprehensive fraud-detection program for Home Relief recipients, producing an astounding drop in the rolls. He is rigorously enforcing the work requirement for able-bodied recipients. Pataki has introduced commonsense regulations requiring homeless shelter clients to refrain from violence and drug use, as well as to contribute a portion of their welfare check to their rent. He has persuaded the legislature to enact a fingerprinting requirement and more rigorous work demands for Home Relief recipients; he also won a measure to dock welfare mothers if their elementary school-age children are truant. But Assembly Democrats shot down Pataki's proposal for time limits on Home Relief. In December, Pataki announced a set of more dramatic reforms that would bring New York's AFDC payment into line with New Jersey's, impose a five-year lifetime limit on AFDC and Home Relief, and allow localities to test welfare recipients for drugs and to require those with positive results to participate in treatment as a precondition of receiving benefits.

The fate of Pataki's reforms in the legislature is uncertain. But their passage is crucial, for New Jersey and Connecticut remain way ahead of New York in reform. New Jersey has implemented a "family cap," so that a client's AFDC grant doesn't go up when she has additional children; Connecticut has enacted strict time limits for AFDC as well as for Home Relief. These changes make New York's more generous system all the more attractive to would-be migrants.

New York needs to challenge foursquare the credo that has guided social work for too long: "Thou shalt not judge." Lacking any moral compass for determining who is most deserving of help, the city has, perversely, spent most on those who act the most destructively, because by definition they have the worst problems. The evolution in the city's day-care programs is a case in point. Fifteen years ago most parents using city day care worked, according to Rhonda Carlos-Smith of Child Care, Inc., an advocacy group. Now working parents are at the bottom of the priority list. At the top are parents who have abused or neglected their children. Between 1989 and 1994, the number of teen parents using day care increased by 94 percent, and the number of homeless families by 21 percent.

It's time for New York to junk the demonstrably false shibboleths of social services as well: the reflexive worship of "community care" or "family preservation." With no real community to go back to, no real family to preserve, community-based drug treatment, pregnancy prevention, family preservation, foster care, and juvenile rehabilitation can do little other than to enrich the coffers of the nonprofits. In an extraordinary development, some juvenile delinquents are now refusing probation and requesting incarceration upstate, recognizing that they need the structure provided by an institution and fearing the mayhem on the streets.

The city ought to restore the distinction between the deserving and undeserving poor. For the poor who do deserve and can benefit from help, especially children, the state and city should consider the use of boarding school–like institutions outside the city. But those who behave the most irresponsibly should no longer have the greatest claim on city revenues. And for the most part, the city should get out of the business of social uplift, which three decades' experience has proved is beyond the capacity of municipal government to accomplish.

[1996]

Welfare's Next Vietnam

BY DECADE'S END, the public may well discover that the great welfare reform debate of 1995 addressed only half the problem. The Rivera family of Boston illustrates why. Eulalia Rivera came from Puerto Rico in 1968 and proceeded to raise a welfare dynasty. Her sixteen surviving children (the seventeenth was shot) and their eighty-nine progeny collect $750,000 to $1 million a year in government benefits. Their main form of support, however, is not AFDC, the program for single mothers and children that has been targeted for reform: it is federal disability payments.

Not that the Riveras suffer from crippling physical illnesses or injuries. Most of the family's disabled members collect benefits for their "nerves." As Eulalia's son Juan, a divorced father of five, told the *Boston Globe*: "I have a nervous condition. . . . There is no way I could work." He pointed to his hands, which were shaking. "Look at this," he said: "I'm having an attack right now."

The Riveras represent the future of public assistance. While AFDC costs have grown 23 percent since 1980, the costs of the federal government's two disability programs have more than doubled. By 1998, they will reach $80 billion a year. In 1993, they already enrolled a total of 8.2 million Americans—more than 3 percent of the population. Disability for the poor is the nation's fastest-growing welfare program, about to surpass both AFDC and food stamps as the main form of support for the non-working poor. Workers' disability is ballooning as well: the Social Security disability trust fund will go bankrupt in 1995 and will be bailed out with money from the Social Security retirement fund.

The explosive growth in disability payments reflects an unacknowledged shift in the function of the disability program. Disability increasingly supports people whose main problem is not a traditional medical impairment but a host of social handicaps that no doctor could cure. Many of these newer beneficiaries may indeed be unemployable, but their unemployability reflects rampant drug use, a chaotic upbringing, and a lack of education and work ethic rather than any physical impediment.

Behind this shift in the function of the disability program lies a revolution in the concept of disability, the crowning achievement of fifteen years of litigation by welfare- and disability-rights advocates. American culture now defines as "mental disorders" behavior that other parts of the world might consider simply antisocial or even criminal. This policy is turning disability into a general welfare system for all the poor, including addicts and alcoholics—even including children with behavioral problems, for whom the designation "disabled" becomes a self-fulfilling prophecy, marginalizing them for life.

Running a welfare program under the guise of a disability program is extremely costly. More important, putting people on the dole for life does nothing to alleviate the social conditions that made them unemployable in the first place. It is time to ask whether the expansion in disability entitlements has gone too far.

The federal disability program began modestly in 1956 to support workers over fifty whose severe disability was expected to last indefinitely, preventing them from ever returning to work. Its history since then has been one of almost unbroken expansion.

Currently, the Social Security Administration (SSA) administers two disability programs: the original Social Security Disability Insurance (SSDI)—now for workers of any age who've paid into the Social Security trust fund and whose disability is expected to last a year or more—and Supplemental Security Income (SSI) for the non-working, disabled poor. Unlike SSDI, eligibility for SSI (which also covers the elderly and blind) requires no work history. Like AFDC and other welfare programs, it is means-tested to make sure that the recipient's income and resources are below a certain level. In 1993, 3.7 million SSDI recipients—26 percent more than in 1989—received $34.6 billion in payments, including payments to dependents. SSI had 4.5 million disabled recipients in 1993—37 percent more than in 1989—receiving $19.9 billion.

Disability is the ticket to an array of government benefits. The federal government pays up to $458 a month in SSI. Almost all recipients can receive an additional $50 to $60 a month in food stamps; most are automatically eligible for Medicaid. SSI also entitles the recipient to subsidized housing, low-income energy assistance, school lunches, and payments from the federal Women, Infants, and Children program. All told, life on disability commonly entails a tax-free income, in cash and other benefits, of upwards of $10,000 a year.

The current disability explosion results from a chain of reactions set going in the seventies. That decade saw the first major surge in disability applications, fueled by liberalized eligibility standards, a declining work ethic, and rising unemployment. The application and award rates for SSDI reached record levels unmatched ever since, though current rates are rapidly nearing those levels.

But the burden on the SSA from the jump in SSDI applications paled by comparison with the massive short circuit caused by SSI. Even today, the start of SSI in 1974 is remembered within the agency as an unmitigated disaster. Caring for the disabled poor had traditionally been the responsibility of state and local governments. SSI moved that entire responsibility to the federal government, saddling the SSA with 3 million applications from 1,350 state and local agencies almost overnight. The agency had never before run a means-tested income-support program: determining someone's eligibility for Social Security is far easier than figuring out the income, resources, and living arrangements of a transient, often marginal, population.

When the agency ran into inevitable delays in processing and verifying the new claimants, chaos broke out. Mobs of angry claimants assaulted and spat upon agency workers; federal marshals or private security officers had to be called in. As Floy Newman, a Social Security operations officer in Santa Ana, California, discreetly explains: "Welfare recipients have a different attitude to government" than Social Security beneficiaries.

Toward the end of the seventies, exploding benefit costs and the looming insolvency of the SSDI fund prompted the SSA to try to tighten eligibility standards. At the time—and still today—a claimant could be found disabled by one of two routes. For a so-called medical allowance, the SSA publishes a list of physical and mental impairments deemed disabling in themselves. A claimant is eligible for benefits under a medical allowance if his impairment matches in severity one of the listed impairments, without inquiry into whether he can work. But if his impairment is not as severe as those on the list, he can still win benefits under a "vocational allowance" if he can show that his impairment nevertheless prevents him from performing either his past work or, in light of his age, education, and work experience, any other work generally available in the economy.

There has always been a tension between the two types of allowance. Critics say that vocational allowances are more subjective than medical allowances and thus result in non-uniform decisions. More important, the vocational evaluation can serve as a cover for importing social considerations—such as a bad or nonexistent education, lack of responsibility and work ethic, and a self-destructive lifestyle—into the disability determination. For these reasons, the Reagan administration once tried to eliminate vocational allowances altogether but was defeated by welfare- and disability-rights advocates, who fight tooth and nail every attempt to reduce the weight of education and work history in disability determinations.

As for the apparently more objective medical listings, many analysts today question whether they actually correspond to the inability to work. Someone who loses both legs below the knee, for example, is automatically eligible for benefits; with current technologies, though, he undoubtedly could hold a job. And under the 1992 Americans with Disabilities Act he could sue an employer for not hiring him.

By 1975, the percentage of vocational allowances had risen to over 26 percent of claims granted at the first stage of the disability award process, up from 1960's 10 percent. Concerned that the decision-making process was losing its objectivity, SSA revised its eligibility standards to reemphasize medical criteria—but still failed to halt rocketing costs. So in 1980 Congress enacted the Social Security Disability Amendments, which required the SSA to review every three years the continuing eligibility of all recipients who were not permanently disabled. When the Reagan administration took office, it seized upon these amendments as part of its campaign to reduce the size of the federal government. From 1981 to 1984, it reviewed 1.2 million cases and terminated benefits in almost a half-million of them.

The government's effort to rein in disability proved one of the great administrative debacles of recent history. The reviews upset beneficiaries' settled beliefs, born of years of lax enforcement, that they were on the rolls for life. In its roll-slashing zeal, the administration cut people who may not have been disabled when they entered the program but had become so after years of dependency on the dole. The press furnished a running account of cripples turned onto the streets and beneficiaries committing suicide.

The courts revolted. By the end of 1984, all the federal circuits had deemed the reviews illegal. Judges had put 200,000 people back on the rolls—often without evidence of disability—and had authorized further lawsuits that could nullify the rest of the reviews.

There is wide consensus that the administration took a meat-ax approach when individualized reviews were in order, but on the central legal point—the SSA's standard for determining continuing disability—the administration was in the right. In requiring a beneficiary to prove that he was currently disabled to continue receiving benefits, the agency was faithfully following a 1976 Supreme Court ruling.

Starting with a 1982 decision by the Ninth Circuit Court of Appeals, however, the judiciary rejected that standard. The lower courts ruled that the SSA had to show that the claimant's medical condition had improved since the initial disability determination before ending his benefits. It was no longer enough to show that he was presently able to work. In fact, the agency itself had employed just such a medical improvement standard from 1969 to 1976 but had abandoned it as unworkable, since for many beneficiaries who'd been grandfathered into the SSI program from the state disability programs, the original evidence of disability, collected years before, no longer existed. The only meaningful standard, the agency reasonably argued, was whether someone could currently work.

Congress, which had started this battle between the agency and the courts with its 1980 mandate to conduct the reviews, stepped in again in 1984. That year, the Social Security Disability Reform Act adopted the medical improvement standard that the courts had imposed on the SSA. Not surprisingly, the agency once again virtually ceased reviewing cases, and now 90 percent of those it does review continue on the rolls. In the SSDI program alone, the cost of not reviewing recipients from 1990 to 1993 will reach $1.4 billion by the end of 1997.

The legacy of the 1980–84 review crisis is enormous, for in the legal counterattack the reviews ignited, advocates brought a series of test cases that successfully challenged and enlarged the SSA's eligibility standards. Ultimately, Congress codified virtually all of these victories in the Reform Act of 1984. With eligibility criteria vastly liberalized by the combined judicial and legislative efforts, the gunpowder trail was laid to produce the explosion in the rolls that ineluctably ensued.

Mental, rather than physical, complaints have fueled the disability explosion, and no legal decision of the early eighties has more affected the current composition of the rolls than one in a 1982 Minnesota suit challenging the SSA's evaluation of "non-severe" mental impairments. The judge held that the agency had been illegally denying benefits to people who, despite their impairments, were able to cope with daily activities such as cooking and shopping. To find such claimants able to work, argued the court, ignores the fact that the work environment poses unique stress for the mentally ill. Chronic mental illness, the decision stated, is "characterized by an exquisite sensitivity to stress and a decrease in coping skills." The court ordered the agency to give greater weight to testimony from claimants' own doctors regarding their ability to work.

The court's holding that non-psychotic mental illness can interfere with the ability to work is unimpeachable, but the chief message of the case was that the agency should evaluate mental impairment claims far more liberally. The decision and its subsequent congressional ratification have given rise to a host of agency rulings and court decisions in which work itself is portrayed as toxic to mental and emotional stability—especially owing to its "competitive nature." The Seventh Circuit rebuked the SSA in 1989 for denying disability to a computer operator who had been fired because of his inability to get along with co-workers. The agency improperly ignored the treating psychiatrist's report, the court held, which had stated that the operator was "unable to work in a competitive environment."

Today, attorneys in disability cases routinely pay $75 for a psychiatric exam for their clients, to make sure that either stress and anxiety or depression is part of most every complaint. Because the agency is now required to defer to the claimant's treating doctor—even if the claimant has seen him only once—it has little recourse when confronted with a boilerplate diagnosis of personality disorder or identity disturbance. "People are playing games because everyone knows we have to follow the treating doctor," complains Arlander Keys, an administrative law judge in Chicago. All over the country, explains Morton Gold of the SSA's Savannah office, attorneys who work closely with certain doctors have made disability into "a budding industry, and profitable."

Many disability claimants belatedly discover mental impairments when their claims for physical impairments are denied. An SSDI claimant in Illinois had unsuccessfully appealed the termination of his benefits after the bone fracture for which he had previously received payments had healed. On his second appeal, he argued that his epilepsy and alcoholism qualified him for benefits. Again he lost. Then he saw a psychiatrist, who diagnosed him with "personality disorder with dependent, antisocial, and passive-aggressive features." This did the trick. A court in 1991 found that his "psychological abnormalities combined with alcoholism lead to the conclusion that he can't meet the minimum standards of a normal competitive work setting." He was, in other words, unemployable.

The 1984 Reform Act further shifted the disability determination process away from objective medical evidence and toward much fuzzier, non-medical indicators, such as a patient's own description of his condition and his participation in "activities of daily living" and "social functioning," in determining his capacity to work. Evidence of the claimant's behavior necessarily comes from family members and friends—many of whom have a direct financial interest in the disability decision.

Because the 1984 act also increased the role of age, education, and work experience in disability decisions, someone who has worked and has some skills can now be denied disability, while someone with the identical impairment but no work history can be found disabled—a clear inequity. In 1991, 31.7 percent of SSDI awards at the first level of the disability determination rested on such vocational considerations, rather than on the medical listings—an all-time high. Though comparable figures are not available, the percentage of vocational allowances in the SSI program is undoubtedly higher still.

As a direct result of the act, mental impairments today constitute the largest portion of the agency's caseload, a radical change from the early years of the program. Fully 30 percent of all SSI beneficiaries are classified as mentally impaired. By comparison, all other categories of impairments—with the exception of mental retardation—are in the single digits. Male SSI recipients between the ages of thirty and fifty have a nearly 45 percent mental impairment rate.

The situation is the same with SSDI. One-quarter of recipients are mentally impaired; for those under forty-five, the mental impairment rate is 37 percent. Since 1982, mental impairments have increased by more than 500 percent among younger SSDI recipients. And in 1992, applicants making mental impairment claims won SSDI benefits 66 percent of the time, as against only 39 percent for physical impairment claims.

The surge in the number of mentally impaired disability recipients not only has swelled the rolls but also has changed the demographics of the beneficiary population. The average age of recipients has dropped. The average SSDI recipient is now under 50. The typical SSI recipient is in his thirties with a high school education or less. Younger recipients stay on the rolls longer; younger recipients alleging mental impairments stay the longest of all. According to the SSA, individuals between the ages of 18 and 34 with mental impairments stay on SSDI for 25.5 years, 39 percent longer than the average for that age group.

The newfound liberality toward mental impairment is placing severe strains on the SSA. "The more claims we pay, the more people apply," laments the chief administrative law judge in Chicago, Stephen Ahlgren. "Our judicial system is not up to dealing with these numbers." There are 450,000 cases backlogged at the hearings level nationwide; the annual caseload per administrative judge in Chicago has jumped in recent years from 250 cases to 800. Such caseloads prevent judges from developing cases sufficiently to rebut boilerplate diagnoses. And judges are resolving more cases without a hearing— which they can do only if they rule in the claimant's favor.

Not surprisingly, frustration with the mental impairment standard is rising. "We're finding a lot of people disabled who can work," says Judge Ahlgren. Jane Ross, associate director of income security at the General Accounting Office, told the *Boston Globe* recently, "For those of us who work and manage stress daily, it's easy to get pretty angry about people who say they can't because of 'anxiety.'"

Though unquestionably mental illness can incapacitate, the courts seem remarkably credulous toward mental illness claims. A 1989 federal court decision in Massachusetts is typical. The court granted the appeal of Linda Zeitz, forty-two, a former sales rep for Coca-Cola who claimed she had suffered from agoraphobia since 1978 because of her consumption of "birth control pills, junk food, and large amounts of Tab." According to court records, Zeitz described her illness and her seven-year effort to get on SSI as "a typical story of a woman who finally starts thinking about who she is as an independent person, rather than as an extension of a man and family." Numerous visits to doctors had revealed no medical basis for the palpitations, backaches, and headaches she said she had experienced while on sales calls before she quit her job. One psychiatrist did note in 1979, however, that she had recently stopped her long-running marijuana habit.

At the time of the appeal, Zeitz said she left her apartment only for doctors' appointments, though she had managed to run up an $11,000 credit card debt. She was ignoring a psychiatrist's recommendation that she attend group therapy, relying instead on health food, vitamins, and solitary reading as prescribed by a "naturopath" she consulted. An administrative judge had denied her claim, finding only slight functional limitations and citing an agency rule that if a claimant fails to follow prescribed treatment that would restore the ability to work, he will be denied benefits. But the district court ruled that Zeitz was under no obligation to follow the prescribed group-therapy treatment because "a psychosomatic anxiety-related disorder such as agoraphobia may defy any generally accepted prescribed treatment requiring the will of the individual to recover." The court remanded the case for further hearings.

The beast that lies beneath the entire mental impairment caseload is substance abuse. Where there is depression, one of the main mental disorders, there is usually also alcohol or drugs. In most cases, it is impossible to separate the effect of drugs and alcohol from that of the alleged illness itself.

Recent press and congressional attention has focused on a small category of substance-abusing disability beneficiaries: those officially acknowledged as addicts or alcoholics, who are required to be in treatment. But the reach of addiction goes far beyond those addicts, even beyond the mental impairment category generally. Dig deep enough and you will find drugs and alcohol throughout the entire disability system, according to David Fiske, an analyst at the General Accounting Office. Fiske tells of a case that focused exclusively on the claimant's bad back. Buried in the medical records, however, was the fact that the claimant relaxed on Friday nights by drinking a case of beer. "You won't deal with the problems of the claimant's back," says Fiske, "without dealing with the problems caused by those cases of beer."

Morton Gold, the Social Security attorney in Savannah, calls addiction the "Vietnam quagmire of the agency." It forces the agency to turn a blind eye to law-breaking and to support destructive behavior. SSA's response to addiction and alcoholism ranges from "enlightened" tolerance, in the case of officially classified addicts and alcoholics, to a sort of willed ignorance in those myriad other cases where addiction is the subtext of other physical or mental disorders.

"Substance addiction disorder" is itself a listed mental impairment. SSA used to give benefits for addiction and alcoholism per se only if the claimant could show irreversible organ damage, but the courts struck down that precondition as too harsh, putting in its place the requirement that the addict have lost the ability to control his addiction. Today, at least 250,000 diagnosed addicts and alcoholics are on the disability rolls, up from fewer than 100,000 five years ago. They receive approximately $1.4 billion annually in benefits.

When Congress established the SSI program, it attempted to allay criticism that paying cash to addicts merely bankrolls their addiction. It required recipients whose primary diagnosis is addiction or alcoholism to enroll in treatment. It also obliged them to have their benefits paid to a "representative payee," who is supposed to prevent the addict from misusing his disability check.

Both requirements turned out to be a farce, however. The agency had trouble finding representative payees as far back as 1976; relatives often balk at agency requests to serve, fearing violence should they try to withhold cash from the addict. In recent years, stories have accumulated of benefits being mailed to the corner liquor store or to fellow addicts.

Of the quarter-million addicts and alcoholics on disability, the representative payee and treatment requirements apply only to those 78,000 SSI recipients whose primary diagnosis is alcoholism or addiction. Of these, however, only 9 percent actually are in treatment. What's more, while an average of 2,000 new addicts entered the rolls each month in 1993, only 75 completed treatment. Even completing treatment, though, doesn't generally mean that the addict has been rehabilitated or removed from the rolls. Indeed, the addict has every reason not to conquer his addiction, since that would mean losing his benefits, including Medicaid.

Because the claims and appeals process takes so long—currently, 155 days for an initial decision, and a year and a half for an administrative judge's decision—addicts, like other disability beneficiaries, often receive huge retroactive payments of $15,000 to $20,000. These usually result in protracted binges.

On ordinary check days, the effect is similar. A director of a homeless shelter in Denver told Senate investigators that his clients call the first of the month "Christmas Day"; he termed SSI "suicide on the installment plan." Addicts and alcoholics who do not die from their subsidized substance abuse simply become more and more disabled, thus staying on the rolls longer.

In August 1994, Congress extended SSI's representative payee and treatment requirements to SSDI recipients whose primary diagnosis is substance abuse. It also put a three-year cap on addiction benefits for both programs. Given the agency's inability to enforce the treatment and representative payee requirements for SSI recipients, it seems likely that the new SSDI provisions will likewise languish. Even if the provisions could be made to work, however, they apply to far too small a subset of the drug- and alcohol-abusing disability population. Drink enough to develop cirrhosis of the liver, or contract AIDS through IV drug use, and your benefits will come with no strings attached, because you are now disabled irrespective of your addiction.

In some cities, claimants with drug and alcohol problems are overwhelming the administrative hearing system. More than half the nation's officially classified addiction beneficiaries are in California and Illinois; 98 percent of the cases heard in Chicago in January 1994 involved some element of addiction, according to Chief Judge Ahlgren. Administrative judges there say they are burning out from the addiction cases.

Classifying addiction or alcoholism as a federally subsidized disability not only is highly destructive to the recipients; it also compromises the government. In 1991, officials of the SSA's Chicago office requested guidance from headquarters in Baltimore regarding a type of claimant, exemplified by "Ronald C.," that they were seeing more and more frequently. An addict who used IV drugs three or four times a day and consumed three pints of wine daily, Ronald had spent his adult life in and out of prison for drug-related crimes. He was currently awaiting trial for shoplifting. The question exemplified by Ronald was: how should the agency evaluate someone's capacity to work if he has resided mostly in prison?

Susan B. Parker, associate commissioner for disability at SSA headquarters, issued the agency's response, and it should gladden the hearts of many a convict: while confinement in an institution does not establish the existence or severity of an impairment, she wrote, it may be "suggestive of factors that are reflective of diagnosis and severity." According to the psychiatrists' *Diagnostic and Statistical Manual of Mental Disorders*, she said, one of the symptoms of "psychoactive substance abuse disorder" was a "great deal of time spent in activities necessary to procure the substance (including theft)." In other words, serving time for drug-related crime works in your favor for getting benefits—and, given the twelve-month retroactivity for SSDI benefits, you can even get paid for doing so.

Parker was quick to realize, however, that in answering one question, she had merely raised another. If someone is able to apply himself to "activities necessary to procure the substance (including theft)," shouldn't he then be presumed able to apply himself to work? Far from it, Parker announced. "In contrast to persons who beg for sustenance or 'criminals' who commit illegal acts for a variety of acquisitive goals, the evidence demonstrates that, in this claim, the claimant engages in these activities solely to obtain and use addictive substances." (Apparently Parker is as uncomfortable with labeling people who break the law "criminals" as she is with presuming that people can work.) "It would be unrealistic," she concluded, "to expect the mental functions that the claimant demonstrates to be successfully employed and sustained in work situations."

Employment within the SSA today often requires just such a nonjudgmental attitude to crime. "Claims representatives have to treat drug dealing as any other type of work and forget that it's illegal," explains Floy Newman, operations officer in Santa Ana, California. "It's not as if we're going to turn you over to the police or your parole officer because you're doing drugs. " Newman had to calm one of the claims representatives working under her supervision who had learned that a claimant was working as a prostitute to support her drug habit. "But that's illegal!" the claims rep protested to Newman, visibly rattled. Newman reassured her that her job was merely to "go through the details to find out how she is meeting her expenses."

In this see-no-evil spirit, the agency recently declared that drug dealing would count as "substantial gainful activity" precluding eligibility for benefits. But the Ninth Circuit Court of Appeals ruled otherwise: it recently found that a claimant had spent so little time and exertion dealing drugs that the activity did not demonstrate the capacity to work.

The government's attitude toward personal responsibility in drug and alcohol cases is as inimical to a stable society as is its nonjudgmental view of crime. Both the agency and the courts bend over backward to find claimants incapable of controlling their drug and alcohol use. "There should be a presumption that someone can control their drinking," says Judge Arlander Keys, "but instead the presumption is the opposite."

The case law bears him out. Appellate courts routinely rebuke judges who hold that claimants can manage their drinking, even though the claimant himself may have testified that his drinking is under control. Such a position, says the judiciary, ignores the fact that the claimant has failed to control his drinking in the past. The 1984 Reform Act mandated that the agency pay greater attention to the "longitudinal history" of mental impairment claimants—meaning that, in the government's eyes, once an addict, always an addict.

The government is equally dismissive of the idea that, addiction notwithstanding, people can be expected to work. Judge Keys is in a distinct minority in the system: "I'm not convinced," he says, "that most addicts can't do simple unskilled work. Who is there that can't clean up a warehouse?" But once a claimant brings in a psychological report showing "antisocial trends" or "borderline personality disorder," an administrative judge or the agency is all but compelled to adopt the treating doctor's conclusion that the claimant cannot cope with a "work-like setting." "Even if we can show that someone lost his job for non-alcohol-related reasons," Keys says, "the doctor's position is always that it would be cruel to send him back to work."

The group of claimants that has stretched the concept of disability the farthest is not addicts, though, but children with behavioral problems. They, too, fall into the capacious "mental impairment" category. Treating a child's violent and disruptive behavior as a disability mocks the idea of individual responsibility no less than treating addiction as a mental impairment does. And both programs create almost irresistible incentives for antisocial behavior.

The question of where disability shades into a general welfare program is especially acute for children's cases. Many observers see children's disability as becoming just one more entitlement that perpetuates underclass dependency. John Wolff, the assistant principal of special education at Park West High School in Manhattan, calls children's disability the "male counterpart of AFDC." The applicants, he says, tend to be sons of second- and third-generation welfare recipients, who are using school "as a conduit to hook up to the system."

Children's disability originated in the 1972 legislation that created SSI. A little-noticed parenthesis extended eligibility to children who "suffer from any medically determinable physical or mental impairment of comparable severity." According to the *Washington Post*, the clause was inserted by a senior welfare official on a personal campaign to better the lot of the poor; the official himself is reportedly uncertain what the clause means.

Nevertheless, until 1990, the SSA had kept the growth of children's disability under control by strictly limiting eligibility to children whose conditions were either on its list of disabling childhood impairments or equivalent in severity. But in 1990, the Supreme Court ruled that this restriction was illegal, in a case called *Zebley v. Sullivan*. Like adults, the Court held, children whose impairments are not as severe as those on the listings are entitled to show that their disabilities impose "functional limitations" deserving of benefits. This requirement revealed the absurdity of the very concept of children's disability payments. For adults, a "functional limitation" is one that restricts the ability to work. But children are not only not expected to work to support themselves; they are legally prohibited from doing so. For them, the usual rationale for disability benefits—that they make up for lost income—doesn't apply. Nor, in general, does another rationale: that needy parents need help with their disabled children's medical expenses. In fact, Medicaid covers most medical costs for children who are both poor and disabled.

How, then, to measure the disabling consequences of an impairment? The Court held that an impairment is disabling if it limits the child's ability to engage in "age-appropriate activities." Evidence regarding the child's behavior could come from parents, teachers, and social workers.

The concept of "age-appropriate activities" is extraordinarily vague. The result, according to Savannah attorney Morton Gold: "It is almost impossible to defend a denial of benefits in a court of law." To make matters worse, around the same time that the Supreme Court decided *Zebley*, the SSA itself added seven vague new childhood mental impairments, like attention deficit hyperactivity disorder, and it required decision makers to give more weight to the opinion of parents and social workers in evaluating childhood disability.

The results of both *Zebley* and these 1990 regulations have been spectacular. Children now account for just under 20 percent of the SSI disability rolls, receiving $4.35 billion a year in benefits. In 1993, more than 770,000 children were on disability, up from fewer than 300,000 in 1989. The rate of growth from 1992 to 1993 alone was 23.5 percent. In New York State, says Lloyd Moses, associate commissioner of disability determinations, *Zebley* has changed the entire disability program. With 500 to 600 new children's cases being added to the rolls in the state every two weeks, children are now a major part of the agency's workload.

The most important effect of *Zebley* and the 1990 regulations was to open the rolls to the vast and growing world of behavioral and learning disorders. "Under the old ways, we didn't think learning disabilities interfered with the main business of life," explains Jack Schmulowitz, chairman of the SSA's Office of Research and Statistics. Now the agency knows better. Mental impairments account for more

than two-thirds of the growth in children's awards since 1990, with behavioral problems now constituting almost one-quarter of all child
mental impairment cases and attention deficit disorder constituting
an ever-rising portion of the total.

Two influences helped fan the rapid rise in children's cases. After
Zebley, the agency embarked on an aggressive publicity and outreach
campaign to sign up more children, sending out brochures to local
welfare offices and schools. Its allowance rate for children's cases also
shot up, initially to around 60 percent. For a period of six to eight
months after the decision, says Abe Anolik, income maintenance program specialist for the SSA in New York State, "If you were a kid and
you knew someone who sneezed, you got benefits."

Equally important has been word of mouth. "This is one that's
really out on the street," says John Hoffman, a Detroit administrative
judge. "It's common knowledge that you might as well try for SSI because it's not that hard to get. I've seen cases where the problems
were extremely minor." Parents have threatened teachers who've refused to fill out applications for their children; mothers have called
the agency trying to get their unborn children on SSI.

The parents' eagerness is understandable. The federal payment
is $458 a month; twenty-seven states also provide a supplemental pay-
ment. The money comes with no strings attached. Though the theory
behind children's SSI is that it compensates for medical costs, there is
no requirement that it actually be used for that purpose. According to
Ann Marie Sullivan, director of the Parents and Children Together
Program at Fordham-Tremont Community Mental Health Center in
the Bronx, some parents simply put their children's payments "up
their nose" in cocaine. A twenty-three-year-old mother in public housing in Boston told the *Boston Globe* that her eight-year-old son, who
had been put into a special needs class for punching and kicking other
children, was on SSI though he "was not really disabled." "I tell him
that he gets us money to help us," she said. "I just think he needs help
in terms of his attitude, and we need the money."

Some of the awards for the original class of claimants in *Zebley*
were as high as $75,000. A mother in Greenville, Kentucky, spent the

$13,000 she got for her hyperactive son on a car, washer-dryer, refrigerator, stove, TV, three jogging suits for him, home repairs, and a $2,500 computer. Some of Ann Marie Sullivan's clients received $20,000 each at age eighteen as a retroactive payment for attention deficit disorder—from which they no longer suffered, and whose treatment had been paid for by Medicaid.

Though professionals worry about the stigma that may attach to the label "disabled," the recipients seem untroubled by that possibility. Sullivan tells of a large family who came to her, each member brandishing his or her SSI check "as if this were a form of prestige." "The kids buy into it," she says. "They see it as a way of having more spending money."

Disability seems to run in certain families. A family in Arkansas with all nine kids on SSI received $3,500 a month; another family with eleven children on SSI got $4,000 a month. Income maintenance specialist Anolik tells of families in New York who are "all dysfunctional together."

As the children's caseload has risen, so too has criticism of the program. Stories abound of parents coaching their kids to misbehave in school or fail their tests. A child in Wynne, Arkansas, asked his teacher if doing well on an exam would affect his "crazy check." According to Savannah's Morton Gold, parents sometimes hold their children out of school to ensure that they will fall back several grades and thus fail the "age-appropriate" test of disability. Eighty-one percent of teachers and special-education counselors polled in Arkansas said that their students had been told to misbehave, and 79 percent agreed that once a child qualifies for SSI, his motivation to comply with schoolwork decreases.

"Teachers are disgusted with it," says Jeff Nussbaum, a special-education music teacher at Park West High School in Manhattan. "A kid gets classified as 'emotionally disturbed': what that means is anyone's guess. He can be violent, really rotten, and he gets on the dole."

John Wolff, the assistant principal of special education at Park West, has little patience for the system: "The same kids who two days before would spit in my eye and call me obscene names are now applying for disability. Some of these students I've dealt with for five years. I know they could work, and now they're seeking to get something for nothing." Though Park West does not yet have a large SSI population, Wolff has seen the cases inch up in the last couple of years. Applications become more prevalent at about the time that students are leaving school. Once a child turns twenty-one, his mother loses her eligibility for the AFDC benefits that have hitherto supported the family; so, as students start aging out of the system, Wolff says, "they start scurrying around looking for their next form of support."

Once on SSI, a child is a good candidate for staying on disability for the rest of his life. Until 1994, there was no requirement that children's cases be reviewed for continuing disability when recipients turn eighteen; Congress passed such a mandate in August, however. This requirement is unlikely to have much of an effect, given the backlog of disability reviews throughout the agency. Moreover, eighteen years is a very long grace period. Children who got SSI as low-weight infants are still on disability as healthy four-year-olds and will likely remain on the rolls at least through their eighteenth year.

Like SSI for addiction and alcoholism, or indeed for every disability that could be remedied, paying benefits for behavioral problems penalizes getting better. It also sends children the wrong message about responsibility. Writing in 1993 in the *Journal of the American Medical Association*, pediatric neurologist Fred Baughman warned that the danger to children misdiagnosed with attention deficit disorder is that they "believe they have something wrong with their brains that makes it impossible for them to control themselves without using a pill." The official stamp of welfare payments can only strengthen that self-destructive belief, leading, in the worst cases, to criminal behavior.

Experts increasingly agree that SSI rewards parents' destructive behavior. Philadelphia psychiatrist Kenneth R. Carroll told the *Washington Post* recently: "Many of the problems these children manifest are largely traceable to parental neglect or abuse. Behavioral and emotional problems, or conduct disorders that are directly attributable to inadequate parenting, are being called disabilities, and the parents are receiving a cash award for having achieved the problem."

For their part, welfare advocates take a laissez-faire attitude toward the possibility that SSI may be bankrolling parental misconduct. "The program is not about only giving to good parents," explains Barbara Samuels, Social Security coordinator for Legal Services for New York City. "You can't legislate against parents who are irresponsible."

Congress established a commission in August to explore whether cash payments are the best response to children's disability and whether the provision of retroactive benefits should be changed. Yet the growing doubts about children's disability have not daunted either the SSA's or local governments' enthusiasm for the program. Since 1990, SSA has funded ten major outreach efforts for children. Local welfare offices actively promote SSI: parents don't receive AFDC for their children who are on SSI; and since states and localities bear some of the costs of AFDC, getting clients onto disability shifts welfare costs to the federal government. For the last two years, the New York City Board of Education and the Human Resources Administration have cooperated on a joint project to get every special-education student receiving welfare onto SSI.

Federal disability continues to play a vital role in supporting people with serious maladies. But its ability to do so is threatened by the overextension of the concept of disability. The House Republican welfare reform plan proposes an overall cap on SSI expenditures, which could reduce or deny benefits for the truly disabled, as well as the elderly and the blind. Better to cut the rolls by adopting a more reasonable definition of disability.

The preamble to the Americans with Disabilities Act claims that 43 million Americans are disabled—an implausibly large number. By contrast, the National Institute on Disability and Rehabilitation Research estimated in 1991 that 3.1 million Americans need assistance with basic activities like bathing and dressing, while 3.9 million need help with things like shopping and cleaning. As John Kiernan of the International Center for the Disabled points out, "The definition of disability depends on where you're coming from and what you want the numbers to do for you."

Numerous other problems afflict the disability program. First, the agency makes too little effort to rehabilitate its clients; in 1993 it spent just $68 million on rehabilitation, and only one in five hundred SSDI recipients returned to work via vocational rehabilitation. Second, the program contains serious work disincentives for low wage-earners, since SSDI replaces a high proportion of their former wages. Third, there is a critical need to revisit the listings of physical and mental impairments to see if they really measure the total inability to work. In fact, many people whose impairments the agency would deem disabling are working. Finally, some commentators suggest taking SSI out of the jurisdiction of the SSA entirely, since its clientele differs so significantly from the traditional Social Security recipient.

But the greatest burden on the agency arises from its having collapsed the categories of social dysfunction and disability. "We don't talk about responsibility anymore," argues Chicago's Judge Ahlgren. "I haven't heard anyone say: 'You've made decisions which are responsible for your condition.'" By awarding benefits for self-destructive behavior, and by treating as a disability what ought to lie within someone's will to control, we have created yet another set of incentives for failure.

[1995]

Foster Care's Underworld

THE NATION'S foster care system has given rise to an unnoticed and deeply troubling reality: not only has it accepted the inevitability of legions of abused and neglected children, but it has made them into an integral part of the inner-city economy. For every child put into foster care, the foster family—which may be complete strangers or only a slightly different configuration of the child's birth family—gets a subsidy two to three times larger than what ordinary welfare pays. Whole communities of grandmothers are living on the money they receive for their abused or neglected grandchildren. Welfare advocates treat foster care payments as just another routine way to pump government money into troubled neighborhoods.

Two vast, obdurate realities fuel this foster care economy. First is drugs. One recent study of foster care in New York City found that about three-quarters of the birth mothers abused drugs. Some 24 percent of children in foster care in the city are born with drugs in their system, a number likely to grow if the national trend of increasing births to crack-addicted, impoverished mothers continues. Mothers waiting for their cases to be heard in family court sometimes nod off or disappear from the courthouse to score.

The other overwhelming fact of the foster care economy is the explosion of the traditional two-parent home into a dizzying array of intersecting family fragments. Family court is where the worst problems of our post-marriage era reach their nadir. Any single-mother household in the system most likely has several different biological fathers attached to it, and each of those fathers probably has children across the city with several different mothers. The mantra of the foster care functionaries is "family preservation"—maintaining children with their abusive or neglectful parents whenever possible. Yet to speak of "family preservation" in this context is fanciful; which combination of fathers and mothers and half-siblings should we demarcate as the family unit? Though married couples are not absent from family court, they are not common; a 1989 British study found that coming from a single-parent home was the most significant risk factor for a child's admission to foster care.

Rather than working to ameliorate these hard realities, the foster care system runs a great risk of enabling them. It allows families to accommodate, and even profit from, their dysfunctions. Self-appointed children's advocates further normalize the culture of single parenting by refusing to make it an issue in children's welfare. The following stories from Manhattan's Family Court illustrate how entrenched foster care has become in certain communities (in Central Harlem, for example, one out of ten children is in care), how rational the calculations of people benefiting from the system can be, and how far the system is from securing the welfare of the children it supposedly exists to save.

"What else would you want them for?" snorts Lucille Murray, in response to the question whether she thinks grandmothers seek foster custody of their grandchildren for the foster care payments. The petite Murray, sporting white tennis shoes and a black straw bowler with a bow, has just emerged from Family Court, seeking to wrest custody of two of her grandchildren (along with the attendant foster care payments) away from their maternal grandmother, with whom they are now living. The mother of these two children, Marla Wish, is "one of those street girls," according to Murray—an appellation that embraces a host of possible wrongdoing, from drug use and child abandonment to prostitution and theft.

Wrongdoing seems evident enough when Murray's son Robert and Marla enter the courtroom in handcuffs, roughly shoved along by prison guards. Robert has been in Rikers since 1996, on charges of assault with a deadly weapon. During the hearing, Marla, razor-thin and wiry, sat mute, her chin tucked low into her gray Guess sweatshirt, her eyes raised warily toward the judge. Next to her sat her mother, who, all told, has four of Marla's children in her care. Robert has another child himself, by another woman.

The case, like virtually all in the Family Court, is impossibly complicated, defying the ability even of the judge to disentangle. The parties present a welter of contradictory petitions to, and custody rulings from, courts in three boroughs, applying to an array of children by various fathers and mothers. Merely trying to figure out where Robert and Marla's two children have been over the years is taxing; the maternal and paternal grandmothers both claim that they have been caring for them. The judge adjourns the hearing without a resolution (like most Family Court hearings), and the case reenters Family Court limbo.

Outside the courtroom, Murray, barely articulate in court, comments on her opponents. "Her daughter and her cooked this up," she sniffs. "They never done anything for [the children], but they're using them for this welfare thing." Murray claims she found burn marks on the children after they were in their other grandmother's care. How do you know that their motivation is financial? I ask. "How could she live without it?" Murray replies. She laughs. "My friends are having a ball with that money and their grandchildren; they're going all over the world. They want that money! If you get the foster children, you get big bucks, you can buy nice clothes. They get the opportunity to go places they never went. They all get food stamps," she adds.

A caseworker at a large foster agency confirms Murray's economic analysis. "For people on public assistance, $500 a month [a typical per-child foster care payment] is a lot of money," she says. "They're not using it totally on the kids. If Section 8 pays for housing, and you're getting public assistance—which is not taxed—you can't spend $500 a month on food. They don't pay for the children's clothing or their medical needs, and we reimburse transportation." If the children are disabled or emotionally disturbed, monthly payments can reach $800 a month. The caseworker recalls a grandmother with five grandchildren who collected $3,000 a month for three years, while living in a "disgusting apartment in a scary building." Thereafter, she bought a beautiful town house, cash down. Another caseworker tells of foster parents under her supervision who have never had a job but who have a Jeep Cherokee and a house in the South. "It's an industry for quite poor people," she concludes.

The Murrays and the Wishes (pseudonyms, like all the names of aid recipients in this story) demonstrate how easily kinship foster care, a humane idea, can produce serious unintended consequences. Kinship care—which child-welfare authorities must try to arrange before finding unrelated foster parents, if at all possible—is meant to decrease the trauma for a child removed from his mother, and undoubtedly it often does so. But it has also become a major financial support system, perversely turning the production of neglected children into a family business. (Relatives receive the same foster care payments as unrelated foster parents.) Children remain in kinship foster care much longer and are less likely to be adopted than children placed with unrelated families, suggesting a possible perverse incentive structure. Poverty advocates well understand the economic role of kinship care in underwriting poor communities. Any sign of flagging kinship-placement rates produces cries of alarm; advocates managed to exempt kinship foster care from the time limits in a recent federal foster care reform bill, thus preserving it as an open-ended entitlement.

By no means do all families see kinship care as a financial opportunity. I spoke with many families in Manhattan's Family Court whose all-consuming goal was to get a troubled relative and her children out of "the system" and into their unsubsidized care as soon as possible. But enough families treat foster care as a subsidy that policy makers had better start paying attention.

Olivia Darwin views foster care as an entitlement. "I haven't been this pissed off in a long time," she fumes, as we go swooping toward the courthouse elevator banks. A strongly built, forceful woman of fifty with short-cropped hair, Darwin is angry because the city won't put her youngest grandchild, aged three, "on the system." She already gets foster care payments for her eleven- and twelve-year-old grand-children, whom she has had all their lives. She is in the process of adopting those two children but admits she may not be doing her part: "They [the city] want medicals so often, it's nonsense." (Foster care workers complain bitterly about the difficulty of getting relatives to comply with foster care requirements, especially medical exams.) Darwin's daughter has two other children who have been placed out-side the family. But the three-year-old, with Darwin since she was six months old, is in a legal no-man's-land, since the city did not officially place her with Darwin.

Now Darwin faces a dilemma. Though she once worked briefly in construction in order to qualify for a HUD-subsidized house, she now gets home relief, the welfare program for childless adults, and food stamps (in addition to the foster care payments), and in return the city wants her to do workfare. She is refusing, on the grounds that she has her three-year-old grandchild at home and should be exempt. As Darwin tells it, the city says that if she puts the child on AFDC—Aid to Families with Dependent Children—she would be exempted from workfare, but she is holding out for the far higher foster care payments. She has been to eight disciplinary hearings in the past three months over her failure to do workfare.

Her daughter is "on the street" but not out of touch. Does Dar-win see her? "Of course I see her!" Darwin shoots back, incredulous at so foolish a question. Such maternal visits almost certainly violate the foster care agreement that put the two elder children in Darwin's care. Darwin won't be seeing her daughter for a few months, however, since the daughter just got sentenced to a year. For what? "Whatever she does to support her habit." In the meantime, Darwin won't be ac-celerating the adoption process; she knows of too many people, she says, who stopped receiving payments once they adopted.

Darwin's open-door policy toward her drug-addicted daughter is typical in kin cases. Caseworkers despair of keeping the mother, who may still be dangerously abusive, away from her children when they are placed with relatives. Sometimes the living arrangements make contact inevitable. A lanky, heartbreakingly passive nineteen-year-old, sitting listlessly on the ninth floor of the courthouse, has been in foster care with his grandmother, along with his brother, since he was one. He has apparently fallen through the system's cracks, for at his age, unless he is in college or a training program, he should no longer be in foster care. Still in the tenth grade, the boy sports a sapphire stud in his ear and a beeper. His two cousins also live with his grandmother, who apparently has a propensity for raising troubled children. His mother visits every day, since she lives "next door, just around the hall," he says; his aunt—the mother of the two cousins he lives with— also visits regularly. "It don't matter who you live with, your mother or your grandmother," he says, summing up the de facto policy in many kin cases.

The prize for efficient and profitable use of the porous boundaries in kin cases surely belongs to the Rodriguez family: Ann Rodriguez, in her mid-forties; her three daughters, Janet (twenty-six), Marisol (nineteen), and Pia (sixteen); and three illegitimate grandchildren, including Marisol's eighteen-month-old daughter. Ann and Marisol are in court for Marisol's yearly extension-of-placement hearing. For the past six years, the outgoing Marisol, her baby, and her younger sister have officially been in the kinship foster care of the older sister, Janet. But while Janet has been collecting $1,400 a month in foster care payments, along with federal Section 8 housing vouchers for a three-bedroom, $1,200-a-month duplex apartment big enough to house herself, the two girls, and the baby, the girls have actually been living in their mother's East New York studio apartment, along with the baby. Janet, seizing the opportunity, has been renting out the room supposed to be Marisol's. The family splits up the foster care money according to an elaborate system of internal payments that also draws on a diverse pool of additional welfare benefits, from AIDS money to food coupons for infants.

However orderly its current internal trading system, the family has a highly troubled, taxpayer-subsidized history. Ann, the matriarch, has used drugs since she was twelve and is now on methadone. Small, high-strung, and good-natured, with two sandy braids down to her waist, Ann has lost most of her teeth to the addict's life, which has also left her with HIV and hepatitis C. In the late 1980s and into the 1990s, she recalls, her husband—now dead—"was shooting heroin like a bandit," as was she. Nevertheless, she was working for the Transit Authority while illegally collecting $500 a month in welfare and food stamps.

Around 1990, the family lost its apartment and ended up traveling from shelter to shelter. Ann's husband ran away but returned; the city rewarded the newly reunited couple with a five-bedroom subsidized apartment in Harlem. The husband was getting Supplemental Security Income payments for AIDS, while Ann was still collecting welfare. "I told him: When your money comes, we can party; when my money comes, that goes into the house," Ann recalls. The family rented out rooms in their subsidized apartment to drug dealers for $50 a week. She maintains that she and her husband shot up and smoked crack only when the children were in school or in bed—unlikely but, even if true, hardly adequate to protect the children.

Ann kept going to jail on shoplifting charges and thought she had an understanding with the oldest daughter, Janet, about child care while she was gone. "I would tell her before I went in," she says, "to take the kids and put them on AFDC"—for which Janet would have been eligible as the girls' non-foster caretaker. In this way, Ann hoped to avoid charges of abandonment and potential loss of parental rights. She undoubtedly didn't grasp the financial superiority of kinship foster care over AFDC at that point.

Ann believes that Janet betrayed her. She claims that during one of her prison stints six years ago, Janet reported her to the city's Administration for Children's Services (ACS) as a drug addict, so that she could get foster care payments for the girls. "Janet knows the advantages of foster care," Marisol breaks in; "she involved ACS because of the money." Ann and Marisol were adamant that Janet not know that they had spoken to me, so I have not confirmed their tale.

For a while after Janet gained foster custody of the girls, Ann, back on the streets, lost contact with all three. Then, about three years ago, Ann's husband died, and Marisol, shaken by the loss of her father, started drinking, stopped going to school, and tried to commit suicide. She entered Payne Whitney psychiatric institute, was put on Prozac, and was discharged to a group home rather than to her sister's. "The group home wasn't bad," she recalls. "They had a closer leash on me— they made sure I made and kept appointments, because these were foster parents, not my family." But Marisol grew homesick, and besides, she says, people at the group home were stealing from her. She went AWOL and returned to her sister. "No one came looking for me," she laughs, with her customary broad smile. "I called my foster care worker and said: I'm not at the group home, you know."

The agency, a Jewish foster care organization, never investigated when Marisol's younger sister, Pia, dropped out of high school, either. Janet's supervision of Pia was almost equally lax. Pia began selling drugs. Her mother blames Janet's poor oversight: "Janet would ask her to do errands, instead of going to school, and she would do drugs." Is she using drugs now that she's back with you? I ask. "Nah," Ann responds, then qualifies her answer. "If she is, it's not like before, when she wouldn't look me in the eye."

In January 1995, Ann, still shooting heroin, got arrested again and learned she had HIV. The good news: she became eligible for the city's Division of AIDS Services' (DAS) welfare programs. DAS found her a series of apartments, rent-free, including her current $553-a-month studio; it also provides her with $120 a month in food stamps and almost $300 a month in cash.

A year or so thereafter, Janet started demanding that Marisol cook and clean for Janet's six-year-old daughter. "'I'm not going for this,' I said," Marisol explains. She moved in with her mother. Pia eventually came, too. The arrangement is highly illegal; besides the fraud of Janet's taking foster care payments for sisters no longer in her care, the girls are not even supposed to visit their mother without agency supervision. Now Pia wants to move back in with Janet, but Janet says she has no space because of her paying lodger. "She's on that system good," marvels Ann. "But she's not a criminal. If she was criminal-minded, she could really make out." It's hard to imagine what further advantage of the foster care system she could take, however.

With the girls at Ann's, the family has developed its own internal economy. Janet gives Marisol and Pia $350 a month each—half of the foster care payments—out of which they give their mother $20 a week for baby-sitting and $40 a month for the phone and food. Janet also gives Ann $40 a month for baby-sitting her six-year-old daughter.

Ann was baby-sitting her three granddaughters—by Janet, Marisol, and a thirty-year-old son—when I visited her one October Sunday in her studio. Janet was at her job as a restaurant manager; Marisol and Pia at their jobs at Kentucky Fried Chicken. The apartment building sits on a wide East New York avenue, next to a high school with a verdant lawn. The entry door is broken; a liquor bottle litters the stairway.

Ann, in shorts and a striped tank top, is making frozen waffles and bacon for her grandchildren in a toaster oven on a card table by the entrance. The children bounce on the two big beds while the TV blares. When the girls become too rambunctious, Ann shouts: "Don't disrespect me, please!" The apartment, though cluttered, appears clean. Boxes and folded comforters are piled up against the walls; a tall, mirrored chest of drawers draped with a Puerto Rican flag separates the two beds, near which hangs a framed and decorated poem: "Before love blooms/ It gets its start/ deep within a mother's heart."

While Ann serves the children at a brightly colored plastic baby table, she explains her most important role in the family economy: as a gofer for federal entitlements. She does the footwork for recertifying Janet for Section 8, providing the necessary documentation proving the (fictitious) continued presence of the three girls with Janet. Ann also takes Marisol's baby in for lead testing, so as to qualify her for the federal Women, Infant, and Children (WIC) supplemental food program. Marisol is "too lazy" to take her, Ann gripes. Ann made Marisol sign up for WIC, she explains, because "we can't afford milk"—in spite of the household's monthly cash income of $1,120.

Marisol's infant bites Janet's daughter on the eye, and Ann starts in on Marisol's other failings toward her daughter. She has procrastinated about having her daughter's eyes checked, Ann says, and now she has misplaced her Medicaid card, so she can't get an appointment. Ann also blames her for sleeping through her baby's crying. "One morning the baby had a mouthful of cat food," she recalls. Now, Ann might not seem like the right person to cast the first stone regarding child rearing, but the family has a penchant for recriminations, especially regarding their foster care entitlements. Marisol blames Janet for ignoring her and Pia's medical rights: "[As foster children,] we have medical requirements, such as eye exams, and my sister is supposed to get braces. But Janet doesn't follow up." Ann blames Janet for buying the girls cheap and shoddy clothes with the foster care clothing allowance.

But despite the sniping, the family seems to have achieved some measure of stability. In the courthouse for Marisol's twelve-month extension-of-placement hearing, Ann and her daughter conspiratorially mock the counseling sessions they are required to attend before Ann can officially get her daughters back. "We're not therapy people," Marisol says, rolling her eyes. When Ann throws a fit after learning that their case has been put off for the next day—an all-too-frequent affront to families in the system—Marisol maternally tries to calm her down. "They're watching you, Mommy; you're not helping your case," she says, adding to me, "They say she's argumentative." Ann keeps screaming in a high-pitched voice that the system is not meeting her needs.

Even so, the family is in no hurry to get out of it. "I'm dependent on money from my sister; my sister is dependent on that money, too," Marisol explains. If Marisol were to leave foster care and go on AFDC, she would get $220 in cash a month, less than she is now making on the system. Their city overseers are in no hurry, either. There is a winking acknowledgment among them of the illegal living arrangements, according to Marisol. Marisol's government-funded law guardian has told her: "You want to live with your mother, right, so why not sign this twelve-month extension and not rock the boat?" Marisol has answered the phone twice when her social worker called her mother's house; the worker told her to go back to Janet's but has not followed up on the order.

Ann never made it to the rescheduled placement hearing the day after their case had been adjourned. "When I go through stress, my body hurts," she explains several weeks later, "so I couldn't get up. I said to myself, 'Let me go to the [methadone] program first.'" By the time she got to court, she had missed the hearing. It has been rescheduled yet again—along with hundreds of other hearings for which the parties never show.

Now, as dysfunctional families go, there are undoubtedly worse ones in the foster care system than this one. I heard no evidence that the parents had physically or sexually abused the girls. And to varying degrees, the girls seem to have landed on their feet more than would have been expected. Nevertheless, as I left Ann's apartment, I saw a troubling sign that the cycle may be repeating itself. Janet's six-year-old daughter, who had been quietly drawing, gave me a poem she had written and cut out in a diamond shape:

my mom is like witch

my granma is glad

my mom is scary

I loue [*sic*] granma and my mom

frfriends.

This family's rigorous calculations are typical; people on welfare, including foster care, are as painstaking as anyone else in weighing their options. Nor is the family's current defrauding of the foster care system unique; overworked or indifferent social workers regularly turn a blind eye to major rule violations in kinship and non-kinship cases. But the kinship system is especially difficult to police, given the blood ties between the birth parent and the foster parent. While thousands of upright kin foster parents are saving their relatives' lives, policy makers must more seriously balance the risks of placing children with their relatives against the advantages. As University of Pennsylvania child-abuse expert Richard Gelles explains, kinship care requires a suspension of academic knowledge regarding the intergenerational transfer of dysfunctionality.

Here in Family Court, the parents of a toddler now in non-kinship foster care illustrate the difficulties of reconstructing family in the postmarriage era—difficulties the foster care system does nothing to address. The mother is in the stairwell of the court, cursing, furiously smoking (despite the NO SMOKING signs), and stomping back and forth, while a sweet-faced caseworker tries to quiet her. "I'm going to get some reefer," the woman threatens. She is small, thin, and toothless; her short hair is tightly waved. She produces a photo of her toddler son; her seven other children, she says, with considerable poetic license, are dead—meaning, in foster care or adopted.

Moments earlier, the judge had been about to grant her visitation rights to this latest son, when she flew into a rage in court. Wholly taken aback, the judge withdrew her order and instead required the woman's attendance at an outpatient drug program and anger-management classes for six months. She also slapped an order of protection against her for the father of her son.

The father, John, is in court, too. He is a walking compendium of excuses not to marry. Tall and gentle-mannered, with a diamond stud in his tooth, he shakes his head at his previous lover's behavior. She once brought a four-foot snake with her to an agency-supervised visit with her son, he recalls, scaring everyone—her son included. Do you intend to marry her? I ask. "Oh, no-o-o!" he laughs, tickled by the preposterousness of the idea. He had been trying to meet her girlfriend at a Narcotics Anonymous meeting, he recounts, but ended up twice having sexual intercourse with her instead. "When I met her," he explains ruefully, "she was not on drugs, and she had teeth." Besides, he has three other kids already, by another two women. The mother of his seventeen-year-old daughter is dead of asthma, and "it's too late" to marry the mother of his other two sons, he assures me. "We knew each other from high school, and we've gone our own way. Now she's stable with who she's got—although her sons don't like him. But it's not up to them," he adds philosophically, echoing the self-justifications of divorced and remarried parents.

Though two of John's children are in foster care, he still considers himself a good father. "At all times I have had a connection with my children," he boasts. His daughter had been placed in foster care first with her half-sister (by another father); now she is in a non-kin foster home. To his disappointment, she refused to visit him in prison, where he spent several years of his early thirties. Now thirty-seven, he has been out for two years and clean for three, he says. He thinks he has patched everything together: "The proudest day of my life was my birthday party; all my children came, and my daughter accepted my sons."

John is presently living at a new girlfriend's apartment but assumes this current relationship is not permanent: "We could have a fight," he says, matter-of-factly. With any luck, that relationship will not produce a fifth child. He expects the city to get him an apartment for himself, so he can get custody of his youngest son, the toddler at issue in today's Family Court proceeding.

Perhaps John, currently working as a mechanic, will prove a responsible father, if granted custody. His effort to retain contact with his children is, sadly, unusual. But he lives in a world where expectations for fatherhood are abysmally low, where the marriage norm is nonexistent, and, as a consequence, where having a few children of assorted parentages in foster care is not particularly unusual. By contrast, if John had settled down and gotten married to his first paramour, the chances that half his progeny would be in foster care would be eight times less, according to a study in the *British Journal of Social Work*.

Child-welfare advocates are almost universally unconcerned about the marriage meltdown's impact on children. Ask if the two-parent family is important to child welfare, and they'll give you a breathtaking collection of excuses and evasions. Equivocates Nilofer Ahsan of the Family Resource Coalition in Chicago, for instance: "It's very important for parents to have the support they need when raising a baby. Having two parents of course makes that easier, but it is not the only solution to a set of problems." Equivocates Betsy Rosenbaum of the American Public Human Services Association: "There's a general issue in child welfare that kids do better in families, rather than raised by the state, but what a family is, is open to a lot of interpretation." Equivocates influential New York City child-welfare advocate John Courtney: "I think marriage needs to be looked at in terms of modern society; it's not the legal and religious fact it once was. That does not mean I advocate having no regard for the relations and people present in the home that can care for children. . . . The idealized concept of the two-parent family is not happening today."

Given these pervasive apologetics for social breakdown, a recent federal foster care reform act faces an uphill battle. The law aims to shorten the length of time children spend in foster care, and to eliminate the worst abuses of "family preservation." Yet even if the law achieves its goals, the foster care economy will be dented, not dismantled. As long as drug use and out-of-wedlock childbearing remain high, children will continue to need out-of-home care. But foster care, whether kin or not, often merely moves children from one troubled home and community to another.

The new federal bill rightly promotes adoption to end the foster care musical-chair game. But not all children can be successfully adopted. Nationally, nearly 25 percent of at-risk adoptions are terminated, according to the Child Welfare League of America. In her 1997 book, *The Limits of Hope*, Ann Kimble Loux gives a sorrowful account of adopting two very young, seriously abused sisters. Despite the loving midwestern family she offered them, the girls sank into delinquency, school failure, pregnancy, drug abuse, and prostitution. Loux concludes that, for disturbed children, a home is not necessarily the ideal salve; a boarding school or group home that does not make emotional demands that the children are unable to fulfill may be the one environment where they can thrive.

Minnesota has recognized this unwelcome truth and has begun to create stable, academically rigorous boarding academies for children from dysfunctional families. The tuition and board, estimated at $18,000 to $20,000 annually, will be paid with money already allocated for a child's public school, foster care, or other social services. New York should emulate this idea quickly.

The advocates will loudly object that, instead of building "orphanages," we should keep the money in the foster care economy. New York's leaders should respond: no government parenting or early childhood intervention program has ever been shown to make a lasting difference in inner-city children's lives, even when those children do not have parents who abuse and neglect them. The notion that more parental services will solve the problems of the city's most unfortunate children is nothing but politics. For example, even if the city were to beef up its drug treatment services—a major demand of parent advocates—no one knows if many more mothers with kids in foster care would use them: currently, 68 percent of such mothers provided with drug treatment fail to cooperate. Rigorous and well-managed boarding schools, by contrast, could give the children of these mothers a fighting chance of success.

For babies born with drugs in their systems, the government's response should be much more child protective. Currently, New York City may not initiate a case for child neglect or abuse if a child is born with positive toxicity but must send the child home with its addict mother. This policy, mandated by a court ruling and a Cuomo-era regulation, is breathtakingly foolish. It sends the message to drug addicts that the state considers them—not their children—helpless victims, unable to avoid either pregnancy or drug abuse while pregnant. And by sending babies home with their coke-addicted mothers, the state is guaranteeing their further developmental impairment. A woman who gives birth to a positive-toxicity or fetal-alcohol-syndrome baby should be presumed unfit, or at least deemed to have abused her child for purposes of foster care placement. If her parental rights are not immediately terminated, she should be allowed to regain custody of her child only if she can immediately go clean and stay clean for six months; any subsequent relapse should terminate her parental rights. Too much is riding on the child's first years to hold him hostage to his mother's habit.

Like so many of the pathologies of child welfare, the foster care economy needs inspired moral example and suasion to change it, and that requires a real change in our national culture. Community leaders can help future parents understand their obligations, so that they come to parenthood with a deep desire to do right by their children. But while we await that cultural renewal, we need to make sure that the foster care system is not unwittingly perpetuating the very conditions that put children at severe risk.

[1999]

Diallo Truth,
Diallo Falsehood

JUST AFTER MIDNIGHT on February 4, four New York City cops
took forty-one shots at an unarmed street peddler named Amadou Diallo and plunged the mayoralty of Rudolph Giuliani into crisis. Within
a day, a powerful morality tale gripped the city and clung there for the
next three months. It ran as follows: "The shooting of Amadou Diallo
exposes the dark underbelly of Mayor Giuliani's world-famous crime
rout: a culture of police abuse that has struck universal fear into blacks
and Hispanics and is now erupting into a broad-based multiracial
protest movement."

Almost nothing in this tale was true. Residents of the city's most
crime-ridden neighborhoods are far more positive about the police
than the press ever hinted. Empirical data show a police department
more cautious with the use of force than at any time in recent history.
And the obsessively covered protest movement consisted only of long-
standing Giuliani foes, whose importance shriveled when the TV
cameras decamped.

The Diallo crisis was a manufactured one—an unparalleled example of the power of the press, and, above all, the *New York Times*,
to create the reality it reports. Some people have good reason to re-
sent the police; many more—especially minority New Yorkers—re-
sent them precisely because of the false charges made by activists and

echoed incessantly by the press. That's why it's critical to rebut the press's mendacious morality tale from the ground up.

The event that sparked the crisis was horrific. As February 4 began, an unmarked car carrying four undercover police officers from the elite Street Crime Unit cruised down Wheeler Avenue in the Soundview section of the Bronx. Under the Giuliani administration, Street Crime officers aggressively seek out illegal guns—dangerous work, but a key cause of the city's breathtaking 75 percent drop in gun homicides since 1993.

The four cops would have been briefed that night about a rash of shootings in the neighborhood, including the murder of a livery cabdriver. The unit was also looking for an armed rapist responsible for up to fifty-one assaults, including ten in the Soundview section, where he probably lived. The four officers have yet to disclose publicly what happened next; the following speculative account, compiled primarily by the *New York Post*'s crime reporter, rests on sources close to the case.

The cops spotted a slender man pacing nervously in the doorway and peering into the windows of 1157 Wheeler, a small brick apartment building. Officers Sean Carroll and Edward McMellon got out of the car, identified themselves as police, and asked the man to stop. Instead, twenty-two-year-old Amadou Diallo, a peddler of bootlegged videos and tube socks on Manhattan's East 14th Street, continued into the vestibule and tried to get inside the building's inner door. Diallo had recently filed a wildly false application for political asylum, claiming to be a Mauritanian victim of torture orphaned by the government security forces. In fact, he was a Guinean with two well-off and living parents. He had reason, therefore, not to welcome encounters with authorities.

The two cops ordered Diallo to come out and show them his hands. Turning away, Diallo reached into his pocket and pulled out what Carroll thought was a gun. "Gun!" Carroll shouted. "He's got a gun!" McMellon, who'd followed Diallo up the stairs, feared he was in point-blank danger and shot at Diallo three times before stepping backward, falling off the steps, and breaking his tailbone.

Carroll, seeing McMellon down and thinking he'd been shot, opened fire.

As bullets ricocheted into the street, the other two cops concluded that a firefight was under way. They jumped out of the car and began shooting at the figure crouched in the vestibule. Diallo hadn't fallen prone, according to the cops' lawyers, because the nine-millimeter copper-jacketed bullets passed through him cleanly without bringing him down.

When the shooting stopped, eight to ten seconds later, the officers had fired a total of forty-one rounds, nineteen of which had hit Diallo, perforating his aorta, spinal cord, lungs, and other organs. Two of the officers had emptied their sixteen-bullet magazines. When they searched Diallo's body to retrieve his gun, they found only a black wallet and a shattered beeper in a pool of blood. Officer Carroll wept.

The killing of Amadou Diallo was an unmitigated tragedy, demanding close investigation into police training procedures, to see if any feasible safeguards could have prevented it. But nothing in the police department's recent history suggests that it was part of a pattern of excessive force. Nothing that is known of the case to date suggests that the shooting was anything but a tragic mistake; the officers acted in the good-faith, though horribly mistaken, belief that they were under deadly threat. "The majority of officers, because they're not in combat often, feel extreme fear," explains Robert Gallagher, a former Street Crime Unit officer and one of the most decorated detectives in history. "They saw Diallo acting suspiciously, and if one officer says 'gun,' the rest will believe him. In the exchange of gunfire, nothing in your mind says: 'I want to kill this man.'"

Every available fact about the New York Police Department (NYPD) shows how atypical the Diallo shooting was. After three years of steady decline, the cops' use of deadly force was far lower last year than in 1993, the final year of Mayor David Dinkins's administration, currently hailed as a paradigm of peace. In 1998, less than 1 percent of the department used their weapons, 25 percent below the 1993 number. Shootings per officer dropped 67 percent from 1993 to 1998. Most impressively, even as police interaction with criminals has risen precipitously since the Dinkins administration, and even as the department has grown by 36 percent, both the absolute number of police killings and the rate of fatalities per officer have fallen. In 1993, the police made 266,313 arrests and killed 23 people, compared with 1998's 403,659 arrests and 19 people killed. In 1990, one year into the allegedly golden Dinkins era, there were two and a half times more fatal shootings per officer than now, while, of course, New Yorkers were being murdered by civilians in record numbers.

Today's NYPD also looks restrained compared with the cops in other cities. Last year, New York's fatal police shooting rate was 0.48 fatal shootings per 1,000 cops, compared with Philadelphia's 0.72, Miami's 2.01, and Washington, D.C.'s whopping 3.12. Washington's trigger-happy and predominantly black cops fire their weapons seven times more often than New York's, thus belying the endlessly repeated claim that a racially representative force is a more restrained force.

Though the absolute number of civilian complaints rose between 1994 and 1996—concurrently with a growth in the force and greater outreach by the Civilian Complaint Review Board—the rate of civilian complaints per officer dropped by 20 percent. And over the last two years, the absolute number of complaints has declined as well, following Commissioner Howard Safir's introduction of civilian complaints into the NYPD's celebrated Compstat (computerized crime analysis) system.

From the day he took office, Rudy Giuliani threatened the foundations of the liberal worldview—denouncing identity politics, demanding work from welfare recipients, and, above all, successfully fighting crime by fighting criminals, rather than blathering about crime's supposed "root causes," racism and poverty. It was a godsend for his opponents that the four officers who killed Diallo were white, allowing the incident to stand as proof of alleged departmental racism, the "dark side" (in *The Economist*'s triumphant headline) of Giuliani's conquest of crime. Now it was payback time.

The Clinton administration jumped in immediately, sending FBI agents and federal prosecutors to the Bronx to help the local district attorney investigate the shooting and probably to start building a federal case against the officers and the department as well. The president denounced police misconduct (implying that the Diallo officers were guilty of deliberate brutality or racism); Hillary Clinton, readying her New York Senate run, let it be known that she was consulting with local Democratic pols about the Diallo case. Both the U.S. Civil Rights Commission and the Justice Department announced investigations into the NYPD as a whole and the Street Crime Unit in particular; the Justice Department inquiry could ultimately—and preposterously—lead to damaging federal monitoring of the city's police. The state attorney general started his own duplicative inquiry into the department's stop-and-frisk practices. One Police Plaza has become a round-the-clock paperwork-processing center for the numerous investigations.

Meanwhile, Al Sharpton and other local activists were experimenting with various protest venues. Sharpton's fellow reverend, Calvin Butts, announced a consumer boycott, whose relevance remained inscrutable. The Reverend Al finally settled on having his followers arrested for sitting in on police headquarters. His big break came when David Dinkins and Congressman Charles Rangel joined his protest and got their picture on the front page of the *New York Times* in plastic handcuffs. Bingo! The civil-disobedience campaign became an overnight sensation.

A wider range of Giuliani antagonists—and a very occasional, much-cherished "celebrity," such as Susan Sarandon—started showing up to be photographed and arrested. Not one objected to the vicious anti-police and anti-Giuliani rhetoric spewed out daily by Sharpton followers, nor did any shrink from linking arms with the city's most noisome racial troublemaker, despite his recent conviction for slander in the notorious Tawana Brawley hoax. After the announcement of almost unprecedentedly severe second-degree murder indictments of the four officers, Sharpton and a coalition of left-wing labor leaders and Democratic activists organized a march across Brooklyn Bridge on April 15 to promote a hastily devised "Ten Point Plan" for police reform.

The more Mayor Giuliani struggled against the net that ensnared him, the more entangled he became. When he burst out in impatience against the media's infatuation with the plastic handcuff charade, his opponents happily denounced his alleged racial insensitivity. His repeated refusals to condemn the entire police department and his insistence on responding to emotion with fact earned him censure for rigidity.

No press organ covered all this more obsessively (with the exception of local news channel New York One) than the *New York Times*. No mere observer of the unfolding events, the *Times* was a major player, enveloping the city in an inescapable web of anti-police Diallo coverage. In the first two months after the shooting, it ran a remarkable 3.5 articles a day on the case, climaxing on March 26—at the height of the Police Plaza protests and when news of the second-degree murder indictment was leaked—with a whopping 9 stories. The paper buffed up Al Sharpton and glorified his protest movement. It covered Diallo's burial with loving detail and sentimental drama worthy of Princess Di. Most important, the *Times* created a wholly misleading portrait of a city under siege—not by criminals, but by the police. In so doing, it exacerbated the police-minority tensions it purported merely to describe.

The unquestioned assumption of the *Times* coverage, as well as of the protests and government investigations, was that the Diallo shooting was a glaring example of pervasive police misconduct. But since in no way could the Diallo facts—the shooting of a peaceful, unarmed citizen—be shown to be typical of the department, the *Times* zeroed in on a different angle. The Street Crime Unit, and the NYPD generally, it claimed, were using the stop-and-frisk technique to harass minorities. The logic seemed to be that the same racist mentality that leads to unwarranted stop-and-frisks led the four officers to shoot Diallo.

The day after the shooting, the *Times* announced its theme: ELITE FORCE QUELLS CRIME, BUT AT A COST, CRITICS SAY. Ten days later, the front page put it more bluntly: SUCCESS OF ELITE POLICE FORCE UNIT EXACTS A TOLL ON THE STREETS. Four days after that, another front-page article declared: AFTER THE SHOOTING, AN ERODING TRUST

IN THE POLICE (big surprise, given the paper's nonstop allegations of widespread police brutality); an op-ed article the same day by a lawyer who makes his living suing the police reiterated: DAZZLING CRIME STATISTICS COME AT A PRICE. Two days later, a front-page article in the Sunday Week in Review announced: BEHIND POLICE BRUTALITY, PUBLIC ASSENT. A later article was headlined: IN TWO MINORITY NEIGHBORHOODS, RESIDENTS SEE A PATTERN OF HOSTILE STREET SEARCHES. The burden of the series was that the Street Crime Unit stops minorities for "no reason," creating terrible fear and resentment in the streets. Uproariously, the paper even suggested that African immigrants are in greater danger from New York police than from the security forces of their homelands.

Unquestionably, the police under Mayor Giuliani have been using their stop-and-frisk power more aggressively than the Supreme Court opinion establishing the power contemplated. That's true of police departments across the country, though. Unquestionably, too, an active use of stop-and-frisk risks alienating people, especially since many officers fail to show appropriate courtesy when no gun is found. That hardly means, however, that the police are stopping people at random.

The *Times*'s own evidence shows something very far from randomness. The Street Crime Unit, the paper says, reported 45,000 frisks in the last two years and made 9,500 arrests, of which 2,500 were for illegal guns. That ratio—one arrest for every 4.7 stops; one gun for every 18 stops—looks pretty impressive, though admittedly the police may not be reporting all stops. Argues Columbia law professor Richard Uviller: "I don't know of any other way to fight the war on handguns—the number-one crime problem in the U.S. today. A system that hits one in 20 is well within tolerance," he maintains. "The ordinary stop-and-frisk is a minimal intrusion."

But to the *Times*, any unsuccessful frisks may be too many. Its gut feeling about the stop-and-frisk issue shone out clearly from a shocked statement in the February 15 "TOLL ON THE STREETS" article: "Nearly 40,000 people were stopped and frisked during the last two years *simply because* a street crime officer mistakenly thought they were carrying guns" [emphasis added]. Why else would the police stop and frisk someone? Can the *Times* think that the police should only stop and frisk people who actually have guns—an impossible requirement?

Missing from the *Times*'s "simply because" conception is any sense of the danger that illegal guns pose or any recollection of the pre-Giuliani reality, when homicides topped 2,200 a year, compared with 633 in 1998. Richard Green, the leader of the Crown Heights Youth Collective, has not forgotten. "I've been to six young people's funerals since January," he says with frustration. "If the Street Crime Unit pats me down because I match a description, and the next guy they pat down has a gun, God bless them. I have a right to privacy, but you have an absolute right to your life and property."

The *Times*'s coverage of police-community relations had no space for leaders like the dreadlocked Green. Instead, the paper conferred glowing profiles on Lieutenant Eric Adams, a strident internal critic of the police; cartoonist Art Spiegelman, who produced a disgraceful *New Yorker* cover drawing of a jolly policeman aiming at citizen-shaped targets at a shooting gallery; and David Dinkins and Charles Rangel, who competed for the most extreme insults they could hurl at Mayor Giuliani and his crime record.

Green has no tolerance for lawless police activity, but he has quite a different perspective on the NYPD's efforts to get illegal guns off the street from anything the *Times* reflected. He recalls a young man shot to death in April inside a Brooklyn movie theater. "If I have to choose between the bad and the intolerable," he says, "I'll take the bad. The intolerable is the mother crying in front of the casket, the father telling me: 'You know, the emergency room tried really hard to save his life.' If the mayor is doing something to stop this, God bless him." Green dismisses the image of the Street Crime Unit as rogue cops itching for a fight. "Those guys are not coming from the Yankee game to beat up some guy. When the SCU comes to a community, they're not there randomly. They're there because a Compstat analysis showed high crime in the neighborhood."

Many minority officers echo Green's observation. Mubarak

Abdul-Jabbar, now a transit coordinator for the police union, came up to the Bronx courthouse one windy morning in March to support the Diallo officers. Are the police targeting minorities? I ask him. "That's a hard question," Abdul-Jabbar says slowly. "Unfortunately, there's a high rate of crime in black and Latino communities. The Street Crime Unit doesn't go where there's crime *per se*, but where there's *high* crime. If there were high rates of crime in Bay Ridge, they'd be there. No one wants to admit the facts," he adds, "that in black and Latino communities, senior citizens have to stay inside." But are the police stopping too many people? "I don't think the police stop and frisk too much," muses Abdul-Jabbar. "The reality is, you have to stop and frisk; no one will announce to you that they have a gun."

Some officers undoubtedly make unjustified stops, but the *Times* rarely bothered to get the police's side of the story (a February 11 article on the dilemma of deciding whether to use one's gun, and a sensible June 20 Sunday magazine article on the controversy over racial profiling were the exceptions). In early May, the bulletin board at the Street Crime Unit headquarters notified officers of the following series of armed robberies in the Bronx:

4/22/99 Blue Toyota 5 MB [male blacks] NFD [no further description]

4/23/99 Blue Toyota Uzi and .45 rev. 3 MB NFD 1 FB [female black] NFD

4/28/99 Blue Toyota MB 27, 5'6", 210 lbs.

These descriptions will be just the starting point for further observation and crime-pattern analysis. A broad-chested Street Crime Unit member from a family of police officers explains some possible additional guides. "We're trained to look for things that don't make sense," he says: "people congregating, turning away fast, or holding or picking up their belts, like an off-duty police officer with a gun." Even so, officers searching for the Toyota robbers may well stop some innocent drivers. Which is worse—stopping four innocent people on the basis of reasonable suspicion to make one arrest, or not making the arrest at all?

A preliminary analysis of stop-and-frisk records in over twenty precincts last year disproves the charge that the police single out minorities for investigation. In fact, police frisk blacks at a lower rate than their representation in I.D.s by crime victims. Victims identified 71 percent of their assailants as black, but only 63 percent of all people frisked were black (and only 68 percent of all arrestees were black). Since the majority of crime is committed by minorities against minorities, inevitably the subjects of frisks will be minorities, too.

In talking to city residents about the police, the *Times* found only resentment and suspicion. An article on March 21 on the Model Block program contained a characteristic touch. The paper had triumphantly discovered one of the city's few neighborhoods to turn down the program, in which police cordon off and intensively patrol a street to keep drug dealers from returning. Noting that some residents doubted whether they could reduce crime and drug dealing on their own, the article quickly added: "These residents are not police boosters, . . . but they like drug dealers even less." Phew, we might have thought they actually supported the police! The *Times* noted that these non-police boosters were worried "over well-publicized reports of brutality against . . . minority groups." It did not stop to consider whether that publicity—its own reporting, in other words—was creating the fear it described.

Undeniably, the sentiment the *Times* reported is real, and dangerous to the city's social fabric. It also long predates the Giuliani administration. Through much of the nineteenth century, police would enter the Five Points area of lower Manhattan—the city's most noisome Irish slum, with a homicide a night for fifteen years—only in pairs, since they were so hated.

But though this animus toward the police still exists, it is accompanied by goodwill in the very communities where the animus is thickest. "I think the community loves the police; the silent majority is happy," says Street Crime Unit captain Harold Kohlmann, and most cops would agree. Had the *Times* visited a Model Block program one street away from where Diallo was shot, it would have found support for Kohlmann's claim. One April afternoon, Dave Rivera was basking in the bright sun and smoking a cigarette on Elder Avenue, drug-infested until recently. Rivera has lived on the block for twenty-five years and works as superintendent in the building across the street. The Model Block program? "Everybody loves it," he says in heavily accented English. "It's good they're here." Having lived under a drug fiefdom, Rivera offers a street-eye view of what the police are up against: "Sometimes the police have to be a little rough, they have to play the game. If you be too nice. . . ." He shrugs meaningfully. Across the street, a slender twenty-two-year-old with sunken cheeks and a red bandana around his head is leaning against a chain-link fence.

Antonio Espinosa, a carpenter's aide, looks like a prime target for police harassment, but somehow the cops have missed him. "I've never had a problem with the police," he says in Spanish. "I believe if you do right, you won't have a problem."

Many people will find this law-and-order view naive. But naive or not, it has many proponents among minorities. Mario has come to a community meeting at the 43rd Precinct, where the Diallo shooting occurred, to ask the police to clean up a drug problem in his neighborhood. Does he think the police harass people? "Sometimes you're in the wrong place at the wrong time, and people think you targeted them. I'm pretty sure that if you were home where you were supposed to be, nothing would happen to you." The city's recently retired chief of police, Louis Anemone, one of the most revered members of the department and a major catalyst in the Giuliani crime revolution, concurs: "Guys out there at 1 and 2 a.m., stopped on street corners—they're not your average Joe Citizen."

A constant *Times* theme was that people had "exchange[d] the fear of crime for a fear of the police," as an April 2 editorial solemnly charged. Some people, mysteriously, haven't picked up that terror. Asked if she feared the police, Freddie, a middle-aged woman attending the 43rd Precinct's May community-council meeting, unhesitatingly answers, No. Are the police racist? "I don't feel they're racist. We have very good officers." Pointing to her grandson and foster daughter, she says: "These two children, I try to teach them the police is their friend. When they come into the neighborhood, we talk, so they know they are there to help them."

This view has advocates even on Wheeler Avenue, where Amadou Diallo was shot. Pushing a cart filled with laundry one day last April, a few houses down from Diallo's former apartment, a boy named Eric says: "The police are here to protect us from bad guys and to stop the drug dealers. Before, parents couldn't let their kids out." Eric is no Pollyanna, however. "Some police are bad guys," he adds judiciously. "They don't know how to react against other people."

It turns out the *Times* had to work pretty hard to avoid people like this. A recent Justice Department study found that 77 percent of New York City blacks approve of the police, an astoundingly high number, considering the relentless anti-police propaganda of activists and the press. The *Times* tried desperately to neutralize this refutation of its own coverage by playing up the paltry 12 percent gap between black and white approval ratings.

On the street, it's not difficult to find a more nuanced view of police-citizen interactions than the *Times*'s simple aggressor-victim model. Sharit Sherrod, a twenty-three-year-old inventory specialist, is standing in line at the 43rd Precinct to report a stolen car. He's had friends who've been arrested, he says—not surprisingly, since he has many friends in the Bloods. "But I don't run into the same problems with the police as the average black man," he explains, "because I know how to talk to them. I don't get an attitude, I don't take it personally. A lot of my friends start cursing, but the way I look at it, the cops carry guns."

Sherrod is onto something. While there is no justification for the police treating peaceful citizens hostilely or rudely, police-citizen relations are a two-way street. Two 1998 studies for the National Institute of Justice found that citizens are more inclined to show the police disrespect than vice versa, and that the most powerful predictor of police disrespect is a citizen being disrespectful first. The nonstop coverage of the Diallo shooting has already increased the taunts thrown at the police on the street, escalating tensions.

No claim of police harassment seemed incredible to the *Times*. A troubling article told of police harassment of students at Rice High School, a Catholic school; one boy alleged that an officer had accused him of personally knitting the school sweater vest he was wearing in order to pass as a student. Perhaps every teen regaling reporters with his police ordeals tells only the gospel truth, but on the streets you hear skepticism about such accounts. "I'm sure the students provoke the police," sighs Lilliam Rosa, the youth coordinator for the Highbridge Unity Center in the South Bronx. "It's the attitude of kids these days: no respect for the police or other adults." Rosa's students are nearly all from Catholic schools; in her youth group, they tell of "looking hard" at the police, whom, she says, they hate. "Then they say: 'What you looking at?' and it makes the police suspicious." The cops have stopped some boys in her group at night to check their backpacks for guns—not a bad policy, she thinks. "The police just check them, then let them go," she says, "but most people react. Then the police react."

John Vargas, a hospital financial investigator and president of the community council in the 43rd Precinct, greets many police-harassment stories with similar skepticism. "I say: 'Tell me what *you* did, not just what the cops did.' People won't honestly admit they did something wrong to provoke the police. People will always say this and that, but when you ask for concrete information, they walk away." The fact that only 5 percent of the complaints filed before the Civilian Complaint Review Board are ever substantiated, with many dismissed for failure to follow up, supports such skepticism.

A recent claimant to police-victim status shows how tenuous such claims can be. At Sharpton's April 15 march across the Brooklyn Bridge, a woman in the high-profile row of police-brutality victims was carrying a photograph of her bruised and cut son, Jovan Gonzalez. It turns out the police never laid a finger on Jovan. But the "racist gang" who did beat him up has "ties," Ms. Gonzalez claimed, to the 47th Precinct. Gonzalez has already entered popular lore as a police victim; no one has ever asked for proof of the involvement of the 47th Precinct.

Like liberal critics of the police throughout the city, the *Times* was *shocked*, shocked by the Street Crime Unit's motto: "We Own the Night." Here was proof of the marauding attitude of this renegade outfit! The *Times* neglected to report that the motto frames a silhouette of an old lady bent over a cane; the unit proudly asserts supremacy over thugs it unapologetically views as evil, in order to protect the helpless.

Fearless of self-contradiction, the *Times* played up the claim that racism causes the police to ignore crime against ghetto residents, even as it trumpeted claims that the police were *too* aggressive in trying to get guns out of the ghetto. A February 17 article quoted minority women who complained that the police were ignoring the serial rapist terrorizing the Bronx and upper Manhattan. If a white woman is attacked, the police are all over the case, complained a West Harlem community advocate, but "when we have fifteen-year-old girls beaten and raped, nobody comes to do anything." A Washington Heights woman bathetically doubted that the police would catch the rapist: "We are Spanish people, poor people. They might care if this was the Upper West Side."

Though in former days the police did ignore ghetto crime, today Compstat's crime analysis does not give extra points to white neighborhoods but targets crime wherever it occurs. The Street Crime Unit had gone to the 43rd Precinct precisely to track down the rapist; had the rapist not been out there, Diallo probably would still be alive. Were there angry demonstrations against the rape suspect when, after clever sleuthing, the police finally arrested him not too far from Wheeler Avenue? Of course not.

So overwhelming was the case against the police, in the *Times*'s view, that Giuliani's unaccountable support for them was front-page news. GIULIANI SOFTENS HIS TONE BUT STILL DEFENDS THE POLICE, the paper reported incredulously on March 24. Instead of reporting the numerous positive data on the police, the *Times* left the task to Giuliani and then implied that his was an advocacy position rather than a statement of statistical fact. "While Giuliani has expressed sympathy and concern over the shooting, he continued to deny a pattern of excessive force in the department," marveled the paper on February 10. But Giuliani "continued to deny" such a pattern because none existed, as the *Times* itself could easily have ascertained.

The nonstop Diallo coverage had its desired effect. A March 16 front-page article smacked its lips at the plunge in Giuliani's approval ratings from 63 percent to 42 percent and announced that "MANY THINK POLICE ARE BIASED." No wonder. Since the dark days of Giuliani's high ratings, noted the *Times*, "one issue has overshadowed all others, the death of Amadou Diallo." But it was a deliberate editorial decision, not an imperative of nature, that made that issue predominate. As Giuliani observed, if the press had been covering a recent murder of a guest at the Waldorf Astoria with the same obsession as the Diallo shooting, everyone would be convinced there was a growing murder problem in New York, even though murders were down 70 percent.

While embroidering its theme of the out-of-control police, the *Times* ran increasingly starry-eyed stories on the protest movement. At first, the paper occasionally noted the demonstrators' advocacy of violence, along with the death threats and obscenities they hurled at the police. But a different theme soon dominated: the heartwarming and progressive diversity of the protesters and the ever-increasing stature and statesmanship of the Reverend Al Sharpton.

In its relentless diversity coverage, the *Times* simply echoed the organizers' line. "In every photo and every event, there would be some sense of a rainbow," former Dinkins aide Ken Sunshine told the *New York Observer*. "If we had to drag someone in at the last minute to complete the photo, then we would do it." The *Times* was only too happy to be spun.

But then, in a cute postmodern twist, the *Times* acknowledged its own spun state and the made-for-the-media nature of the protests. "The carefully scripted parade has drawn unflagging press coverage," reporter Dan Barry confided in an extraordinary March 19 front-page article, with the most extraordinary front-page headline of the whole affair: DAILY PROTESTERS IN HANDCUFFS KEEP FOCUS ON DIALLO KILLING. Here was a completely self-referential piece posing as news: the paper covering itself covering the Diallo protests. The article might as well have been headlined: WE KEEP FOCUS ON DIALLO KILLING. Further signaling his postmodern awareness of the media game, Barry commented on the staged nature of the events: four of the day's prominent black arrestees, he wrote, "made a striking image for the scrum of news photographers."

If anything, Barry understated how completely media-driven the civil-disobedience campaign was. As I chatted with a Sharpton follower one morning at One Police Plaza, a woman in a sleek suit paced nearby, casting impatient glances at me. Finally, I asked her what she wanted. State Assemblymen Richard Gottfried and Pete Grannis were getting arrested that day, she portentously announced, then disappeared to spread the word among other reporters.

The ratio of cameras and reporters to protesters on the plaza easily approached one-to-one. Commissioner Safir needn't have made his ill-timed trip to the Oscars; he could have imbibed the same air of media-fabulousness outside his own workplace. The unreality rivaled any Hollywood production: here were Sharpton attorney Michael Hardy and Giuliani basher Norm Siegel of the NYCLU backslapping and sharing jokes with top police brass, while the "NYPD=KKK" signs bobbed nearby. Here were the allegedly brutal officers politely informing people where they should go to get arrested.

An eager swarm of reporters encircled Sharpton upon his arrival each day, climbing over one another like drones trying to get to the queen bee. Then the day's high-profile arrestees would link arms with the Reverend, about 50 yards from the entrance to police headquarters, and wait patiently for the signal, while Sharpton stared wordlessly at the building with a noble faraway look, like Telemachus faithfully scanning the horizon for the long-vanished Odysseus. Finally, the glorious march began, past the rows of cameras, down the brick walk to the revolving glass doors, and Sharpton would hand his current batch of arrestees off to the police like an usher presenting guests to a receiving line. Some high-profile arrestees found ways to make the moment even more meaningful: the *Times* noted reverently that Susan Sarandon "walked to her arrest singing 'We Shall Overcome' quietly."

Meanwhile, the *Times* tried out a little historical revisionism regarding the early protests. A March 26 article recalled that the protests were "small and sporadic at first, quiet prayer vigils or sub-dued marches involving only a few dozen supporters of the Diallo family." Quiet prayer vigils? How about the warning issued by the vi-ciously racist Khalid Abdul Muhammad at the February 12 homego-ing service for Diallo: "You shoot one of ours 41 times, we shoot 41 of yours one time. One shot, one kill." And the paper stopped listening to the regulars who showed up every day to wave banners at One Po-lice Plaza—people like the man who yelled at officers that he'd kill them, or like Carol Taylor, a Sharpton groupie in a yellow African hat, who every day screamed hoarsely at the nearest cop: "P.U., I smell something blue!"

So the *Times* never noticed that the "rainbow" message that Ken Sunshine and other organizers worked so assiduously to convey didn't trickle down to the troops. When two Sharpton followers learned that one pro-police demonstrator, Gloria Horsham, had a white son-in-law, they could not contain their contempt for the sixty-seven-year-old Trinidadian. "You're filled with self-hate, so you taught your children to go after Caucasians," sneered a middle-aged woman from New Jer-sey. "Go back to Trinidad; don't bring that stuff here!" An older man, unfazed by Horsham's retort that if she is so filled with self-hate, how come her other children had married blacks, chuckled condescend-ingly: "You want to bleach yourself out." Bill Lord, a former Sharpton campaign manager, hadn't gotten that rainbow feeling, either. He coolly told me that while I couldn't understand him, he could under-stand me. "I'm a specialist on white people," he assured me, "because they're the deceivers."

For all the determined spinning, the protests were hardly inte-grated. Politically, they were monochromatic, ranging from the unions opposing Giuliani's welfare reforms on the right flank to the Young Communist League on the left. The groups that sent members to get arrested at One Police Plaza represent every interest that Giuliani's ef-forts to dismantle poverty and identity politics have offended, from the NAACP, the National Congress for Puerto Rican Rights, Jews for Racial and Economic Justice, the CUNY faculty, and the National Lawyers Guild, to ACT-UP, the Committee Against Anti-Asian Violence, Housing Works, the Center for Constitutional Rights, the War Resisters League, Workers to Free Mumia, the Working Families Party, Lesbians and Gays Against Police Brutality, New York Lawyers in the Public Interest, and various unions. The most strident members of the City Council turned up at One Police Plaza, as did the state legislature's Black, Puerto Rican, and Hispanic caucus. Few left-wing causes couldn't be piggybacked onto the Diallo episode. A poster outside Sharpton's headquarters denouncing Giuliani's workfare program read: "Shooting people like Amadou Diallo is one way to commit murder, starving people is another!"

Too bad former mayor Ed Koch, who had intended to get arrested with Susan Sarandon, never made it to One Police Plaza. His arrest would have been the icing on the protest movement's hypocrisy. Not that he hadn't gotten in his media licks against Giuliani already, labeling him "nasty" on New York One and admonishing him to start speaking out about "racism" in the NYPD. In the *Times*, he had pontificated that being mayor "requires a willingness to hear. So we're saying to the Mayor: 'Listen.'"

The phrase must have brought a certain feeling of *déjà entendu*, since in 1983, during an episode eerily foreshadowing Giuliani's current problems, a *Times* editorial had commanded then-mayor Koch to "Listen" to complaints of police brutality. Koch had had the temerity to question an account of police harassment then in the news. Such intolerable candor brought the Feds rushing up from Washington for hearings on police brutality and racism; familiar figures from the Diallo episode included Charles Rangel, Reverend Calvin Butts, and Jesse Jackson.

Koch fought to head off the planned hearings tooth and nail. Look at the facts, he argued with acerbity: the department has a far better record on brutality than elsewhere. It didn't work. "Listen!" admonished the *Times*. Facts are not appropriate; empathy is: "When people rush to pour out their stories," the paper editorialized, "what they want from their leaders is not an argument but an ear." A parade of witnesses launched the identical charges of racism and insensitivity against Koch that Giuliani would face fifteen years later.

Today, Koch has come round to the position that, in attacking the police, data don't count. "There's a greater number of corrupt and brutal cops today than ever before," he told me. What does he base his conclusion on? "I talk to people," he said. But don't the data show that police use of force is way down? "You're an advocate," he snapped.

What judgment should we make of current public officials who went to One Police Plaza to get arrested? By blocking police head-quarters, they implied that the department was illegitimate and so should be prevented from functioning even at the risk of imprison-ment—a message both false and irresponsible. If officials such as comptroller Carl McCall, the third-highest elected official in the state, feel that the legal regime they administer should be disabled, they should resign. (McCall declined to be interviewed on his decision to get arrested.)

That so many Democratic politicians so lightly tripped over to One Police Plaza for arrest shows how debased the currency of civil disobedience had become in Sharpton's hands. No pol seriously be-lieved that the NYPD was so unjust that it required civil-rights-style demonstrations to resist it, and no pol expected any penalties—cor-rectly so: there were none. Instead, "arrestees" grumbled over the time spent in booking. A student of Richard Green's correctly called the charade "designer arrests," noting that real arrests entail sitting in a holding cell for two days, eating bologna sandwiches, and coming home only if you're lucky. Green fumes: "The youth saw the [black] leadership marching in handcuffs; it legitimates being in handcuffs."

For all the hyperbole surrounding the arrests, the final tally—1,166—hardly adds up to overwhelming support for Sharpton's cause. A second test of Sharpton's drawing strength, the April 15 march across the Brooklyn Bridge, came up even shorter, considering the re-sources behind it. The planners drew on the massive capacity of the health-care workers union, Local 1199, headed by Dennis Rivera, an implacable foe of Giuliani's efforts to privatize the city's dinosaur pub-lic hospital system. To recruit marchers, Rivera's state-of-the-art pub-licity machine printed hundreds of thousands of posters and leaflets;

his phone banks made 150,000 calls. The Dinkins administration-in-exile took over the union's media center, with Dinkins's ex-chief of staff, Bill Lynch, directing operations, while former aide Ken Sunshine managed the media. Union media expert Bill Batson gave tours to reporters of the march's command center, around whose huge paper- and takeout-food-covered table political operatives, on loan from various City Council members, planned strategy. Batson, youthful and high-strung, with a chrysanthemum mop of dreadlocks and dental braces, proudly pointed out the operatives' gorgeous diversity: here's the former Black Panther (duly noted by the *Times*); here's the aide to City Council member Christine Quinn, whose recent swearing-in ceremony, attended by David Dinkins and Senator Charles Schumer, featured readings from the lesbian play *The Vagina Monologues*.

The anticipation of a kill was palpable. "A month ago, people were scared to say anything bad about the mayor; now he's being compared to Bull Connor in print," marvels Batson, in his tiny office crammed with posters like "10 Things You Can Do to Free [convicted cop killer] Mumia." Leaning back in his chair, Batson gossips on the phone with Elinor Tatum, editor of the *Amsterdam News*, while carrying on a second conversation. "I want you to know, Ellie, I was grandfather of the ads," Batson boasts, referring to a slanderous anti-police television commercial the union and other funders had just released. "I'm glad those 'Fooliani' pieces [a vituperative anti-Giuliani series in the *Amsterdam News*] started up again," he says. "And that *New York* piece—oh my God!" he crows in delight, referring to a blistering cover story on Giuliani.

The recent TV commercial, portraying two ominously angry white cops and one very terrified black boy, put its sponsors on the defensive. As a portrait of Rigoberta Menchu, the patron saint of political fibbers, looked down from the wall of 1199's reception room, the tightly coiled union boss Dennis Rivera ducked reporters' questions comparing the ad to the Willie Horton commercial. But the little flurry of negative publicity around the ad may have been welcome. The official propaganda—the flyers, the ads—is not the real point, reveals Batson conspiratorially. "The meat of this," he says, "is the free media. We're managing the media consciously, because we have no fucking money"—a plea of penury that's hard to swallow sitting in 1199's gleaming headquarters. The result, in Batson's view, was triumphant: "We have captured the imagination of the city of New York."

If so, most people decided to imagine at home, rather than come out to march. Days before, at Sharpton's headquarters, attorney Michael Hardy had envisioned "20,000 to 50,000 people coming across the bridge." In fact, police estimates of the march ranged from 4,500 to 10,000. A media consensus emerged toward the lower number. And a visitor from another planet would have concluded that the protest was a joint effort on behalf of Diallo and cop killer Mumia, so numerous were the "Free Mumia" signs bobbing in the crowd. Once the cameras went home, the movement against police brutality collapsed. Two weeks after the April 15 march, a Sharpton-endorsed anti-police group held a meeting, and seven assorted socialists showed up.

Of all the stories the *Times* wove into its Diallo morality tale, none strained credulity more than the maturing of Al Sharpton. While virtually ignoring his past history of racial slander, the *Times* portrayed Sharpton as having been pushed into the Diallo case only by the appeal of a supporter (Sharpton gave the same story to the *Village Voice*, but changed the identity of the supporter). It also presented him as the passive recipient of the Diallo family's appeal for help: never has his "renown and resourcefulness . . . been as clear as this week," marveled the paper, "when a bereaved family from another continent turned to [him] for help."

In fact, Sharpton tried desperately from the start to capture the Diallos for his own use. He raged with resentment when he heard that the mayor had reached out to Amadou's parents: "Oh God, what are they trying to do here?" he recalled for the *Village Voice*. Giuliani, of course, was trying to offer his condolences and help, and had he met with the parents, the next three months might have been different. But Sharpton dispatched a brigade to the airport to try to get to the parents before the Giuliani people. To the great detriment of the city, he captured his quarry. The mother rebuffed Giuliani's assistance, and from then on, Sharpton used every opportunity to rub the mayor's nose in his defeat and to use the photogenic Mrs. Diallo to advance his cause. He made Giuliani wait for over an hour for the parents on the day of Diallo's funeral and then disclosed that the family would not see him at all. "I hate to blow the mayor's bubble here," Sharpton triumphantly announced, "but they are not preoccupied with the mayor."

A falser statement was never uttered. Sharpton, who scripts what the Diallos are preoccupied with, is obsessed with Giuliani. Ever since the mayor refused to meet with him after an ambush of the police at a Harlem mosque in January 1994, Sharpton has fumed at being denied access. "You've been running from me for the last four years. But now it's me and you, Rudy," he declared after the savage police assault on Abner Louima in 1997, "and I'm going to whip you all over town."

Speaking to supporters at his National Action Headquarters, a large, low-ceilinged room in Harlem with a plaid carpet and large portraits of himself and other black activists on the walls, Sharpton erased any ambiguity about the real political agenda of the Diallo movement. Addressing Giuliani in absentia, he vowed: "All that barking and talking will come back to haunt you. Only God could arrange for this trial right before your run for the Senate," he roared. "I think the mayor needs a long rest and I intend to help give him that. . . . I'm going to march until I march up those steps [of City Hall] and take my seat inside."

If Sharpton ever does reach City Hall, he will get an adoring reception from the City Council members, among the silliest of the Diallo case's anti-police critics. It was a remarkable experience to watch them lecture Commissioner Howard Safir on how to police during an April 19 Public Safety Committee hearing. Stephen DiBrienza, the council's most histrionic grandstander, bellowed for more community policing and less anti-crime activity. Safir responded acidly: "The time you referred to, when there was allegedly more community policing, there were also 2,240 murders in the city." Amazingly, DiBrienza replied: "I'm not sure of the relevance of that." Shot back Safir: "It's of relevance to the people killed."

Council members spent most of their energy excoriating various breaches of political correctness. Many took wallops at the department's allegedly inadequate diversity. Too bad they didn't witness a one-sided exchange between three black toughs and a young black police officer at the April 15 march, which might have challenged their facile assumptions about police diversity and community relations. "Yo! Fuck you! You want to put a plunger up our ass?" the self-identified "hip-hop producers" spat at the impassive officer.

But nothing produced quite the excitement as an exchange between Councilwoman Ronnie Eldridge and Safir. After announcing imperiously: "Our children are being taught to fear the police," Eldridge threw down the gauntlet: "Is there not a way to keep crime statistics down without violating civil liberties?" Safir would have none of it. "Is that like: 'When did I stop beating my wife?'" he snapped.

Oooh—not just racism, but sexism! Christine Quinn, of *Vagina Monologues* fame, sputtered: "I don't think domestic violence is anything to joke about, Commissioner." And the commissioner's alleged insensitivity to women then became the leitmotif of the rest of the hearing.

Quinn and her colleagues found a perfect partner for their staged distress in Lieutenant Eric Adams, the persistent police critic and head of 100 Blacks in Law Enforcement Who Care. Adams signaled his readiness for the game in his opening statement. "I'm appalled that the council allowed the police commissioner to make light of women being beaten," he declared. He had brought along a hooded witness, a former member of the Street Crime Unit, to testify to the unit's brutality and racism. He hustled the witness in and out of the council chamber with great drama, including loud allegations that police spies were in the room. But it later turned out that the former officer, a woman, had an abysmal record on the force, including an assault on a superior, psychological instability, and malingering, and Safir had fired her a week before her anti-police testimony.

It's hard to top such anti-police foolishness, but the U.S. Commission on Civil Rights came close in its May 26 hearing in New York. The exchange between Mayor Giuliani and a row of Sharpton hecklers, led by "P.U. I smell blue" shouter Carol Taylor, provided an unparalleled duet between rationality and prejudice. Every fact Giuliani presented about the police, the Sharpton devotees met with closedminded contempt. Do the police now shoot far fewer people than in 1990, even though there are 8,000 more officers? "What's the relevance of that?" Are fatal shootings by the police way down? "Oh, yeah, only blacks." Do FBI statistics show that New York is the safest large city in the country? "Stop it please, you make me sick!" One supporter shouted out the theme of the entire hearing: "I'm tired of statistics. He doesn't talk about the reality of racism."

Commission chairwoman and longtime practitioner of race politics Mary Frances Berry adopted the David Dinkins method of crowd control: let them vent. While the hecklers were virtually drowning out Giuliani, only once did she ever so delicately tap her gavel, grinning broadly at the Sharptonites. When they interrupted her, however, "BANG!" went the gavel.

With no more interest in the facts than the Sharpton crew, Berry cut off Giuliani's recital of data about the NYPD's low use of force to ask her all-consuming question: "Do you believe the NYPD fairly represents the population of New York City?" Berry should have known how irrelevant the query was. The new chief of her local police force in Washington, D.C. recently *begged* the Justice Department to investigate it for civil-rights violations, even though the force is majority black.

From then on, it was all uninformed second-guessing and attempts to trivialize the Giuliani crime rout. "Isn't it the case that bias crimes, brutality, and allegations of domestic abuse by police officers went up at the same time that crime went down?" she asked portentously. More police insensitivity to women! Not surprisingly, Giuliani did not have the figures on police domestic abuse at his fingertips.

Before dismissing Giuliani, Berry made clear how little of what he had said had made any impression on her. "Some of the choices appear stark, listening to you," she intoned gravely. "We could protect safety by ignoring civil-rights protections." Everything Giuliani had said, however, emphasized that the department insisted on improving police respect for citizens even as it fights crime. But Berry made sure that the record reflected the specious claim that Giuliani's crime turn-around had a "dark side," making New York, in effect, a police state. And though Berry couldn't ensure the mayor the courtesy of a re-spectful hearing, she was all graciousness to another figure in the drama. "I recognize that the Reverend Al Sharpton has already ar-rived," she beamed. "I just want to acknowledge the work he has been doing"—"work" that consists of keeping race tensions as high as pos-sible.

The Diallo follies have damaged the city enormously. The 23 per-cent of black New Yorkers who do not approve of the police have grown angrier. Street Crime Unit officers, well aware of the increased hostility toward them, have pulled back: their felony arrests fell 47 percent in the first four months of 1999, compared with 1998. Shoot-ings and gun homicides are ticking up in the neighborhoods where the unit patrols; citywide, murders were 10 percent higher from February 4 to May 23, 1999, compared with the same period of 1998. And needless to say, the four Diallo officers have almost surely lost the chance of a fair trial.

What should we do? Commissioner Safir is right to reject the claim that crime in New York is low enough, so the police should change their mission. Continuing to bring crime down is the best civil-rights program he can offer, since blacks make up four times the num-ber of homicide victims as whites, and the streets of minority neighborhoods have until recently been less safe for their law-abiding residents to walk than other parts of the city. Safir is also right to push the cops to show more respect for civilians. Too many officers have a rude, contemptuous attitude, and Safir's excellent, and unfairly ma-ligned, Courtesy, Professionalism, and Respect training program for cops is a good antidote.

But if the police bear a heavy responsibility for maintaining cor-dial community relations, the community shares that responsibility, too. It is a travesty that Sharpton and his eager new followers focus all their energy on stigmatizing the police. If they spent half their lung and media power on stigmatizing criminals, and the other half on helping young people compete in the job market, they could transform the city.

[1999]

Index

A NOTE ON THE AUTHOR

Heather Mac Donald received her B.A. in English from Yale
University, graduating summa cum laude with a Mellon Fel-
lowship to Cambridge University, where she earned her M.A.
in English. Later she received a J.D. from the Stanford University Law School. A nonpracticing lawyer, Ms. Mac Donald
has clerked for the Honorable Stephen Reinhardt in the
United States Court of Appeals for the Ninth Circuit; has
been an attorney-adviser in the office of the general counsel
for the United States Environmental Protection Agency; and
has volunteered with the National Resource Defense Counsel
in New York City. Her writings have appeared in *City Journal*,
the *Wall Street Journal*, the *Washington Post*, the *New York
Times*, *The New Republic*, *Partisan Review*, *The New Criterion*, *The Public Interest*, and *Academic Questions*. She is currently a John M. Olin Fellow at The Manhattan Institute and
a contributing editor to *City Journal*. She lives and works in
New York City.